THE BOYKIN BOY

a memoir

DENNIS L. BOYKIN

The Boykin Boy
A Memoir
by Dennis L. Boykin

Published by
GREAT PLAINS PUBLISHING

First published in 2003

Most names have been changed to protect the privacy of others.

Edited by Ruth Bramall
Original cover design by Debbie Riley • aesopF@msn.com
Production by Gary A. Rosenberg • TheBookCouple.com

ISBN: 978-0-69284-178-5

Printed in the U.S.A.

Also published by Dennis L. Boykin
Carson's Lease
© 2004 • ISBN 978-0-69284-178-5

This book
is dedicated to my children,
Kellie Jo, Patrick, and Donovan,
and to the memories of their loving mother, Allison.

ACKNOWLEDGMENTS

My heartfelt appreciation goes to Ruth Bramall—friend, former classmate, and editor extraordinaire, for her careful reading and editing of the first edition of this book, and her sincere kindness and words of encouragement and constant expressions of enthusiasm toward my work.

A special thanks to my friend, Debbie Riley, for her work on the cover design, and her constant expressions of approval and support.

To my children of Allison K. Mills (Boykin) who are named in the dedication.

FOREWORD

The Boykin Boy . . . is an unforgettable, unique, and sometimes humorous true story that exemplifies that good old American credo of pulling oneself up by his/her own bootstraps. In this vivid memoir of a boy striving to transcend his social environment, we meet Dennis Boykin. Dennis was born in the middle of the Great Depression. During his childhood, he struggles to overcome polio, brutal physical attacks from his father, the loss of his eleven brothers and sisters, and total desertion by both of his parents.

At age eleven, Dennis finds himself alone on a Wyoming ranch, left by his father in the care of a bewildered old ranch couple, with no hope of ever seeing any of his relatives again. Never having attended school, totally illiterate, Dennis dreams of learning to read and write, attending school and being accepted by other children.

The old couple grants Dennis board and room in exchange for ranch chores, teaches him the rudiments of reading and writing, and he starts school, for the first time, ever, at age thirteen. Tall, lumbering, labeled retarded by some, handicapped by a severe speech impediment, mastering only the basis of reading and writing, he doggedly fights his way through his first year of school.

For six years, Dennis stubbornly clings to his dreams of finishing high school, conquering his speech impediment, gaining self respect and identity, and becoming a normal boy. He survives clashes with classmates, teachers, local police, broken bones, and harassment from those he tries most to impress.

Dennis's memoir, set in the cotton fields of Texas during the Great Depression era, and later on a Wyoming ranch, vividly reveals to us the emotions, trials and conflicts of every growing boy, but his story is made unique by the degree of emotional and physical strife few children have ever successfully confronted.

—Ruth Bramall

ONE

Six months had passed. Six months of bad dreams and anxious thoughts about the possibility that this day would come. And now that it was here, I sensed it was just the beginning of something even worse than I had known before. As I stood on the frosty porch, with all of these feelings rushing through me, the hurt from losing my dog, Queenie, when I was just a small boy, came to mind, and it struck me that losing her had to be a close second to what was happening to me right now. I knew, sure as the world, that once I ducked into that big black car and closed the door, that I was caught in my own second-worst nightmare, and there was no way out anymore, for sure, no way of my own choosing.

I closed the door to the house and buttoned my jacket. The light frost made a crunchy sound under my feet as I stepped off the porch and trudged across the narrow boardwalk. Mr. and Mrs. Valliant were waiting in their 1942 Chevrolet with the motor running.

A flash of pride shot through me as I opened the yard gate and took in the freshly shined paint of the family car. Just the day before, Mrs. Valliant had parked the mud-splattered Chevrolet near the creek, gave me a box of Oxydol, a brush, and a hand towel. "Dennis Boykin," she said, in a profound tone, as if her next words were to be remembered forever, "If you can scrub just half the mud off of old Betsy, it's worth a silver dollar to you." Then she gave out a little chuckle. A dollar (a silver dollar at that) seemed like a lot of money for washing one car, but I didn't say anything. I worked most of the afternoon, carrying buckets of water from the creek, scraping mud from the running boards, and polishing the paint with a hand towel, all the while dreading what I feared would be my last ride in the big, black sedan.

Opening the car door, I shoved my suitcase in ahead of me and settled myself in the back seat. Mr. Valliant drove a short distance north along the hilltop road, then circled back to the south around the steep hill and down into the barn area. Driving past the corrals, the car bounced over a little bridge near the barn. I noticed the stream with only a trickle of water. I glanced toward the Sierra Madre mountain range to the south and saw thin clouds hanging on snow-capped Bridger Peak. I thought back to last October when my dad and I first came to the ranch, when the creek was too wide to jump across, and I thought about how the peaks looked with their first blanket of snow. I wondered if I would ever see these mountains again.

Coming out of the creek bottom, Mr. Valliant drove north out of the ranch and stopped at the wire gate at the corner of the horse pasture. He cracked his door only slightly before I was out of the car and hurrying toward the gate. The four ranch saddle horses were standing near the fence. Their heads came up, and glanced in my direction before lowering their heads again in search of a stray blade of old grass on the thinly frosted ground. My favorite horse, Red, was with the others. While holding the gate, waiting for the car to pull through, I watched the white steam rise from his nostrils. I closed the gate and hurried back to the car. Mr. Valliant flashed me a smile as I opened the door and settled myself in the back.

In the front seat, Mr. and Mrs. Valliant talked quietly, leaving me to ponder my fate awaiting me in Chillicothe, Texas, where I was going to meet my father. I sat composed in the rear seat with my suitcase beside me, careful not to reveal my fear and nervousness. I had told them little about my previous life. They didn't know that ever since I could remember I had wanted to be anywhere out of sight and hearing distance of my father, or that I was already planning ways to escape from him and return to the ranch.

The date was March 26, 1946 just two days after my twelfth birthday, and almost six months, to the date, since Dad had left me on the ranch in the care of Mr. and Mrs. Valliant. Now, I was returning to Dad, because he had sent them a letter, explaining that he had quit drinking and could care for me and send me to school. And only I knew the real truth: he wanted me back because having me along made it easier for him to hitch rides from town to town and earn more money from panhandling and odd jobs to buy liquor. The other miserable particulars about living with my dad I also kept locked inside my shell.

During the long car trip to Rawlins, my emotions were on a roller coaster. On the high side, I knew I no longer had to be kicked around like a stray dog. I'd learned there was a different way of life. On the Valliant ranch, I had experienced learning in a way other than having my tail worn out with a cotton switch, and I couldn't get enough of this new way of life. I knew if I could survive Dad's physical abuse long enough, I could run away and experience another way of living. I could fork hay, harness and drive a team of horses, and do other work required on a ranch.

I had seen how other children lived and I felt an overpowering confidence that I could change my life if I could only escape, and find my way back here, or to some another ranch where I could work and go to school. I felt hopeful. Coming off my high, I knew I was going to a strange place, I had no idea how I could escape, and I was nervous, and scared.

My suitcase was packed with two pairs of new pants, two new shirts, two pairs of socks, and an assortment of other items. It also contained my most priced possession, a .22 caliber, single shot rifle, which was my birthday present from Mr. Valliant. The little rifle was broken down into two pieces, fitting neatly into my suitcase.

We arrived early at the Greyhound bus depot. Mrs. Valliant went inside to buy my ticket. Mr. Valliant looked in his rear view mirror, and he must have noticed my hopeless expression, because he turned around in his seat to face me. "We'll keep ol' Red in the pasture, just in case you find your way back from Texas," he said, grinning. Red was the horse that Mr. Valliant and the sheepherder, Pete, had taught me to ride; the horse I claimed as mine.

Boarding the bus, I seated myself next to an old woman with a lap full of knitting. She started talking immediately, only stopping long enough to catch her breath from time to time. I was relieved to learn she was going to do all the talking; I was shy, and I didn't think where I was going was any of her business. Anyway, by not really listening to her I was free to do my thinking and try to figure out how things might be when I arrived at my destination.

Desperate to believe my dad, I tried to convince myself this time would be different—that he really had a job and would treat me like something other than another object and a punching bag. Deep down, though, I knew his promises meant nothing. But for just a moment, I allowed myself to fantasize a little about how it could be, and how I wanted it to be. Anyway, it kept me from thinking of all the bad things I could remember from living with him in the past.

As the bus pulled away, I pressed my face to the window, waved and watched the Valliants disappear into the distance.

The old woman got off the bus some time after dark. I was relieved and went right to sleep, as I had the full seat to stretch out.

The next morning it was much warmer. Some of the passengers had their windows open. We were rolling across the Texas Panhandle on a bright and sunny day and I alternated between the excitement of the trip and the dread of being at my father's mercy again.

The sun was high in the sky and I was hungry and thirsty before a small town came into view, and the driver announced, "Breakfast," as he pulled into a little restaurant. The bus picked up a Mexican man and woman at the stop. One sat next to me and the other across the aisle. Again, I didn't have to speak as they maintained a lively conversation in Spanish, and I was left with my thoughts.

TWO

With the drone of the bus engine in the background, I relaxed my head back on the seat, and relived another experience that took place seven months ago, when my sister, Mary Lee, and I experienced a similar adventure. The trip with Mary Lee started the change in my life, which would see me on the Valliant ranch, from which I had just left. Our journey began in Memphis, Texas. Our destination was Rock Springs, Wyoming.

Life was good living with my grandmother and my four uncles, where Dad had left me. He said he was going to look for work, and would send for me later. I wasn't there long until Mary Lee arrived. She was a year older than me, and had been living at St. Joseph Orphanage in Bethany, Oklahoma, not far from Oklahoma City. Mary Lee had sneaked away from the orphanage and hitchhiked to Grandma's.

We were at Grandma's place about two months when she received a letter from Dad. He told Grandma he had a job working in the coal mines in Reliance, Wyoming—a small mining town ten miles north of Rock Springs. He asked Grandma to put me on a train, and said he would meet me in Rock Springs.

In early August 1945, Mary Lee and I boarded the train for the long trip to Wyoming. Grandma paid for our tickets and gave us extra money for meals. Neither of us had ever traveled any farther north than Oklahoma; the countryside was all new to us. 'Our house is going to look just like that one,' Mary Lee would point and say, as we passed one ranch house after another. Or, 'look at those beautiful hills, I'll bet our house is going to be right in the middle of one of those.' Her endless chatter kept me awake and, as the train rattled on, mile after mile, I joined in her make-believe games.

Mary Lee and I were always close. We trusted each other and she was the only other person who knew the secret about Dad.

We ate in the diner, drank Dr. Pepper and RC cola until we nearly burst, neither of us giving much thought to the real world that awaited us.

Dad met us at the train station in Rock Springs. He hadn't known about Mary Lee coming, and I could tell by his sour expression that he wasn't pleased at seeing her. With Dad was a woman, which neither of us had ever seen or heard about. He simply said, "This is your new mother, Mollie." Mollie looked a lot younger than Dad. She was tall, with blonde hair. She was not fat, but solid, and I thought at the time that she could probably do a good job of swinging a switch, if she ever decided to. Mollie wore a big smile and hugged both Mary Lee and me as we stepped off the train. We liked her instantly, and she proved to be a friend from the first day.

Together, we hitched a ride the ten miles to our new hometown—two rows of run-down rambling shacks, with dirt streets, and a line of outhouses behind. This was a coal mining community, and the shacks belonged to the mining company.

Our house had two rooms for sleeping, each containing one bed, a kitchen area with one table and benches for eating, and a coal-burning stove for cooking. We had electricity for lighting but no refrigerator or other electrical appliances.

The mining camp was about evenly divided between whites and Mexicans. By choice, or by chance, the camp was pretty much segregated. But, our house was located in the Mexican section, along with two other white families.

Within the camp there were two gangs—Mexican and white. I learned early that the kids in the white gang were considered wimps by the Mexicans, and the whites were careful to keep their distance from Mexican turf. I also quickly learned that the Mexican kids called themselves Spanish, but the white kids said that was a damn lie; they were all from Mexico. To be heard calling a Mexican kid a Mexican was grounds enough to get your ass kicked right on the spot.

If you were a kid living in the camp, you either belonged to the Mexican gang or you didn't get out of your own yard unless your dad or mom was with you. The Mexicans didn't like me from the start. Twice they caught me away from the house, roughed me up, and threatened to do a lot worse.

It was a bright, sunny day. Mary Lee and I were on our knees, playing marbles in our yard, when a group of Mexican kids (maybe six or seven) slowly walked toward us. I froze. Mary Lee jumped to her feet and ran into the house to get Mollie. I felt a hand grasp me by the collar of my shirt and pull me to my feet. I recognized the face behind the grimy arm as Hector Sanchez, the big Mexican kid with a menacing smile and yellow teeth that were too big for his mouth—the same kid who had roughed me up good a few days before. He was smiling, as he held me at arms length. I couldn't hide my fear and they were all laughing now.

"Whattaya want?" I managed through a long stutter.

"Hey, honkey, relax, we ain't gonna hurt you," Hector said, releasing his hold on my shirt. "You scrap pretty good. You wanna join our gang? You don't look like a real honkey, anyway."

"Yah, sure," I said. "What…what…do I have to do?"

They all laughed, again. "Well, honkey, there's 'nitition you gotta do first. But it ain't nuthin' you pass or flunk, like in school. If ol' Ortiz don't kill you, you're in, just like that." He snapped his fingers. There wasn't a white kid in the camp that didn't know who Victor Ortiz was—the legend—the Mexican kid who strutted around the camp, fearing nothing, saying almost nothing. I'd never seen Ortiz in a fight, but I never for once doubted that he was the toughest kid in the camp, maybe in the whole world.

What it came down to, I could either fight Ortiz, and try to stay alive long enough to join the gang, or continue getting my ass kicked every time I stepped out of my yard, beginning right now, I thought. I cast a pleading look toward the doorway, where Mollie was standing, holding a coal shovel with both hands, watching.

"I wanna join," I said, through another long stutter. "Can I fight somebody else?" They laughed, passed cigarettes around, and shared a kitchen match to light up.

Ortiz took a long pull on his cigarette, covered my face with smoke and asked me how old I was. I told him I was eleven, going on twelve.

"You wanta fight him?" Ortiz said to Sanchez. "He's scrawny as a stray dog. I'd waste the little bastard with one punch."

"Yah, I can do that," Hector Sanchez said, reaching a hand out to shove me in the chest. "Saturday night, six o'clock, honkie. In the street in front of my house. You better be there."

———

Saturday came too soon for me. For two days I moped around the house, dreading and expecting the worst. On Friday, I finally told Dad about the fight. He smiled. "You can whip that damn Mexican, son. Just keep your head down, lead with your left, and when you have him off-guard, kick him in the balls." I'd never been in a real fight, and I'd never kicked anyone in the balls. I wasn't at all sure that anything Dad had told me would work for me. Or that Hector wouldn't just laugh at my feeble attempts to fight back. For sure, I wasn't going to try anything tricky, like kick him in the nuts, or anything else that would really set him off.

Word spread about the camp, and as time came for the big fight, parents and kids gathered in the dirt roadway in front of our house. Dad and Mollie were there. Dad and some of the men were sharing bottles, cigarettes, talking and laughing.

I was scared, but I tried not to let on. Sanchez looked about half-grown to me, with his confident swagger, and long, black hair slicked straight back with gel. But there was no way out, and I just figured that in a few minutes I would either be dead, or a live member of Victor Ortiz's gang. That's all I had to look forward to.

The fight started and I could hear Mary Lee cheering me on. His first punch landed square in my mouth, and knocked me down. A burst of pain shot through my head. I wanted to cry, but, instead, I got mad as hell. He let me get up before landing another punch to the side of my head, and I went down again. He was smiling as I got up, and I sensed he was toying with me. I rushed him head-first, my fists flailing. I didn't hurt him with my fists, but I took him to the ground. They separated us, and we were toe-to-toe, again. I landed one punch to his midsection before he hit me in the nose and knocked me down again. My nose started to bleed, and Dad called the fight.

I was hurting and I could barely stand up. But despite the beating I'd taken, I felt proud; I didn't cry, or break and run, and I wasn't dead. The gang formed a circle around me, patted me on the back, and assured me I was now one of them.

There were ten to twelve members in the gang, sometimes more. At least once a week we hitchhiked into Rock Springs. Before the picture show started in the evening, we roamed the streets, stole candy, turned over garbage cans in alleys, and threatened other little kids without parents. I had learned the grab-and-run method of stealing from my Uncle Marvin, and won instant approval from the gang members. Even though I was the smallest one in the gang, I felt safe and protected. After the picture show we split up into groups of three or four and hitched it back to Reliance.

After winning approval from the gang, I felt secure at the camp. Mollie cooked good meals, laughed and joked—and then there was the hard candy from the company store, which she warned us to keep secret from Dad. But I knew things would soon change. I worried if I would get to say good-bye to the gang, or would we just walk out the door in the middle of the night.

In less than two months at the camp, Dad announced one night that we would be moving on come morning. I went out and tried to find some of the gang, but they had all gone to Rock Springs. I told one of the parents I would be leaving the next morning and asked her to say good-bye to the others. The next morning, with nothing to pack, we walked out the door into the bright, yellow sunrise.

When we were on the highway, Dad said, "We can't all catch a ride together. Mary Lee will go with Mollie....Dennis, you come with me. We'll meet at the Salvation Army in Rawlins and stay there until I can find a job." I never saw Mary Lee or Mollie again.

Dad and I caught a ride to Rawlins, only to learn there was no Salvation Army. After two days of staying drunk, all his money was gone. Through the employment office, he learned Shannon Sharpe was looking for a ranch hand. We met the ranch owner in Rawlins and he drove us to his spread located near Elk Mountain, Wyoming.

Mr. Sharpe owned a large ranch located about ten miles west of Elk Mountain. Dad's job was feeding hay to the cattle. I stayed in the bunkhouse all day, alone. I didn't like the loneliness and was glad when he decided, late one night, that we should leave. It was a clear, cold, October night. With a full moon to guide us, we walked the ten miles on a dirt road to Elk Mountain, a town even smaller than Memphis, Texas, where I'd lived with my grandma.

From Elk Mountain we hitchhiked to Saratoga, Wyoming. Inquiring around town, Dad learned the Grimes and Valliant ranch was looking for a hired man. Claude Grimes, the bachelor brother of Anna Valliant, met us in town, and Dad was hired.

Right off, I noticed how Anna and Booth Valliant smiled at me, when they didn't really have to. I kept returning their smiles, and not many days had gone by before Mrs. Valliant asked me if I wanted some books to read. She didn't know that I couldn't read. I didn't tell her right then, either, because I was afraid she would think I was a dummy, which I was. Later, though, I had to tell her something, so I just said that Dad changed jobs a lot, and I hadn't learned to read very good.

Dad and I slept in the bunkhouse, but I spent most of my days in the house with Mrs. Valliant. I'd never seen a book, and became fascinated with the stories she read to me every day. She often played the piano, and taught me some keys and how to play a simple tune. Some days Mr. Valliant and I would ride around the ranch in his black Chevrolet. He didn't talk much, but from what little he said, I could tell he was proud of the ranch. I wanted to ask questions, to learn more about ranch life, but I never did.

After one month, Dad collected his pay and decided to move on. I said good-bye to the Valliants, and Grimes left us on the highway in Saratoga. We hitched a ride to Rawlins, arriving about sundown. Ambling down the street, we entered the first bar, and Dad started drinking. When the bar closed, he was broke, and falling-down drunk. We had no place to sleep, and we hadn't had a bite to eat since leaving the ranch. The bar owner allowed us to sleep in a tiny room located in the back. He gave us some blankets and we curled up on the floor.

The next morning, while I was rubbing the sleep out of my eyes, Dad tried the door. It was locked from the outside. Dad was hung-over and grouchy, and I was hungry and thirsty. The bar owner finally arrived to unlock the doors, and we were on the streets again—broke, hungry, dirty and cold. Dad said he would place a collect call to the Valliants for some help.

I didn't hear any part of Dad's conversation with the Valliants, but in about two hours they arrived. Dad and Mr. Valliant quietly negotiated for quite awhile before Mr. Valliant reached in his pocket and handed Dad something. Dad walked away without a backward glance. The Valliants and I went to a restaurant for breakfast.

"Your Dad said he's going back to Texas to look for another job," Mrs. Valliant said, smiling at me from across the table. "Mr. Valliant gave him fifty dollars. He promised to pay us back and send for you when he gets on his feet."

Living on the ranch with the Valliants became an all new life experience for me. Learning my ABC's, playing with the four ranch dogs, having my own horse, desserts every night for supper, sledding on the iced-over meadow, learning to harness and drive the team, and riding with the hired man, Pete, on the hay wagon. Then there was Thanksgiving, and Christmas—holidays I had only heard mentioned until now.

Even though I had thought about it every day, and felt the eerie sensation that Dad was out there, somewhere, ready to snatch me back, it didn't seem like half a year had passed. Mrs. Valliant went to town for groceries and the mail. I was through eating supper, excused myself and started to leave the table. "Dennis," Mrs. Valliant said, laying her hand on my shoulder, "We received a letter from your dad today. He didn't send any money, but he wants you back."

THREE

As the bus pulled into a rest stop, I was jolted back to reality. My brain was exhausted from reliving the past. And it was high time I started thinking about how to survive whatever Dad had planned for me in Chillicothe, Texas.

Except for several more stops, and more donuts and milk, the rest of the day was just boring; I couldn't read a book, or a magazine, or anything, as I could see most of the other passengers doing. When it turned nightfall again I started to worry: *what if Dad had gone on a binge and forgotten about my coming, or what if he got into a fight and was thrown in jail, or what if he simply decided to move on and ignore the fact that I was arriving that night?*

All these thoughts, and many more, plagued me as the bus roared into the night. Also, I knew I was to get off at Chillicothe, but I couldn't read the signs, and I was afraid to ask the bus driver to let me off at the right place.

I didn't sleep at all. At some point during the long night, the bus stopped, and the driver turned and looked directly at me. "This is where you get off, kid."

The town was silent and dark when I stepped off the bus; not a person was in sight, the streets noiseless and empty. Only a small glow of light was visible through some of the store windows.

With my suitcase in hand, I walked the two-block length of the town, hoping the bars would still be open. I didn't know the time of night, but since the lone town bar was closed, it had to be very late. I didn't know what to do, but for sure I didn't want to sit on the street until daylight.

Thinking I could find a road culvert to sleep in, I started walking. When I was almost out of town, I noticed a used car lot. My mood brightened. *One of those cars is going to be my bed for the night,* I thought. From past experience, I knew that none of the older makes of cars had door locks, and it didn't take me long to find an unlocked car. I crawled into the front seat and fell asleep immediately.

The sun was high when I woke, and I was hot and sweaty. The windows were up, and the sun was shining directly through the windshield on me. For a brief moment, I didn't have a clue where I was. The sounds of men talking in the distance refreshed my memory in a flash, and a sense of urgency jolted me to my senses: I didn't want to be caught in the car—and I needed to find Dad.

Crawling out of the car, I kept low until well beyond sight of the men. Walking the two blocks back into the main part of town, my thoughts turned to what I was going to do if I couldn't find him. I only had a few dollars left from my eating money— maybe enough for one more meal—but what then? I worried. I walked the streets again and found the bar locked and empty. I glanced at a clock hanging from a bank building, and breathed a sigh of relief; it was too early for the bar to be open.

I was standing on a nearly deserted street, holding my suitcase in one hand, looking first one way, then the other. The aroma of fried bacon caused my stomach to do a flip-flop. I followed the smell to a doorway, just a few steps from where I had been standing. Before going inside, I reached into my pants pocket and pulled out a crumpled dollar bill. The restaurant had no menus, just hand-lettered signs taped on the walls, and the register, nothing that I could read. The waitress came and I asked her if one dollar would buy two eggs and a glass of milk. She smiled. "For you, I'll even throw in a coupla pieces of toast, and an extra glass of milk." While I was waiting for my eggs to arrive, I tried to remember if I had eaten anything but candy and donuts since leaving the ranch.

Breakfast revived my spirits, somewhat, but I knew I must continue searching. Most of my money was gone, and I didn't want to sleep in the used car lot another night. I thought of asking someone on the street, or perhaps a shopkeeper if they knew of my dad, but I convinced myself he hadn't been in town long enough to be remembered by any of the locals.

Some time during early morning, the bar opened. I pushed the door open and walked into a musty, foul smelling room. Dad and another down-and-out type were cradling beers at a corner table. I recognized Dad immediately: a big, craggy-faced, broad shouldered man, with a bushy head of red hair.

Dad had an unkempt, grubby look about him, as if he hadn't slept in a regular bed for a long time. "Hello, Son," he greeted me, without leaving his drink, or touching me. His eyes were blood-shot, and he reeked with booze and days-old perspiration. "This is my boy," he said, to his drinking partner. "I'm gonna buy him a new pair of boots and a cowboy hat."

After Dad and the other fellow had a couple of more beers, we left the bar and walked out on the street. "I don't have a job anymore, and I'm broke," he said, with a hopeless gesture. "Do you have any money?" I wasn't prepared for his question; I had planned to keep my silver dollar Mrs. Valliant had given me as a good luck piece, and the rest of my pennies and nickels for candy and ice cream. Without answering, I slowly reached deep into my pants pocket and gave him the pennies and nickels first; then, feeling a flush of guilt, I dug a little deeper and handed him my silver dollar.

We weren't on the street very long until Dad searched my suitcase and found my .22 caliber single shot rifle. After selling my rifle at a second-hand store, and drinking a few more beers with his friend, we were back on the street and walking out of town. As we hiked along the roadway, I could see the heat waves in the distance and feel the hot asphalt on the soles of my feet. But I was in a world of my own, not thinking about the hot sun, or losing my rifle, or how bad things were going to be when we got to wherever it was we were going.

FOUR

I was born in Nueces County, Texas, March 24, 1934. But it was the winter of 1939, and I was five years old, before I was jolted into any awareness of life. The country was waist-deep in the Great Depression. Thousands of people were dying from typhoid and flu. Countless others were hungry and jobless—and I was lying on my back in a damp railroad car that we called home, paralyzed from the waist down.

The Depression had drained the spirits and livelihood of nearly everyone in the country, and we were just one of those families without much to show for anything. My Dad, Mom and eight of us kids were living in a cold, damp, railroad car in Childress, Texas. I was the oldest boy. I had four older sisters: Pearl, Mary Lee, Ola, and Frances. My younger brothers and sisters were: Deola, Frank, and John. With Joe, who was born at the camp, there were nine Boykin kids.

Used and battered railroad cars—delivered and placed on the site—were available for purchase from the Texas and Pacific Railway Company for fifty dollars. The wheels on the railroad car had been removed before the big crane arrived to place the car on a railroad tie foundation. My parents bought one of these ready-made homes and had it set in a field near several other railroad-car families.

Our car was equipped with a wide, creaking, sliding door, and furnished with one bed, a table, and a few wooden chairs. Grandma and her family were living in another railroad car located not far from us in the same, bare, treeless field.

It was the dead of winter in 1939. I had been paralyzed for several days, unable to move my body below the waist. My parents and Grandma couldn't agree as to what was causing it. They argued for several days, with Dad insisting that I had hurt my legs while carrying water from the cistern, Grandma doggedly holding to her conviction that I had infantile paralysis. Finally, it was settled and everyone agreed with Grandma. Grandma wanted Dad to take me to a doctor. Dad refused, saying there was no cure for infantile paralysis, and I would never be able to walk again, anyway.

That settled, Grandma insisted upon taking charge of my treatment and was soon whipping up one terrible tasting concoction after another to force down my throat. I told Grandma it all tasted like Castor oil to me, but she swore they were her own special homemade remedies. My sisters carried water for Grandma to heat on an outside fire. She used the warm water to bathe and massage my muscles several times a day. My toilet was a flat pan pushed under me, and later carried away by Grandma.

When I first learned that I couldn't stand or walk, I was only puzzled. For several days I was cold, shivering, sick at my stomach, unable to hold anything down. After Grandma looked at me the first time, she said I had a fever and would be okay when the fever went down. In time, the fever went away, but I still couldn't move my legs, like everything below my waist was a wobbly mass of skin and bone. That's when I got scared for the first time. But, I trusted Grandma, and when she said she would be doctoring me, I relaxed as much as possible on the cold floor, and enjoyed the extra attention from her and my older sisters.

It seemed like forever that I lay on a quilt, shivering on the floor, unable to move my lower body. As time went on, Grandma insisted that I could learn to walk again. Day after day, with my arms drooped over the shoulders of my older sisters, they half-dragged me around the hard-packed dirt behind the railroad cars until, gradually, I regained some motion in my legs. Each day the muscles in my lower body gained strength. Before winter faded into spring, I was able to start playing on my rubbery legs.

After I got sick, Grandma wouldn't let us play with other kids in the camp. She said most of them were sick, and she didn't want us getting whatever they had.

We lived in our railroad car until spring. Dad and my two older uncles busied themselves digging new pits for outhouses, and doing other odd jobs for a little money to supply our camp with beans and flour—and for the occasional luxury of buying a bottle of Listerine from the town drugstore. The Listerine probably being more to their liking than the home brew and bathtub gin they bottled in fruit jars and sold to hobos and bums passing through.

During our last days at the camp, Mom went away for a few days and returned with my new baby brother, Joe.

When the days turned warm, Dad and Uncle Fred left the camp to look for work in the cotton fields. They returned the next day driving a battered, Model-A Ford. I ran over to check out the car, and that's when I heard Dad telling Mom they had found work for all of us on a nearby farm. There wasn't room enough for both our families to travel in the car, so Grandma and her family gathered their belongings and moved first. The next day Uncle Fred returned.

I couldn't count numbers, but as I anxiously waited for Dad and Uncle Fred to finish cramming our things into the dusty old machine, I became concerned about how we would all get into the little car. My curiosity was satisfied soon after the little car was loaded. "Dennis, Momma wants you to come first. You can sit by me," Uncle Fred said. "There's enough room for your dad, Pearl, Ola, and Frances. I'll come back for your Momma and the rest after we unload." I felt important standing in the seat next to Uncle Fred, waving to the curious barefoot neighbor kids, as we slowly drove out of the camp.

It didn't seem very long until we turned off the main road. The old car bounced along a narrow dirt road for a short distance before two little shacks appeared, sitting in the middle of a newly planted field. The camp we had left was smelly, with flies everywhere and no place to play because of all the trash and litter. I was excited to see our new home; my sisters and I would have endless room to play, and we wouldn't have to share our outhouse with half of the world.

Grandma, her current husband, and my four uncles had already moved into their new home. My sisters helped Dad clean the little clapboard shack, Uncle Fred returned for the rest of our clan, and I explored my new playground.

At our new location, Dad, Mom, my four older sisters, and three of my uncles disappeared during the day to hoe cotton in the freshly seeded fields. Mary Lee and I played under the mesquite trees, or made red clay mud pies in the shade of the house, under the watchful eyes of Grandma. Sometimes, Uncle Marvin, who was sixteen-years old, would stay around the house, help Grandma, and hang out with us. Uncle Eugene always stayed at the house. He had been run over by a car when he was a baby. My sisters and I were scared of Uncle Eugene, because he walked with a terrible limp, smoked cigarettes, and one of his arms was shriveled-up and flopped when he walked.

Spring and summer flew by, and it seemed like no time until the cotton was ready to pick. Even though I still had some problems with my balance and coordination, I had all but forgotten my bout with infantile paralysis. I had turned six before we left the camp, and this would be my first year to pull a real cotton sack. I was anxious to get started.

The first day we started picking cotton, I hurriedly ate my mush and fried bread, and waited impatiently for the rest of the family to finish breakfast. I couldn't wait to try on my new cotton sack, and impress Mom and Dad with how much cotton I could pick. My older sisters had been picking cotton since they were my age. But I wasn't convinced by their stories about how hard it was, and how I would be begging to lie under the cotton wagon.

I looped my strap around my shoulders, draped the loose sack over my back, and with half of it dragging on the ground behind me, I skipped ahead of the others to the field. I begged Dad to let me have a whole row to myself, telling him I wanted to prove how fast I was. "You go on up ahead of me and help me pick my row," Dad said, "and we'll see how good you do." Dragging my sack, I ran ahead of him until he was out of sight in the tall cotton, and started to pick—feeling sure I would have my half of the row picked before he reached the cotton wagon. Two hours later, I could see Dad's head bobbing up and down behind me, and I was hungry and dead tired. I felt like crying. I hadn't advanced ten feet, and there wasn't enough cotton in my sack to make even a small bulge.

Long before the end of the first picking season, I understood the words of warning from my older sisters—picking cotton was hard work. I longed for the shade of the house and the mesquite trees. Some days I would be too tired to work after our meal break, and Dad would let me lie under the cotton wagon. After a short rest, I'd get bored, grab my sack, and return to picking cotton.

When the first picking season was over, about the end of October, I was hoping for a rest. But the green boles left on the stalks from the first picking had blossomed like endless rows of cotton candy, and we were back in the fields the next day.

The cotton was picked for the second time. The days were brisk and the nights were cold. Some nights we would be chilled to the bone, all huddled together under our quilt on the floor to keep warm.

It wasn't long after cold weather set in that Grandma and my uncles packed up and left; they were moving to Dallas, where my uncles could find other jobs until spring. Waving my uncles and Grandma good-bye, sadness crept over me, and I was frightened, because Grandma was the one I clung to for love and security. In her quiet way, she always had an answer to my problems.

Soon after Grandma left, Dad became restless and decided to join Grandma in Dallas, where he said he would find a job, and then return for us. Mom was expecting another baby, but Dad promised to have us all in Dallas before the baby came. Early the next morning, he kissed Mom good-bye and allowed me to walk with him on the little dirt road until our house dipped from sight below the brown cotton stalks. "You get on back now," he said. "You have to be the man in the family, and look after your Mom until I return." I watched him until he was out of sight, before I whirled and raced back to the house.

———

I helped my sisters gather dead mesquite tree limbs for firewood, and played among the brown cotton stalks and the barren mesquite trees. Mom and my older sisters kept busy breaking limbs into small pieces to fit into our cook stove, cooking beans, making bread, and changing diapers.

After dinner, my Mom and older sister, Frances, would sit around the kitchen table by the light of a kerosene lantern, smoke cigarettes, and talk about the new baby coming into our family. All our lives Mary Lee and I had watched farm animals hump each other and stared with amazement as cows and sheep dropped babies from their behinds. We discussed all this at length when we heard about the new baby coming, but we still weren't completely certain where our new baby would come from, or how it came to be.

———

It wasn't long after the weather turned warm that Mom gathered us kids in a circle and told us she and Frances were going to town; they would bring back a new baby. Ola, Mary Lee, Pearl, and Deola would stay with the rest of us until they returned.

Even though I had never spent much time with Mom, I was lonely during the several days she was away. Mary Lee and I spent our days playing in the shade of Mesquite trees, or wandering in the fields, walking barefoot in the newly plowed ground. We inhaled the fresh, moldy dust created by the big green tractors that pulled strange-looking contraptions, and laughed with excitement watching birds swoop down into the dust clouds behind the tractors to pick up insects.

Mary Lee and I were teasing bugs under a mesquite tree, not far from the house, when we heard Ola calling our names, over the excited screams of the other kids. Running as fast we could, our hearts were pounding when we reached the house. Ola and Pearl were jumping up and down, yelling, "They're coming they're coming!" Straining my eyes, looking down the dirt road, I could see the heads of Mom and Frances bobbing in the heat waves. We all started to run at the same time. As we drew near, I could see Mom was wearing a big smile, and noticed Francis cuddling a white bundle.

The little hands protruding from the bundle jerked frantically as Frances pulled back a portion of the blanket to reveal a wrinkled, red-faced little creature. "This is your new baby brother, Bernard," Mom said, with a broader smile. Bernard didn't seem any different than Joe, whom I'd seen when Mom first brought him to the camp last year, and I reflected that Joe *still* didn't look like a real person. Our house was already full of kids, and I couldn't understand what all the excitement was about.

Dad returned about two weeks after Mom brought Bernard home. I was riding my stick-horse in the field, near the main road, when I spotted him scuffling down the little trail that led to our house. I ran to meet him. He was carrying a sack of groceries in one hand and a jug in the other. I hugged his leg, and I could smell alcohol on his soiled pants. Right away, I told him about Bernard. "Let's go see your new brother," Dad said, smiling.

I ran ahead of him to spread the good news. Mom and all the kids (who could walk or run) hurried to meet him. I stepped back and watched as they gathered around him—all talking at once. Lingering behind, I watched as they slowly walked toward the house. Dad had his arm around Mom. They laughed and swayed from side to side as they strolled ahead of me. I knew at least part of the swaying was caused by whatever was in the jug he carried. I hadn't missed him much, but, for now, it seemed okay that he was back.

FIVE

As time passed, Dad and Mom drank more and more. The more Dad drank the more vicious and brutal he became. Luckily, he was gone much of the time during the off seasons. I was always happy when he left, because when he was home, he and Mom drank, argued and beat the tar out of each other almost every night. This time was no different.

Late that night, when the fight broke out, Frances and Ola joined in, trying to protect Mom. Mary Lee and I ran to hide under the house.

While hiding down there in the dirt under the house we heard all the frightening screams of the younger kids and Mom and Dad cursing, yelling, and stomping their feet. "I'll kill you, you Bitch," Dad bellowed, and we covered our ears to muffle the maddening screams from Mom and my sisters. A loud thud on the floor, and Mom screamed, "You son of a bitch, you're killing Ola." This went on until we heard Mom and my sisters run out of the house, screaming and crying, leaving Dad to finish his drinking and nurse his own wounds.

We didn't go to school, and only the two oldest girls, Ola and Francis, were allowed to go with our parents on their Saturday afternoon shopping trips. Mom said we couldn't go to school, or even go to town, because the kids in town had flu and typhoid. We'd get sick and die if we played with other kids, Mom said. From the way she described them, I had nothing but fear and contempt for kids in town. In my mind's eye, I pictured them as sickly, hungry, and weak.

We didn't go to town or play with other kids, but we rarely went hungry when we were picking cotton. We literally ate our way up and down the cotton rows. For reasons I never understood, a few watermelon, carrot, cantaloupe, and other vegetable seeds, were planted with the cotton seeds, and they all matured about the same time. It was our favorite trick to lag behind, hide between the rows, and stuff ourselves with watermelons and cantaloupes.

———

Time passed as we moved from farm to farm. The days, months, and finally years faded into one another, and our lives revolved around the cotton fields. It had been almost three years since I'd seen Grandma. While town kids were going to school, getting sick, and dying, I was either hoeing cotton, picking cotton, or playing with my sisters in the barren cotton stalks—waiting for warm weather and another season of work.

Two more babies were born into the family (Tommy, and Mary Ann), and by the time I was nine-years old, our little shanty was bursting to the seams with kids.

SIX

My Mother's name was Clara (no middle name). Her maiden name was Mitchell. She was born in Muskogee, Oklahoma, in 1911. She was, at least, one-half Cherokee Indian, but could be more, as my grandmother swore that Grandpa was part Indian. As nearly as I could tell, Mom's only purpose in the family was to cook, work in the fields, sleep with my father, and have babies. The only clue that she had any rights or power in the family was that she fought back fiercely when physically attacked by my father.

Aside from her obvious black eyes, fat lips, and bruises dished out by Dad, Mom didn't seem to have a care in the world about her health, and she never missed a day in the field. She was about five-feet-four inches tall, small boned and petite, with high cheekbones, dark skin, and coal black hair. She always wore a flowered cotton dress, hand-sewn from flour sacks. Several times I overheard Dad telling Mom how pretty she was. Mom wasn't bashful, but seemed quiet, like my grandmother.

Mom wasn't good at discipline. She might fling a piece of firewood at me, or chase me for a short distance striking at my back with a cotton switch, but, unlike Dad, whipping me wasn't all she thought about. If I'd done something really bad, she'd usually grit her teeth and say, "Just wait 'til your dad gets home. He's gonna wear your ass out with a switch." Then she'd go on about what she was doing, and I'd hang around asking if I could help her with something. Sometimes that worked.

My father's name was John Andrew Boykin. He was born in Baytown, Texas, in 1898. I remember Grandma saying once or twice that Dad was Irish. And that's about all I know about his life before I was old enough for my memory to start kicking in. I remember him as being very tall, probably over six feet, raw-boned, broad-shouldered, and long-legged. With his tall frame, and lanky walk, he had a casual arrogance, and exaggerated command that helped conceal his true station in life. As I think back on him now, though, probably what you would notice first about him would be his large shock of dark red hair. On several occasions, I heard my grandma remark that Dad had a good education and was from a nice family. From her perspective, though, that could mean he finished the third grade, and none of his family were presently serving jail terms. Grandma said Dad had a good job as a welder, but was laid off when the Depression hit.

SEVEN

By the time I was eight-years old, I had eleven brothers and sisters. I was the oldest of six boys. There were two younger, and four older sisters. My brothers were: Tom, Bernard, Frank, Joe, and John. My sisters were: Frances, Ola, Pearl, Mary Lee, Deola, and Mary Ann.

The houses we lived in as a family of farm workers were clapboard shacks, with three rooms—two rooms for sleeping, and a small room for cooking and eating. The kitchen was very small, just big enough for a wood stove, a wooden table, and two benches. The floors were wooden with wide cracks between the boards and knotholes large enough for snakes to slither through. Mom and Dad slept in one room and us kids slept in the other.

Our household furnishings included a kitchen table, two benches, and a mattress for Mom and Dad. Our house was always tin roofed, bare wood, and usually located near the cotton fields. There was no grass around the houses, just a ring of packed dirt, and a packed clay path to the outhouse, which was usually the only distinguishing feature of the landscape.

In some ways our family was very structured, but only in the sense there were strict rules, and severe punishment for violations. Even the very youngest in the family knew the rules. All twelve of us kids slept in one room, huddled together on the floor, with a quilt under us, and whatever covers were necessary to keep warm. We were assigned our positions on the floor—big kids on one end, little kids on the other—and we knew better than to trade places. I was the oldest of the little kids, and I usually didn't wet the bed. But the hardest part was, even on a cold night, I couldn't snuggle with anyone for fear of getting soaked.

Every morning, about an hour before daylight, I could smell coffee brewing and cigarette smoke. All the kids were awake by this time. We could hear Mom and Dad talking, but we didn't dare whisper or make a sound until they had their coffee, cigarettes, and breakfast. Just before daybreak, Dad would come into our room and shout, "Y'all get up, now." Breakfast was always fried bread, karo syrup or molasses, and cornmeal mush.

After breakfast, Mom fixed lunch for the field—pinto beans, sometimes hominy, and more fried bread. Everything, except the bread, she poured into an empty molasses can, which one of us kids carried to the field.

———

We never did any work unless it was in a cotton field. We were either chopping cotton in early spring, or picking cotton in the fall. Depending on the season, when we started for the field on foot each morning we carried hoes or cotton sacks. All kids old enough to carry a hoe or a sack worked. The babies sat in the shade between two rows of cotton, under the cotton wagon, or in the shade of a tree, if there was one nearby.

When picking cotton, we arrived in the field each morning at the first light. Somehow, the boss knew exactly where to position the cotton wagon, because Dad and Mom's sack was always full when they reached that point. The manager, or owner, was in charge of the scales, which hung from the end of the trailer. Dad looped the straps over the hook on the bottom of the scales, and I'd stand back and watch the needle spin around like the hands on a large clock. The boss then recorded the weights in a small book wired to the wagon. After weighing, Dad shoved the cotton sack even higher to be emptied into the wagon. The empty sack was tossed back on the ground. After all the sacks were emptied, we selected another row and disappeared for another two or three hours.

When he was picking cotton, Dad's hands and arms moved in a mechanical-like motion, which reminded me of the wheels of a slow moving steam locomotive. After fastening the cotton strap around his shoulder, he rarely straightened up until his sack was full. Twelve hours of bending over pulling a sack weighing sixty pounds when full, and he never seemed tired at night, when the rest of us were dragging our feet toward the house at sundown.

Time stopped when we were in the cotton fields. The days dragged on, each yielding, ever so slowly to the next. We weren't allowed to express an opinion, but given a choice, I preferred to pick cotton over hoeing. I made it a game to hide from Dad in the tall cotton, and I could usually find watermelons growing in the rows. Also, picking cotton was made easier because Mary Lee and I always worked side-by-side, laughing and teasing when the others pulled ahead of us. Kids each pulled a nine-foot cotton sack. Mary Lee didn't have a quota, but Dad expected me to pick forty pounds a day.

I couldn't read, write, or do arithmetic, but I could do "cotton math." Had I been asked, I couldn't have explained how I arrived at the figures, but I knew, at one dollar a hundred, I was earning forty cents a day. Dad pulled a twelve-foot sack and, on a good day, he could pick five-hundred pounds of cotton. He'd never say anything as he weighed that last sack at the end of the day, but I could always tell by his mood if he'd reached his quota.

Usually, there were kids from other farm workers in the field. Most of the other families were white. There were some Negroes (Dad called them niggers), and a few Mexicans. Anyway, we weren't allowed to play with them.

Just before sundown we'd walk back to the house, sharpen our hoes, or mend cotton sacks before dark. Dad lit the kerosene lamp, gathered wood, and made coffee, while Mom fixed supper from pinto beans, potatoes, hominy, collard greens (or some other variety of greens) and fried bread. We rarely ate any meat unless it was pig's feet, hog jowls, or salt pork. Once in awhile Dad would steal a chicken, which Mom boiled and made dumplings.

Our sleep, eat, work routine never varied—except on Saturdays, when all work stopped at noon. If we were picking cotton, the foreman (or boss) pulled the cotton wagon into town with a tractor for delivery to the cotton gin. Mom, Dad, and my two older sisters, Frances and Ola, hitched a ride into town on the cotton wagon to buy food for the next week. If we were hoeing cotton, they walked or thumbed a ride into town. Knowing our fear of the dark, they'd say over and over, with a happy smile, "Don't worry we'll be home before sundown." But never once did they keep their promise. They said they'd bring hard candy, which made me feel a little better, but I knew (we all knew) that they wouldn't be home before dark, and it would just be another night of trying to keep the bogeyman out of the old house.

The last hour of sunlight you could find us (all the kids who could walk) tramping down the dirt road, away from the house, looking as far down the road as the eye could see. Huddled together, we'd stand there until nearly sundown, searching, searching for any sign of movement in the distance. Finally, the wailing and whimpering would begin and we'd trudge back to the shanty. I didn't wail and whimper-like the rest of the kids. Choking back tears of frustration, I'd curse loudly, stamp my feet, and damn Dad and Mom all to hell.

In the fading light, we'd barricade ourselves inside the little shack. I was just as scared as the rest, but I couldn't let on. I was the oldest and they were depending on me to protect them from getting killed or kidnapped by the bogeyman. There was no lock on the door. So the best I could do was light the kerosene lantern, put a bench against the door, try to keep everyone quiet, and stay awake and on guard until Mom and Dad returned.

It's just another Saturday night, my brothers and sisters are asleep, and I'm sitting on a lard can by the door holding a broken Mesquite branch, waiting for the bogeyman to show himself. Suddenly I hear voices from a distance. Dad is cursing and yelling at Mom. I shudder, because I know by the sound that he's drunk and in a bad way.

I remove the bench from the door, put out the lantern, crawl into bed, and pretend to be asleep. No one dares show signs of being awake. It isn't long before he starts pounding on Mom with his fists, and she grabs whatever she can to defend herself.

The fighting goes on for what seems like hours. With my eyes half-open, I see Mom bust a beer bottle over Dad's head then gouge him in the face with the broken end. Then there's blood everywhere.

The next morning I try not to look at either of them, but it's hard not to notice that Mom has a black eye, a fat lip, and bare spots on her head where hair should have been. Dad's face is still bloody, but I'm careful not to stare. They act like there hasn't been a fight at all, and I'm just glad it will be a whole week before it will happen all over again.

I had no reason to believe that one day would be different from the next. The cotton fields would always be there, and there was Saturday nights and the bogeyman to worry about. But, my life wasn't completely without excitement and adventure. One morning when, instead of awakening to bright, sunny skies, our house was covered with overcast clouds and fog. It looked as if it would rain any minute, but Dad didn't seem to notice. He ordered everyone to grab their hoes and go to the field.

It was only a short walk to the field, and, since it looked as if it would rain soon, Mom didn't take the lunch bucket, and Dad forgot to take the files used for sharpening the hoes. Shortly before noon, Dad called to me, "It ain't gonna rain today, so Dennis, you and Mary Lee get your butts back to the house and get our lunch…and bring the files."

We lit out toward the house at a fast clip, because that's what Dad expected us to do. When he was out of sight, Mary Lee looked at me and we both laughed, and slowed to a walk. This is just what we always did. Whatever he told us to do, we tried our best to do just the opposite.

By the time we reached the shack, it was raining buckets full. The rest of the family would be on their way to the house, but we were told to get the lunch and files, and return. We also knew, even though it was raining, he'd wear us both out with a cotton switch if we didn't meet them part way. It was still raining hard as we left the house, carrying our hoes and lunch bucket—

slipping and sliding in the Texas clay soil. Soon our bare feet and ankles were covered with mud.

Carrying the molasses bucket in my right hand and hoe in my left, I kept walking. Now and again I'd raise a foot and kick the mud from between my toes. I was carrying the hoe with the blade down when I gave a huge kick, hitting the top of my left foot, where the foot and ankle bends, on the blade of the hoe. The kick caused me to lose my balance, and I fell backwards into the mud. The lid on the molasses can flew open and the beans went every which way.

My ankle throbbed with pain, but I didn't cry; I was thinking about the licking from Dad when he saw the injured foot, muddy britches, and empty bean bucket. We continued to walk, hoping to soon meet up with the rest of the family. Mary Lee promised not to tell Dad about my foot and the spilled beans until we arrived back at the house. It wasn't long before we saw them coming.

I was limping and trying hard not to cry, but Dad didn't notice my foot until we were all inside the house. By then the rain had washed off most of the mud from my clothes; I had only to worry about a whipping because of the cut and spilled beans. I braced myself for a good one, especially when Mom showed him the empty bean bucket. But he didn't say a word about the beans and he didn't whip me.

Dad chewed Days Work tobacco and he could fix almost anything that happened to you with a wad of that stuff. I watched him as he took a chaw from his mouth, and packed the deep cut. Then he told me to hold my hand on it until the bleeding stopped. After several days, the wound healed, leaving only an ugly scar to remind me never to kick mud from between my toes.

It was hard to remember all the rules Dad set out for us to live by. He said if we'd just do what he said, we wouldn't get hurt so much, and he wouldn't have to wear us out with cotton switches all the time. I knew he was right and I really tried, most of the time. But it still wasn't easy for me to stay out of trouble.

Like, at one place, we lived within walking distance of another farm worker family. There were at least six boys in the family—all white kids and older than me. Sometimes on Saturday afternoons and rainy days, when we couldn't work, they'd come over and get me to play. I knew part of the reason they were at our house so often was to act crazy around my older sisters, but that didn't bother me any. We lived near a river, and one Saturday afternoon they asked me if I wanted to go swimming with them.

The river was wide and slow moving, with a dirty red color. We all stripped our clothes and waded into the shallow water. I'd never been swimming before; this was the most fun I had ever had. Being accepted by the older boys just added to my enjoyment.

After a time of playing in the shallow water, one of the boys noticed a tree that had come loose from its roots and fallen across the river. Soon they were all performing a circus act, walking out on the fallen tree, diving into the deep part of the river, and swimming to the shore. I was scared, but I didn't want them to think I was a chicken, so I followed them out on the tree limb. I'd never been in water over my head before, and the fact that I couldn't swim didn't cross my mind, not until I fell off the limb into the deepest part of the river.

I hadn't gone under more than once or twice until I felt myself being dragged to the shore by two of my friends. I'd swallowed a lot of muddy water, and was coughing and having a hard time breathing. But that wasn't the worst part of it. I thought I was either dead or would be soon, because they were all excited and ready to cry and calling to each other to do something or what would they tell my dad.

EIGHT

After Grandma and my uncles left Childress, I didn't see them
again for three years—I was nine-years old. It was near sunset on
a Saturday afternoon. Dad, Mom, and my sisters, Ola and
Frances, had ridden the cotton wagon into town. Pearl and Mary
Lee were helping me make plans to keep the bogeyman away
when we heard a car rumbling toward our house. As it grew
nearer, I recognized Uncle Marvin behind the wheel. He braked
to a stop in front of our shanty and jumped out with a wide grin.
After teasing us for quite awhile, saying he had the wrong place,
because we didn't look like any Boykin kids he knew, he finally
said, "Mom and I saw your folks in town. We're working on a
farm not far from here. Mom said I could come out and see you,
but I have to go back before dark."

The sunlight was fading and the mesquite trees were already
casting their frightening shadows when Uncle Marvin said he
had to leave. I clung to his pants and begged him to stay.
"Mom's waiting for me," he said, "but I promise to find your
Dad and tell him to come home before dark." Uncle Marvin
would keep his promise, but that still didn't leave me much hope.

Uncle Marvin left and we hurriedly prepared for the
terrifying darkness and the double threat of an approaching
thunderstorm on the near horizon.

After a long night of drinking and fighting, Mom and Dad
didn't get up at their usual time. Mary Lee and I were up early
and sneaked out of the house to keep our eyes on the road.
Grandma would be coming for a visit and Mary Lee and I were
going to be the first to beg to live with her.

Grandma wasn't a busy-body, but she had a scornful,
concerned look about her that would cause a biting dog to tuck
its tail and run. And she could tell with a quick glance how
things were in the family. Dad was scared of Grandma. I could

tell, because he always faked good behavior when she was around.

Mary Lee and I had played on the road, far from our house, since early morning. It's almost noon now, and we are about ready to give up hope, when we see a dust cloud in the distance. Then, the old Ford suddenly pops over the hill.

I wanted to be the first to soften Grandma up for the big question, and I was hugging her before she could even get out of the car. You had to look closely at Grandma to tell if she was happy or sad. That day I knew she was happy because she looked at me with one of her rare thin-lipped smiles.

Grandma was full-blooded Cherokee Indian. Her birth date would be about 1885. She had a very slender, willowy, gaunt frame, high cheekbones and a sad face. Her skin had a dark brown, scorched look to it. Her married name was Mitchell, and although, she remarried at least four times after my grandfather died (or ran away) she never changed her last name. She confessed to me of not having any schooling and she could neither read nor write. Her long, black hair was always pulled back and tied with a string. She had a firm set to her mouth and a permanent sadness in her eyes—as if she had gone too many years without something to smile or be joyful about. With Grandma, there were no pretenses, everything was either black or white, and her word in the family was law.

Grandma's face reminded me of weathered rawhide, which I'd seen lots of times on cows lying dead in the fields. I never once saw Grandma laugh, but she often cracked a thin smile when something touched her funny bone. She always wore the same cotton dress, hand-sewn from flour sacks. She dipped Garrett snuff, packed a .38 Special in her purse, and kept a cotton switch in every corner of the house. As scary as she looked, her heart was pure gold. I was happier living with her than any place in the world.

I was convinced if anyone messed with Grandma they wouldn't live to tell about it. She was my hero. She didn't talk much, and one day I asked Uncle Marvin about that and he said she had strong silence. And I wasn't sure what that meant until later. Even my dad kept his mouth shut around Grandma. She never used a switch on me and neither did Dad when she was around.

It must have been hard for Grandma, because she was superstitious about just about everything. She would sit patiently for as long as necessary for someone else to cross the path of a black cat. She did not own a mirror and she would not allow anyone to bring one into the house for fear it would get broken and give her seven years of bad luck.

Grandma had four boys: Marvin, Melvin, Fred and Eugene—all schooled by whatever they learned in the cotton field. My uncles were all tall, square-jawed, broad-shouldered guys, and of a good nature—always laughing and cutting up. Marvin was the youngest. Fred and Melvin each had little kids. They either all lived in one household or two migrant houses located close together.

Grandma did the cooking, and everybody ate at one table in her house.

All the boys worked and Grandma kept all the money. Every Saturday, about noon, the boss would come to Grandma and hand her a fistful of bills. Grandma would reach down into her dress where her breasts once were, drag out a roll of bills, untie the string around them and add the new ones.

Grandma always had a man, but I didn't know my real Grandfather. His name was Ben Mitchell. Since he wasn't around, I just figured he was dead, but I never knew for sure. She said he was part Indian and a good man. Grandma never had a problem finding a husband, though. She had been married, and outlived (or chased off) three husbands. They all died (or ran away) very young, and I never heard her say why.

———

In the Mitchell family, none of the wives worked in the field. When our family was working the same farm, I usually lived with Grandma and picked cotton or hoed with my uncles. They shared their lunch with me, told dirty jokes, and didn't care how much I goofed off.

I was nine-years old and living with Grandma. It was a cold frosty morning. I was pulling a sack in a row next to Uncle Marvin. I looked back as my cotton sack was rolling over what looked like a large log. I was slightly ahead of Uncle Marvin, and about the time I noticed the rolling object, Uncle Marvin jumped and yelled. My sack was rolling over the largest Diamond Back rattler I had ever seen. It was easy as big as a fence post. His belly was big and bulgy in places, as if he had swallowed something whole. I guessed he had slithered across the row, right on my heels, and I pulled the sack over him. Uncle Marvin said the snake would have bitten me, anyway, if it hadn't been cold and full of rabbits.

Eating with grandma at her communal table was always an exciting experience. The families ate at a long wooden table with benches for seating. Grandma sat at the head of the table and served herself first, the women and small children were served next. Then it was every man for himself. Grandma never said a word over all the laughing, commotion, and grabbing for the last few biscuits.

Grandma always cooked chicken and dumplings for Sunday dinner. We'd just be finishing supper, on a Saturday night, when Grandma would turn to Uncle Marvin, and say "Marvin, we need two chickens for tomorrow." Uncle Marvin would get up grinning, and motion for me to follow him out the door. Aside from his other responsibilities of stealing gasoline, tires, batteries, and other items to keep their old black Ford running, he was assigned the task of stealing the chickens for Sunday dinner.

Uncle Marvin was the best chicken thief in the family. I was excited to learn everything and make Grandma proud. Uncle Marvin was a good teacher, and it wasn't long before I could have easily got the chickens myself. We would case a neighbor's chicken coop before making our move. We'd walk right up to the door, and if someone came out, it was a lost dog we were looking for. Uncle Marvin said we needed to know the best approach to the chicken house, how many and what kind of dogs were around, how far the chickens were from the main house and if the people in the house were too old to chase after us. If everything looked safe, we would simply approach the chicken house from the back way, grab two chickens by the neck and run.

So I thought stealing chickens would always be a cinch. But it wasn't, as I learned early on in my training. We scouted the farm, just like we had done all the other times. We were lying low, just watching for any movement about the place, when we saw a car leave the main house, which was clearly a sign that we had it all to ourselves. Always before, Uncle Marvin had grabbed the chickens by the neck to keep them from squaking, and that's why I was surprised when he lifted two hens off the roost by their legs. It wasn't long after the hens started flapping and carrying on that I heard the sound of running feet, then a shotgun blast. Uncle Marvin dropped the chickens, grabbed me by the hand, and, half-dragging me, we ran for the woods. Several more shots rang out behind us. We made it through the woods and back to our house. That night we stole chickens from the farmer employer.

We didn't tell grandma about our close call with buckshot. Uncle Marvin said it would for sure bring on a scolding for being so careless. Grandma didn't want us to feel any guilt about stealing, though. I knew that, because she reminded us more than once: "It ain't no crime to steal from white people 'cause they've stole from us Indians for a hundred years, or more."

I never lacked for excitement while hanging out with Uncle Marvin. Sometimes, in the back of my mind, I could feel the danger, before it all went down, as surely as I could feel my breath quicken, but I never once thought about stopping it—like the day Uncle Marvin asked me if I wanted to drive the truck on the main road. I was nine year old and could barely see over the dash, which told me something right there—the thing in the back of my mind.

It was a hot summer day. Uncle Marvin and I were returning to the house to get the crew some lunch and more water, just cruising along in the farmer's old red pickup. Uncle Marvin was doing the shifting and I was doing a good job of keeping it on the road until we came to a downhill grade—then I punched it. Uncle Marvin had allowed me to steer the pickup on the field roads several times; it seemed so easy. But I wasn't prepared for this. I couldn't even *reach* the brakes, and in seconds, I knew I was over my head. There was no time to think, or even wonder what Uncle Marvin was thinking or doing. I had already over-corrected and we were barreling toward a barbed-wire fence, and the little pond just beyond. I ducked under the wheel, and I could hear Uncle Marvin laughing as the pickup came to a sloshing halt. I didn't know why Uncle Marvin was laughing because, even without looking, I knew the truck was buried to the axles in mud and water.

Uncle Fred was following us on a tractor. We weren't far from the house and, after looking the situation over, he continued on to the house and brought back a chain. The tractor easily pulled the pickup back onto the road. We didn't want the farmer to know, and for a while it looked as if we were safe. The farmer pulled up in another vehicle while we were still scraping the mud from the pickup. I saw the storm coming, and I went over to stand close to Uncle Marvin.

He was a big man, wearing bib overalls that bulged at the waist. He had a huge head, bushy eyebrows and a big nose, partially shaded by a floppy straw hat. As he stepped out of his truck he turned directly to me and shouted, with a voice that sounded more like a growl, "Hey, dumbhead, did you wreck my pickup?" He was standing almost on top of me, and I could smell his horrible body odor. My eyes were level with his belly, and I was afraid to say anything. "You stupid asshole, did you let this dumbhead drive my pickup?" The farmer shouted, looking at Uncle Marvin.

Uncle Marvin had a quick temper. I could almost see the hairs bristle on the back of his neck as he stepped between the farmer and me. I didn't say anything, but I was praying Uncle Marvin would slug him. "I was driving the pickup and letting Dennis steer," Uncle Marvin said. "And don't you talk to him like that again, and don't you ever call me a stupid asshole again."

At that moment I was glad Uncle Marvin and I had been stealing his chickens. Uncle Marvin returned to the pickup and continued scraping mud. Without another word, the farmer got in his pickup and spun off. I never forgave him for calling me a 'dumbhead,' and from that day forward, Grandma was never without farm-fresh eggs.

NINE

We usually stayed on the same farm from planting time through the harvest. After the cotton was weeded in the spring, Dad sometimes left to find work elsewhere until cotton-picking time.

It was during one of his work trips that I acquired my first dog. We had never had a family pet. One afternoon a Negro man drove into our yard in a beat-up old Ford truck, with a broken windshield and one fender dangling. He got out of the truck with a jug in each hand. In the back of his truck were two full-grown greyhound dogs. I was playing in the yard. He walked toward me with a big smile. "Is your Daddy home?" He asked.

"Dad ain't home, but Mom's in the house," I said. He kept smiling and continued walking toward the house.

My attention immediately turned to the dogs. I ran to the house and asked him if I could play with them. "Why sure," he said, with a little chuckle.

After talking to Mom, the Negro man returned to his truck and watched me play with the dogs for a long time. "How would you like a puppy?" he asked.

"Can I really have one?"

The man laughed. "Boy, I got a puppy about your size. If your momma says it's okay, I'll bring her right on over."

Mom was sitting on the bench, rolling a cigarette. I was out of breath as I explained the puppy offer. She lit her cigarette, blew a puff of smoke to the side, and gave me a fierce look. "Ain't we got enough mouths to feed without you bringing in a damned dog?" She turned away from me and sipped once on something in a tin cup.

I wanted that dog worse than anything in the whole world. I wasn't giving up. The worst she could do was switch me a little, and threaten to tell Dad when he got home. "He can have part of my food, and the Negro man said she can catch rabbits. Please,

Mom." I just stood there and watched her, with her cigarette in one hand and the cup in the other, puffing and sipping, as if she were all alone in the house.

I didn't move, except to shuffle my feet a little. Finally, without looking my way, she said, "Keep the damn dog, but you know your daddy's gonna have something to say when he gets home."

The minutes dragged like hours until the Negro man returned with my puppy. It was white, with tan markings on the chest, and strips of tan on the legs; the most beautiful dog I had ever seen. I immediately wanted to hold the skinny Greyhound that was choking, and straining at its lease. "She's four months old and pretty wild," the black man said. "Just keep her tied up and be good to her, and she'll start likin' you."

The black man walked to his pickup, then turned and looked back. "Her name is Queenie. My name is Josh," he said, wrestling with the door handle on the old truck.

Mom wasn't pleased about having another mouth to feed and told me so after Josh left. We all agreed to give her some of our portions, but I let them know Queenie was *my* dog. It was only a few days until Queenie and I were inseparable, eating out of the same plate, taking naps under the house, and roaming the fields in search of rabbits.

Josh came by often to check on Queenie. Sometimes we'd sit on his truck bed, legs dangling, and talk. He said his dogs were used to catch rabbits; they helped feed the family. I could feel myself smiling, picturing me and Queenie bringing home our first rabbit.

———

About three months later, Dad returned from his outside work trip. Queenie and I met him as he walked up the lane from the main road. He smiled when he saw Queenie. "Whose dog is that?" he asked. I told him the story about the Negro man giving me Queenie, and that he had moonshine when he came to our house.

"I know Josh," Dad said. "You can keep the dog….for now."

The cotton was ready to pick. It was work time again for all of us. Queenie had grown to almost adult size. She had already chased several rabbits, but it was disappointing to watch her. She was always so far behind it didn't make any difference, and the rabbits seemed to be teasing her.

Queenie followed me to the field and walked beside me all day, while I pulled my cotton sack up and down the rows. At noon I shared my lunch with her. Sometimes she would get hot and exhausted and lie down under the cotton wagon for an hour or two, then wander back to me and follow along until she was hot and tired again. Saturday afternoon, when Mom and Dad left for town, Queenie and all of us kids hunted rabbits. She was a disappointing failure, but we didn't give up on her. Queenie rarely barked at anything, but I just dared the bogeyman to come around when Mom and Dad were gone.

Josh visited our house several times during the cotton season. He and Dad sat on the bed of Josh's old truck, drinking moonshine, and talking. Mom didn't drink much moonshine; Josh always remembered to bring a separate pail of home brew for her. I was envious of Dad's time with Josh because I wanted to tell him about Queenie and hear about his rabbit hunting trips.

We finished picking cotton some time in December, and that's when Dad decided to leave us again and look for work off the farm. I was glad to see him go. I had Queenie, and I didn't care where he went. She had grown and learned from our Saturday hunts, and I was sure she would provide all the rabbits we needed while Dad was gone.

Josh visited our house a day or two after Dad left. I had developed a special feeling toward this scrawny black man, and I was thrilled to see him again. Now we could be together without interference from Dad. With him were two little kids, about three or four years old, his two greyhounds, and another dog that I hadn't seen before. It was smaller than his other dogs and definitely not a greyhound. His color was mixed red, brown, black and white and I could tell he wasn't full-grown. Josh said the dog wandered into his yard. He was going to try him at rabbit hunting with his other dogs.

I was just standing there staring at the new dog when Josh asked me if I could bring Queenie on the hunting trip. I guess he could tell by the look on my face, because before I cold even answer, he started toward the house. I knew this meant he was going to deal with Mom himself.

When Josh came back, he sat his two little kids in the shade under the truck. He told them not to leave and called for the dogs.

We jumped our first rabbit and Queenie proved she could run—not as fast as his dogs, but not far behind. The new dog ran behind Queenie by some distance, and seemed to enjoy the chase. The dogs caught two jackrabbits, and Josh gave one of them to Mom.

Josh was talking to Mom when I heard him say, "That new dog ain't no good to me. Maybe Dennis can keep him and train him to be a rabbit dog. Queenie will be a better dog with another dog to run with."

Josh could see I'd heard their conversation. "He ain't got a name," he said, turning to me with a big grin. I wanted to grab Josh around the waist and hug him, but, instead, I grabbed the no-name dog, hugged him and laid my face on his back.

For the next four or five months I lived in a fantasy world with Queenie and my new dog, Red; my life revolved around them. Red wasn't as fast as Queenie, but he was more ferocious when the catch was on the ground. Even during bad weather, I didn't spend much time inside the house; I wasn't comfortable any more unless I could be with Queenie and Red. After everyone was asleep, I would sneak out of the house and stretch out between the two hounds. If I stayed warm, I would sleep there all night.

———

Dad arrived back from his work trip driving a crumbling old Ford flatbed truck. "I found a new place for us to live," Dad said, talking to Mom and sipping moonshine from a tin cup. "We'll move tomorrow," I heard him say.

I didn't ask any questions, but I pictured a place where my dogs and I could run through the fields and hunt rabbits. I really didn't care where the new place was or what it looked like. I had Queenie and Red, and I knew they didn't care either, as long as I was there. I thought about my friend, Josh, and several times I was on the verge of asking Dad if Josh knew we were leaving.

It was after all our things were loaded and Dad gave the order for everyone to "get on," that I learned that Queenie and Red were not going with us. I was lifting Queenie onto the truck when Dad grabbed my shoulder. "There's no room for the dogs at our new place," he said. "We'll leave them here and they'll find a new home."

At that moment, I didn't care how much Dad beat me. I ran around the yard crying and screaming. He grabbed me, threw me onto the truck and ordered my sister, Frances, to hold me down. I don't know how long I screamed and flailed my arms. I wanted to jump off the truck, but I couldn't escape her grip. The truck was slow and Queenie and Red chased us for at least a mile before I lost sight of them in the dust.

After losing Queenie and Red my life became a painful void. Life had never been this bad, and I didn't think it could get any worse. Our new place was no different than any of our other houses—a rundown shack with three rooms and an outhouse. The only difference being, this was the beginning of the end of my world as I had known it for ten years.

Dad and Mom went to town for their usual Saturday afternoon shopping and drinking spree. They returned late that night. With them was a man about Dad's age. The next morning, listening to their conversation while they drank coffee, I understood them to say this stranger would be living with us and working the fields.

Some time later, I learned the new member in our household was Bob Muse. Muse didn't look much different than any other drunk I'd ever seen: medium build and height, slope-shouldered, pale pasty complexion, as if this was his first time in direct sunlight. At first glance though, I could tell he wasn't from the country. His clothes were definitely store-bought and not worn or dirty from field work.

For the next three weeks after Muse's arrival, he was always near Mom—and he didn't work much. In the field, he pulled an empty cotton sack in the row next to Mom while they talked and laughed. I watched them closely and became suspicious, without knowing what I was suspicious of. I didn't understand what they were doing, but I sensed it was wrong, and it scared me. He never once looked at me, or any of my younger brothers and sisters.

Muse kept Dad out of the field by supplying him with all the moonshine he could drink. The only time I saw my dad was when we came home after work, and before leaving for work at dawn. He would be falling-down drunk at night and too groggy and bleary-eyed to recognize anyone the next morning.

The showdown came on a Saturday night, about a month later. They all went to town Saturday afternoon. I was still awake, late that night, when I heard them coming down the road that led to our house. The cursing and name-calling was louder than usual. I could sense something big was going to happen.

Their quarreling continued after they came into the house. Over the maddening noise, I heard Muse call Dad a son of a bitch. The words were barely out of Muse's mouth, when Dad swung a powerful punch, striking him in the face. Muse fell against the wall with such force it shook the whole house. Muse slid to the floor, covered his face, and begged for mercy. Dad ignored his screams and kept hitting and kicking him until he was silent—and motionless. Bob Muse lay in a heap, with his blood spilled everywhere. Then Dad turned on Mom until she ran out the door into the darkness.

Dad dragged Muse out the door, leaving a trail of blood. Coming back into the house, he grabbed his jug and drank himself into a stupor.

When I woke the next morning, Dad was still sleeping. Bob Muse, Mom, my three older sisters, Ola, Pearl, and Frances were gone. I never learned what happened to my sisters, and I never saw them again.

TEN

Dad rose from his sleep a few hours after sunrise. He didn't look good, even worse than usual. After making coffee, and staggering around the wrecked house for a while, he tried to fix something for us to eat. Later that morning, without saying a word, he walked off, down the dirt road that led away from our house. He returned about dark that same day. The next few days were a repeat of the first day. He always left first thing in the morning and returned in the early evening. I didn't see him drink any moonshine during this time.

My brother, Tommy, was the youngest—about two years old—still in diapers. Mary Lee was one year older than me, but Dad left me in charge. It took both Mary Lee and I to change Tommy's diapers, but she refused to help me wash out the shitty ones. He only had one diaper, and while it dried, he ran around the yard or played in the dirt under the house, crying, either from hunger or his raw bottom. There wasn't much to eat in the house except beans and flour. Neither of us knew what to do with the flour, but, once a day, I chopped wood, made a fire and cooked beans for everyone. Mary Lee mashed the beans for Tommy. He ate them with his hands, leaving a good portion on his face.

It wasn't many days after Mom left that I heard Dad say, more to himself than anyone else, "We're leaving today." Carrying Tommy in his arms, and the rest of us following, we walked down the road. He didn't say where we were going. When we were on the main road we caught a ride, and, through a succession of rides, we ended up in Bethany, Oklahoma, early that evening. Bethany was a small town, not far from Oklahoma City. We went directly to St. Joseph Orphanage, where he left all the kids for the night, except me.

Dad and I spent the night in a mission and returned to the orphanage the next morning. A Nun met us at the door. She said something to Dad, then we all walked down a long hallway before she stopped, and lightly tapped on a tall door. They were all there, except Tommy, sitting quietly at a long table, watched over by another Nun. Dad told me to stay with the others and left the room with one of the Nuns. After awhile, Dad returned with a Priest. "You'll be going with me," Dad said. "The others will stay here until I can find a job." We walked to the outside gate, Dad still holding my hand, my brothers and sisters following, with a nun by their side. The nun closed the gate behind us. I could hear the others whimpering and crying behind me, but I didn't look back.

_____

Dad and I hitched a ride to Oklahoma City, where we bummed a meal and a bed at the Salvation Army. The next morning we were on the highway. By late afternoon we were in a small town some place in Oklahoma—tired and hungry. He bought lunch meat, a loaf of bread, some bone scraps from the butcher, and asked the storekeeper for some empty cardboard boxes.

We left town with our food and empty boxes and followed a railroad track until coming to a bridge over a small creek. It was getting dark when we joined several other men under the bridge. They had a fire going and something boiling in a pot. One of the men told me they were cooking hobo stew. He said everyone was expected to throw something into the pot if they wanted to share in the meal. After some small talk, Dad threw our butcher bones into the stew pot, then they all settled back and passed a jug around. Later, we ate our bread and lunch meat—sharing some with the others. I ate some stew from a can loaned to me by one of the hobos.

Dad and I each had part of a cardboard box to lie on and one for covering, but I thought I would freeze before I felt the warm rays of the sun strike me the next morning. After they all drank some coffee brewed in the same pot as the evening stew, we caught a slow moving freight train. This was my first experience riding the rails, and I was excited. The train was moving very slowly. With help from another man, Dad threw me into an empty boxcar, and then all the others jumped on.

We arrived back in Oklahoma City after dark that evening. Why we returned to the place we had left the day before I didn't know, and I didn't really care. Again, we stayed at the Salvation Army for the night. The next morning they fed us mush, and Dad left me there for the day. Returning that evening, the pastor gave Dad some money and he rented a room at a hotel. The hotel desk was on the second floor of a wooden building. As we climbed the steps to the office, Dad held my hand, guiding me over and around several bums, clutching bottles, or sleeping on the stairs.

Our hotel room smelled of stale cigarette smoke. It was gloomy and dark, with one bed, a dresser and a washbasin.

The next morning, I was still in bed, and Dad had one hand on the doorknob when he told me that he was going to work. He'd be back before dark. He smiled. "There's a bathroom down the hallway, but don't leave the hotel."

Every day Dad returned to the hotel about the same time. He'd be carrying a paper sack with bologna, a loaf of bread, and, sometimes, an RC cola as a treat.

———

It was Friday night. I was getting anxious because my stomach was telling me Dad should have been home long before now. Hours later I finally admitted to myself what I'd known all along: Dad had received his first paycheck from his new job and he was in a bar getting drunk.

I was asleep, with the door locked, when I heard a loud banging. I opened the door and stared up at a pair of cold eyes, full of rage. Without warning, he grabbed me by the hair with one hand, slugging me in the face with the other. By the hair of my head, he threw me against the wall, nearly knocking me unconscious. I slid to the floor before he grabbed me by the hair again, throwing me against the other wall. I wanted to scream and yell, but I was too scared. In a whimper, I kept saying, "Please, I didn't do anything." After beating me on my head and body with his fists until he was exhausted, he picked me up by the hair and threw me on the floor, where he left me.

I was still on the floor the next morning, when I heard him stir. On his way out, he told me not to leave the room, not even to use the bathroom down the hall.

After he left, I looked for a mirror. I didn't find one, so I couldn't see my face, but my body was covered with black and blue marks and bruises. He didn't bring the usual bologna and bread meal home with him last night, and I was getting hungry and thirsty.

Since he forbade me to use the bathroom, I made do with the washbasin and threw the contents out the window. It occurred to me that some people on the street might be getting a bath, or worse, but I didn't aim the stuff at anybody.

When darkness came I lay in bed without sleeping, not knowing what to expect. Dad returned late in the night, his breath reeked with booze, and again he beat me until all I could see was red stars, spirals and explosions. Through it all, I could hear his labored breathing and wondered if he would ever stop. "Stop crying, you little bastard," he'd shout, and I choked it all back. When he grew tired from pounding on me, he threw me on the floor, which had become my permanent bed.

The next morning I nervously ate the bologna he had left on the dresser and drank some water.

I didn't know how many days or weeks we had lived in the hotel room, because after awhile I was past feeling or thinking any real thoughts, but the routine never changed. My legs and arms were a combination of yellow and brown—dark rings of purple bruises, faded on top of fresh rings of blue bruises.

The door was always unlocked, but he had told me not to leave the room. I constantly thought about running away, but where? I didn't have any money, I didn't even know where I was, and I was terrified that the cops might find me and return me to Dad. Then he'd kill me for sure after causing him so much trouble.

I could see glimpses of his face while he beat me, and it reminded me of the way Dad once told me to identify a mad dog: red eyes and frothing at the mouth. He yelled and cursed while beating on me, saying things like: "You caused all of this." As time went by, I started blaming myself for his punishment and believed I was the reason Mom left and the sole cause of all of his miseries. After that, I quit blaming him so much, but none of this kept me from being scared all the time.

The beatings stopped a few days before we left the hotel. The first night, I quietly lay awake on the floor all night, wondering if he would awaken and remember that he hadn't beaten me. For the next few days, I slept during the day and stayed awake all night.

It was during our stay at the hotel that I had my first horrible dream—a nightmare more terrifying than I could ever conjure up in a conscious state: I feel something touch me. I open my eyes to see a Glob—a mass of something—with arms and legs of screaming children protruding from its slimy, lumpy, ball-like bulk. It has no arms or legs of its own. It moves by rolling its lumpy self over and over—arms and legs of children flailing. It starts to chase me. I run, but there is no place to go or hide. I curl up in a ball and scream. This slime-ball creature doesn't catch me, but there's not a doubt in my mind that it will be waiting for me when I sleep again.

It was a cold, windy morning, a few days after my last beating, when we stepped out of the hotel and onto the street. The sun was shining and it felt good just to be outside in the fresh air, and away from the stillness of the smelly air of the hotel room. The black and blue parts of my body had turned to yellow blotches, and most of my pain was gone. Waiting for a traffic light, he bent down with his face close to mine, gave me a cold stare, and said, "We're gonna hitchhike out of here." He put a hand on my shoulder and gave it a good shake. "I wore your ass out back there because you earned it, but you better not be shooting off your damn mouth about it. And don't be rolling up your sleeves when we catch a ride…or else."

We caught several rides that day. By nightfall we were in Amarillo, Texas. Neither Dad nor I had a coat, and we were both shivering in the cold, chilly air. Dad stopped several men on the street, asking about the location of a mission. Finally, one pointed in the direction we were walking, and said some words that I didn't understand. Soon we were warm and cozy inside a Salvation Army building, where we received a meal and a cot for the night. The next morning they served us pancakes with syrup. I ate the serving offered to me and finished off a plate of pancakes left by a man sitting next to me.

Before leaving the mission, they fit each of us with a winter coat.

Dad stepped more lively than usual when we left the mission. He seemed to be in a cheerful mood. I was suspicious, but thought it was probably because of a good night's sleep or the pancake breakfast. "We're going to Houston to visit my sister," he said, as we neared the outskirts of town. "She lives in a nice house and we will be staying with her for a while."

ELEVEN

I didn't know Dad had a sister. No one ever said anything about his side of the family, and it never occurred to me that he could be related to *anyone*. But going to a real home was good news to me; the thought of any place but another hotel room brightened my day. After a series of rides, we arrived in Dallas before sundown. That night we stayed in another Salvation Army mission house.

Early the next morning, a middle-aged couple gave us a ride. Luck was on our side; their destination was Houston. They bought us a meal at a little café, and we arrived in Houston before dark. At a truck stop on the outskirts of Houston, Dad made a phone call.

We waited at the truck stop over an hour before a car pulled up to the curb. Dad immediately walked over and shook hands with a man about his age. We were driving through a nice neighborhood when the man pulled over in front of a house with a white picket fence. A woman met us halfway to the house. She hugged my dad and then looked at me. "This is your Aunt Ola," Dad said. She pulled me into her large body and buried my head deep into her huge stomach. It occurred to me that I might smother before she released me. She held me at arms-length, smiled broadly, and looked me over good. "Well, I'll bet you're hungry," she said, guiding me toward the house with one huge arm around my shoulders.

Aunt Ola wore a long, blue apron over a yellow, flowered, cotton dress, which probably made her look bigger than she really was. The man who picked us up at the truck stop was a skinny little man, about half the size of Aunt Ola. No one said it, but I guessed him to be her husband.

Dad seemed restless around Aunt Ola. He left the house right after breakfast and didn't return until almost dark. He hadn't been drinking and I suspected it was because Aunt Ola didn't approve of alcohol.

Although there were only four of us to feed, Aunt Ola seemed always to be cooking something. I delighted in watching her bake cookies. Her arms were as large as a man's, and when she pounded out cookie dough the whole kitchen shook. Her cooking habits suited me just fine, because I was always hungry. I followed her around the kitchen listening to her constant chatter. She never talked about Mom or my brothers and sisters, and I got the strange feeling she knew everything, but probably very little of the truth. She talked about Dad some, but I didn't understand much of what she said. The only part of her monologue that registered with me at all is that Dad was raised in Houston, where he went to school and had a good job before leaving.

The three of them talked throughout our evening meals, but I stopped trying to understand anything they said. And that's because no one ever mentioned Mom, or my brothers and sisters. It was like they didn't exist.

I had no special feelings for Aunt Ola, or anyone for that matter. My terror from the hotel room was still with me; an angel couldn't have won me over. But Aunt Ola always made me feel loved and wanted. She didn't talk about her family, and I felt a little sad for her, thinking that Dad was probably her only relative.

We had stayed with Aunt Ola about a week when things turned for the worst. I was asleep in the bed shared with my dad when awakened by loud sounds from another room. The whole house vibrated with booming voices—everyone talking at the same time. I couldn't understand much of what was being said, but, I understood enough to know that we would be leaving come morning. I moved as close to the wall as I could and wished with all my heart I was somewhere else.

Aunt Ola hugged me good-bye before she opened my car door. Without saying anything to Dad, she walked briskly back to the house and slammed the door. The little man they called Paul drove us back to the truck stop where he had met us a week earlier. They shook hands and Paul drove away. Dad and I went into the truck stop café, where he had coffee and I had milk and donuts.

It was easy to tell that Dad was in a bad mood. His jaw was set, and his head thrust forward. I was sure it was because Aunt Ola had thrown him out of the house when she'd caught him drinking. But that didn't surprise me any, because every bad thing that had ever happened in my life had been caused by Dad's drinking.

We finished our coffee and donuts and walked out into the sunshine. The weather was warm, and I was thankful, because I'd left my coat at Aunt Ola's. I followed closely, as Dad slowly walked on the roadside, jerking his thumb at passing cars. He did this for quite awhile, until a man in a pickup truck stopped to give us a ride. Our driver was another skinny little man, with several days growth of whiskers, and an unwashed look about him. Dad bummed a cigarette. They smoked, carried on a steady conversation, and acted as if they had known each other for a long time.

I was about half-asleep when the driver wheeled the pickup into a dirt driveway. A bird of a woman met us in the yard, with a cigarette dangling between her lips. She was barefoot and her legs were as skinny as twigs. Following her were three, dirty, potbellied little kids with nothing on but their sagging diapers. The woman gave her husband a kiss, and he introduced her to Dad. "I'll bet yawl'r hungry," she said. The woman smiled down at me with two teeth showing, one on each side of her upper gum. She disappeared into a tumble-down little house with the screen door dangling from the hinges and soon emerged carrying a loaf of bread, mustard and a package of bologna.

After eating a bologna sandwich, Dad left me with the woman and her kids and drove off with the man. They weren't gone long until returning with a case of beer and a sack of groceries. Throughout the afternoon and into the night, the three of them sat on benches at a wooden table, drinking beer and talking. The woman left the table only long enough to make more sandwiches, change diapers, and yell at her kids to stay in bed.

I was sitting in the dirt, leaning against the house, dozing off, when I felt a foot tapping my leg. The skinny man was standing over me. "Hey kid, if you're sleepy you can crawl in my pickup and take a nap," the man said, pointing his beer hand toward the truck.

I stared up at him and thought about that for a minute. I had to sleep *some* place. But since the hotel room I had been having my nightmare almost every night, and the thought of sleeping alone made me break out in a cold sweat. I crawled in the pickup—just for a place to rest—determined to stay awake.

The next thing I know, Dad is horsing me along on his hip, with one arm around my waist. I was kicking and screaming—not yet awake—with the Blob still chasing me. I must've been running pretty fast because I was surprised at how far we had to walk back to the house. He was angry, but he didn't whip me. "Go back to sleep," he said, as he slammed me back onto the truck seat.

I awoke to Dad shaking my leg. I stared at him for a long while. He looked as if he'd been rolling on the ground and I tried to guess where he had slept.

During our visit with Aunt Ola was the first time I noticed that I stuttered. Other than "yes" or "no," I hadn't said anything to my dad since leaving Oklahoma City, and he didn't know that I could hardly speak any more. During my first day alone with Aunt Ola, she had asked me several questions. When I tried to answer, my throat and face muscles tensed, and nothing would come out. She looked at me as though she'd been talking to a sluggish child. She always had plenty to say, but, after that, I never doubted that she was just talking to herself.

Dad found out that I had stopped talking like a normal kid when we started walking away from the house where I spent the night sleeping in the pickup truck. I made the mistake of trying to ask him where we were going. After the word "where" my face contorted, I blocked up, and I could say no more. He gave me a strange look. "What the hell's wrong with you?" he blurted, bending low, as if to see if something was wrong with my face.

I tried again. "Spit it out!" he demanded. I grunted something that sounded like a word to me. Dad kicked a rock across the road, and said, "What the hell's got into you?" And that's the last time he asked me a question that couldn't be answered with a simple yes or no.

We left the skinny man's house and walked into the small town. Dad told me to stay on the sidewalk, while he checked outhouses in backyards. After finding an outhouse that needed a new pit, he motioned me to follow him as he walked to the door of the house. A short, chunky woman pushed the door open. "My boy and I are hungry and broke," Dad said. "I see your outhouse is full, can we dig you a new pit for a little money?"

The woman looked him over for most of a full minute without speaking. Then she turned away from Dad and fixed her gaze on me. "How long has it been since this boy had a bath?"

Dad moved his lips, but he didn't say anything.

"There's a shovel out back," The woman said. "You go start digging the pit. This boy is going to get some food and a bath."

Instantly, I formed a picture in my mind of this fat woman, wearing a big, toothy smile, pulling my pants off, and I didn't want any part of it. I was hungry, though. I would eat, then bolt out the door and hide some place. She put her arm on my shoulder, as if to guide me into the house. I hesitated. "Git on in there with the lady," Dad said, pushing me toward the door, with a heavy hand.

The lingering smell of fried bacon eased my fear a little. She told me to sit in a chair at the table, and I did. I watched her closely, and I didn't try to hide my concern when she put a tub of water on the stove. Every now and then she glanced my way with a little smile. I kept my eye on the tub, while she fried bacon, removed the bacon to my plate, and cooked my eggs in the bacon grease. She put a full plate in front of me, then she fixed a plate for Dad. When she started toward the toilet with

Dad's breakfast, I hurriedly stuffed two pieces of light bread into my pants pocket, and finished gulping down my eggs.

I bolted for freedom, almost running her down in the doorway. She took hold of my arm when I tried to squeeze past her. "Just a minute, son," she said, smiling. "You haven't had your bath yet. Come...help me carry this tub into the pantry." I looked toward the outhouse, thinking Dad might see how scared I was and tell her to let me go. He didn't look up from bending over the shovel. Then I tried to say *no,* but I couldn't push the word out.

I wasn't sure what she had in mind, but I'd for sure made up my mind that this woman was not going to take my clothes off.

I made my face as sour as I could, while I helped her put the tub in a little room off the kitchen. "Get your clothes off", she said, "and I'll bring you a towel and some soap—then I want you to scrub." I waited until she returned with the soap and towel before dropping my pants.

The last thing I wanted was a bath. I'd never taken a bath, except in a creek or a river, or a horse tank, and the tub didn't look near big enough, anyway. I felt like stomping my feet and yelling at the top of my lungs. But, I finally decided that was all useless. There was no escape.

After scrubbing the best I knew how, I put my clothes on and returned to the kitchen. She inspected me carefully. Before I knew what was going on, she grabbed a kitchen cloth and rubbed my ears and neck raw. She threw the cloth in a bucket on the floor and reached for the cookie jar on a shelf. She smiled, and said, "You are such a handsome boy now."

Dad finished digging the new outhouse pit, and I helped him move the little building to its new location. He covered the old pit with dirt from his diggings before going back to the house. She came to the door fumbling for some change in a little purse, while talking down at Dad for letting me get so dirty.

She smiled. I smiled back. We waved good-bye, and I was glad to be going.

We left the outhouse job and walked out of town, Dad hitching as we ambled along the street. He had a way of thumbing that I hadn't seen other hitchhikers use—leaning forward, hand in the air, thumb making quick jerking movements in the direction of our travel. Every vehicle that blew past us was a 'son of a bitch' or a 'dirty bastard.'

A truck loaded with chicken cages pulled over. I jumped in the middle and the driver flashed me a friendly smile. He looked older than Dad, with gray hair showing under his well-worn cap. He was a big, burly man who looked as if he had outgrown his bib overalls. "You're a big boy," he said, "What's your name?"

I didn't answer.

"This is my boy, Dennis," Dad said, jabbing me hard in the ribs with an elbow.

"My name is Bob Willet. You can call me Bob," the man said.

"How far you going?" Dad asked.

"Not too far, I live just up the road a few miles. I own a farm, and mostly I raise chickens and hogs, because I can't seem to make any money farming. I sell chickens to the butcher shop and eggs to the grocer. If it weren't for my chickens I would starve."

I could mouth Dad's next words: "I'm out of work, and the boy and I are pretty hungry. I can do anything on a farm if you need any help."

"I can't afford a hired man right now," the man said, "but I might be able to give you a few days work cleaning chicken houses. I got six houses that haven't been cleaned for about a year. You can sleep in a little house near the barn, and the Missus will see that you don't starve."

Long before the farmer pulled into his driveway, I started feeling good about the job—a place to sleep, food, and a job for Dad. And I had a good feeling about Mr. Willet, too. I tagged along and listened to Mr. Willet's every word as he showed Dad the six chicken houses and explained what needed to be done.

"There's a shovel, fork, and wheelbarrow in the barn," Mr. Willet said to Dad, with a broad smile. "You can start any time you want. The Missus will bring you something to eat."

In all of my life I'd never seen so much chicken crap in one place. I looked toward Dad, waiting for him to shake his head and just walk away. But he didn't.

I helped Dad all afternoon in the smelly chicken house, and we hardly made a dent in the pile. Long before sundown, I was having more second thoughts about the job offer.

About sundown, Bob Willet came over and pointed toward a little shack, not far from the chicken house. "It ain't been used for anything but storing feed. It's empty now, though. You can make do there for a few nights." I ran over and peeked in the door. It was disgusting—one room, with a dirt floor, which the rats were calling home, no electricity or stove. That evening we swept out the rat dung and collected a mattress and blankets from Mr. Willet. Throughout the night the room moved with rats. I covered my face with blankets, tucked the covers around my feet, and prayed they would find Dad an easier target.

We cleaned chicken houses for six days and fought off rats every single night. We both had chicken crap on our clothes and body from head to toe. Dad didn't seem to mind, and I sure didn't—as long as I never saw another chicken again.

Dad collected his pay and we hitched a ride, sharing the back of a beat-up old truck with two large dogs. I guess the man with the dogs was going hunting, because he let us off near a creek, and we walked the extra mile into a little town. It was getting dark when we walked into a dingy-looking hotel. The room reminded me of the place in Oklahoma City.

About that time, Dad looked at me and smiled. "Go run some water in that tub down the hall and let's scrub some of this chicken shit off, then we'll get something to eat." He pulled a rumpled shirt and a pair of pants out of a tow sack and threw them at me.

———

The tavern had a jukebox and a dance floor. Dad ordered hamburgers for both of us. We ate our hamburgers in silence and listened to some music from the jukebox, while Dad eyed some women sitting at another table. Dad smiled at the women and they smiled back, and that's when he moved to their table and left me sipping on an RC cola. Before leaving our table, Dad took off his hat and placed it on a chair before going to the women, which I thought was strange because of his long scraggly red hair which looked like a shock of maize, even when it was combed, which it wasn't now. Soon Dad was laughing and joking with the women, as if this was the most fun he'd ever had.

It wasn't long before Dad was on the dance floor. I was still sitting at the table where we had eaten our hamburgers, sipping on my cola. A man walked by the table, grabbed Dad's hat off the chair and kept walking toward the door. I stood up and waved at Dad, still on the dance floor, but he had already seen the man with his hat. Dad ran for the door. I ran after him.

As the man opened a car door and threw the hat inside, Dad grabbed him and landed a punch that sent him to his knees. With a knee to the face, the man sank to the ground—unmoving. Dad reached into the car to get his hat. When he came up from a bent position, another guy was poised with a beer bottle. Dad saw the bottle in time to turn, and the bottle caught him on the shoulder. He kicked the man between his legs, then backed up and landed a foot to his face. I was watching the fight, and yelled as another man dashed from the bar with something in his hand. He was charging Dad like a biting dog. Stepping aside the rush, Dad kicked the guy in the belly, which sent him to the ground on his hands and knees, groaning and cursing. Dad kicked him several more times, until he quit moving. A knife had dropped to the ground during the scuffle. Dad picked it up, shoved it into his pocket, and we walked away.

TWELVE

The next six months Dad and I traveled from one little rural town to another—in our journey to what seemed like nowhere to me. We'd traveled a long ways, slept under bridges, and ate tons of bologna and white bread, but to me it didn't seem like we were really going *anywhere.* He worked odd jobs, and we were never in one location more than one month at a time. The money he earned he either used to buy a bottle to drink under a railroad bridge, or to buy drinks in a tavern. I never knew if we would be sleeping under a bridge, in an abandoned building, or in a highway culvert. Drunken brawls, knife fights in taverns, and getting the tar beat out of me whenever he felt like it were my daily expectations.

When our clothes were falling off as rags, we went to a Salvation Army mission, where we'd be fitted with another set of worn discards. Dad always smiled with satisfaction, and thanked the man with the white collar. I didn't say anything, because my new clothes were always full of holes, mismatched and too big.

As a family member isolated on the farm with my brothers and sisters, I never thought even once that our tattered clothes and bare feet caused us to be different from other kids. Traveling with Dad, I could see how city kids dressed and lived, and I was suddenly painfully aware of my ragtag appearance. My most humiliating experiences were walking past schoolyards and playgrounds. I always walked so Dad was between me and the kids, and prayed they didn't see me. When meeting kids on the street I lowered my head to avoid eye contact—and hoped they didn't notice me.

It was a hot day. We had been standing on the roadside hitching for a ride all morning. Walking to a house near the road, Dad asked the woman who answered the door if we could have a drink of water. She brought us a water bucket and a ladle. After drinking our fill, we ambled back to the highway and sat down on the roadside. Dad took off his hat, wiped the sweat from his brow, and gave me a long look. "I'm taking you to live with your grandma," he said, then turned and looked straight ahead.

"Grandma?" I whispered to myself. I hadn't thought of her for such a long time. The name almost seemed strange.

I straightened up with excitement. In my mind, I started reliving all the good times at Grandma's and the fun times hanging out with Uncle Marvin. Then I started to worry: how can he know where grandma is living? They're farm workers. They live wherever there's cotton to hoe or pick. We haven't seen them forever...we'll *never* find them. When I was almost crazy with worry, I remembered something my sister, Ola, once told me: 'Dad has a nose like a coon dog when it comes to sniffing out free meals, or moonshine.' Then I stopped worrying and went back to thinking about the fun times with Uncle Marvin, stealing chickens and shooting rabbits.

Two days of thumbing rides, one night sleeping under a bridge, and we were walking into the little town of Memphis, Texas. The streets were crowded with farm workers, and that's how I knew it was Saturday. We were standing on a corner, just loafing, when I saw Grandma's black Ford slowly coming toward us. In my excitement, I ran into the street, directly in their path of travel, waving my arms and screaming, even before I recognized Uncle Marvin's big grin through the windshield. I glanced at Grandma and she flashed me a thin smile. I ran up on the sidewalk, while Uncle Marvin parked the old Ford against the curb. Uncle Marvin got out first, and I hugged his waist. I grabbed Grandma just as she stepped out of the car. "What are you doing here, boy?" she whispered, holding me close to her body.

"I've come to live with you, Grandma," I whispered. I whispered the words because Grandma was close, and I had learned that I could whisper most any word without stuttering.

Uncle Marvin looked at Dad, without saying anything to him, and motioned for me to follow as he walked away from the car.

"Are you going to stay with us?" Uncle Marvin said, when we were a short distance away from the car.

I knew I would look silly whispering since we were not real close, but in the worst way, I wanted to bust out and tell Uncle Marvin that Dad had brought me here to live with Grandma. The muscles in my throat contracted, and the only sound that came from my mouth was something like, "Ahh, ahh." Uncle Marvin gave me a strange look, then he dropped his head to stare at his shoes. I shook my head and stomped my feet in shame, disgust and frustration. I really was a voiceless half-wit.

Dad and Grandma were standing by the car in serious conversation. We were close enough that I could see Grandma wasn't happy, but too far away to understand any of what was being said. "I think John is trying to bum some money from Mom," Uncle Marvin said, laughing. "It would be funny if she got her pistol out and ran him off." I thought it was funny, too, but I didn't laugh. I was still puffed up, angry, and cursing myself because I couldn't tell Uncle Marvin why we were here. We watched as Grandma reached down with her hand in front of her dress for something. "She's going for it, Dennis!" Uncle Marvin whispered.

I knew Uncle Marvin was full of it, because I'd seen the pistol lots of times when she reached in her purse for a nickel or a dime to buy me an ice cream cone during one of our Saturday shopping trips. Coming out with a roll of bills in her hand, she untied the string that held the money together and peeled off some bills. She handed the bills to Dad without even looking at him. Dad whirled and hurriedly walked the opposite direction.

Before starting her shopping spree, Grandma retrieved her roll of money, tore off a dollar bill and handed it to Uncle Marvin. "Buy Dennis some ice cream," she said.

Eating ice cream and drinking RC cola, we wandered around town, staying close to where we last saw Grandma enter a store. Uncle Marvin and I spent the whole dollar on ice cream, candy, and cola. We were still eating when Grandma stepped out of the store and motioned for us to load the dry goods into the old Ford.

We were all loaded and ready to leave, when Grandma put her hand on my shoulder and turned me toward her. She was looking at me really strange, as if she had never seen me before. "You don't look good," she said. "Where did you get those clothes? And you need some shoes."

I looked down at my bare feet.

"Let's go," she said.

Uncle Marvin and I followed her up the street and into a different dry goods store. Uncle Marvin stood aside with a big grin as Grandma told the clerk what I needed. Fitted with new shirt, pants and shoes, the clerk handed me a mirror and I looked at myself for the first time with new store-bought clothes. And it didn't bother me at all when Grandma gathered my old rags off of the floor and chunked them into a trash can.

I walked along staring at my feet, listening to the soles sounding out a loud clacking noise on the pavement. I kept my head low, because I knew people were looking at me, the same way they looked at my Uncle Eugene when he walked down the street.

Uncle Fred was standing in the doorway of the house when we pulled into the yard. "Dennis came back with them!" he shouted. All the Mitchell family gathered in the yard, hugging me like they'd really missed me.

Uncle Marvin and Uncle Eugene lived in one house with Grandma. Uncle Fred and Uncle Melvin lived in a separate house located a few feet from Grandma's house. Fred was married to Nellie. They had three small kids. Melvin was married to Hattie. They had two little kids.

Grandma was stacking the groceries on some wooden shelves on the wall, when she looked at Uncle Marvin, and said, "We need some chickens for tomorrow."

Uncle Marvin reached for his shotgun on the wall and started out the door. "Don't worry about the chickens, Mom. I wanta take Dennis rabbit hunting, and, anyway, I can't get the chickens until it gets dark."

Uncle Marvin and I hiked through the mesquite trees and down the hill toward the cotton fields in the fertile river bottom. We crept between the crop borders and the trees. A jackrabbit jumped up ahead of us. Uncle Marvin shot him on the run, and it wasn't long before he zeroed in on another one. "We got rabbit for supper, Dennis," he grinned, picking up the second dead rabbit.

Trudging up the hill, dragging my feet with my new shoes, I felt as if I were carrying an extra ton of weight. Uncle Marvin glanced toward me and laughed.

As we neared the house, I saw Uncle Eugene coming to meet us. He handed his sack of Bull Durham smoking tobacco and cigarette papers to Uncle Marvin. I watched as Uncle Marvin rolled a cigarette and handed it to Eugene. Uncle Eugene was the only one of my four uncles who smoked, but he couldn't roll a cigarette. Uncle Marvin looked at me, and leaned his head close. "You remember your Uncle Eugene from before, Dennis. He ain't been right since that car ran over him when he was a baby. He still can't hardly hear nothing at all. I reckon he does best he can with what sense he's got, but he sure don't get no better."

Uncle Eugene put the cigarette in one corner of his mouth and grinned at me with the other side. With his eyelids at half-mast, he reached in his pocket with his right hand for a kitchen match, scratched it on his pants, lit his cigarette, and covered my head with a big cloud of blue smoke.

Uncle Marvin let out a little chuckle. Then in a real loud voice he said, "Eugene, you'd probably be rolling your own cigarette if that guy hadn't backed up to see what he'd hit."

I could remember Uncle Marvin saying those exact words when I lived with them before. Uncle Eugene knew it was just a tease, but even then, I didn't think he knew exactly what it meant.

A broad smile broke across Uncle Eugene's face, and we all laughed. Eugene enjoyed the goading from Uncle Marvin, but no one else within arm's length, or rock-throwing distance, could tease him about his handicap.

Aside from his noticeable limp, with his left leg going one way and his body going the other, and the manner in which he carried his left arm—turned up, flopping like an injured chicken wing—Uncle Eugene's physical appearances were not much different from Uncle Marvin's: dark-skinned, tall, broad shouldered, high cheekbones, square jawed. Uncle Eugene always talked so loud that anyone within five miles could hear him, and he had a little slower wit than the others. But he was usually in a good mood and could occasionally come back with a booming, simple little one-liner of his own.

Grandma went all out for my first meal with them—fried rabbit, mashed potatoes and gravy, pinto beans, and fried sweet bread. After dinner, Uncle Marvin and I scouted the barnyard and chicken house with his two dogs, Jake and Louie. The chicken house was just a short walking distance from the main farmhouse, with our house located in-between.

Not long after it got dark, Uncle Marvin and I visited the farmers' chicken house again, and Grandma had a pot of boiling water waiting. We dipped the chickens in the hot water, picked off the feathers, cleaned them, and fed the guts to Jake and Louie.

When the chickens were put away, Grandma retired to her rocking chair, enjoying a fresh chew, spitting at a coffee can on the floor. Uncle Marvin and I were sitting on the floor eating some hard candy she included in her items of shopping, and sneaking a grin when she missed the can. "You'll sleep with your Uncle Marvin tonight—now git!" Grandma said, while drying her mouth with the back of her hand. We already had the sleeping part figured out, and now we figured out it was time to stop our tomfoolery.

That night I forgot about the Blob chasing me and fell asleep before Uncle Marvin even had his boots off.

It was Sunday, and as nearly as I could figure, about the middle of June. The cotton was weeded, and cotton harvest didn't start until September. During the week my uncles were busy cultivating and doing odd jobs around the farm. Unless it was cotton-picking time, no one worked on Sunday, and today was a day of rest and play.

I'd been watching Grandma off and on all morning, and I just knew she was going to make an extra special meal just for me. And she didn't disappoint me—fried chicken, dumplings, pinto beans, and a blackberry cobbler. Grandma didn't talk much, and rarely showed affection, but I could see the half-smile and twinkle in her eye when I thanked her and told her how good everything was.

Afterwards, my uncles and I laid around in the shade of the house in a groggy condition. The sun was overtaking our shade by the house when Uncle Marvin stood up and stretched. "Let's go swimming," he said, through a long yawn. I couldn't believe my ears; I hadn't seen any water since Dad and I slept under our last railroad bridge.

My uncles and I loaded into the old Ford and drove to the dry riverbed about a mile from the house. We left the car at the river and walked another mile or two before coming upon a clear, blue pond—about half as big as a football field. We stripped off our clothes and spent the rest of the afternoon playing in the water.

THIRTEEN

Every day I rode the tractor to the field with Uncle Marvin. While keeping him in sight, I hunted snakes in the trees and shot at birds with my slingshot.

My speech was very bad the first few days I lived with Grandma. I rarely even tried to speak in anything but a whisper. With great effort, which included stamping my feet and waving my arms, I could speak one or two words before my jaws completely locked shut. Gradually I learned to say a few single words without stuttering. No one criticized me, pressed me to talk, questioned me or made me feel different. It seemed so easy watching them, with their words flowing smoothly. I knew that something was badly wrong with me, because the harder I tried the less I could talk, which only frustrated me more.

I tried talking aloud to myself, or to the dogs, that's when I was alone, or just walking through the Mesquite bushes with Jake and Louie. Some words came easy, even when I didn't whisper them, but the tough ones, the ones I really wanted to say, just wouldn't come. I was just thankful that I could talk like any normal boy when I whispered, or when I sang the words. And I was glad that Uncle Marvin was patient with my whispering, but he would never hold for singing.

It was late Friday afternoon. I had lived with Grandma one week. Uncle Marvin and I were returning to the house on the tractor. As our house came into view, I could see Grandma standing in the yard and a small child standing next to her. I could tell it was a girl, but she was too big to be one of the Mitchell kids. When they turned to look our way, I recognized my sister, Mary Lee.

Uncle Marvin and I exchanged glances, and I guess he read my thoughts. "Don't worry," he said, "I won't let him take you."

Uncle Marvin stopped the tractor and I ran to Mary Lee as fast as my new shoes would take me. "Where's Daddy?" I whispered, while keeping a sharp eye on the house, expecting him to explode through the door at any minute. She was excited, and my words didn't register with her.

"I'm so glad to be here," she said.

I cupped my hands and whispered directly into her ear, "Where's Daddy?"

"I don't know," she answered, "I haven't seen him. I ran away from the orphanage and came here by myself."

My panic instantly disappeared, and I hugged her until she laughed and pushed me away.

For the next two months Mary Lee and I spent almost every waking hour together. It was a carefree time, of which neither of us was used to. Sometimes we followed Uncle Marvin to the field on his tractor and played in the Mesquites, between the cotton rows, and hunted birds. Other times we just hung around the shade of the house and talked. She told me about the orphanage and how much she hated everything about the place. In my whispering, halting speech, I told her about Dad and the way he treated me in Oklahoma City. She swore to secrecy because I told her Dad said he would kill me if I told anyone.

It was after supper, and everyone was out of the house except Mary Lee, Grandma and I. Grandma was sitting in her rocking chair holding her purse. I was watching when she unsnapped the weathered black pouch and removed a white piece of paper. I was puzzled by the bleakness and despair in her expression, as she rocked and stared straight ahead, both hands in her lap, holding the paper. "A woman in the dry goods store read it to me," she finally said, without looking our way. "It says your Daddy wants Dennis to meet him in Rock Springs, Wyoming."

Mary Lee covered her face with both hands, started crying, and ran outside. I knew she was afraid of the dark and would stay against the house where we always go to play in the shade.

Grandma put the letter back in her purse, and we sat for a short while without speaking, then I ran outside to find Mary

Lee. She was sitting with her back to the house, sobbing. I sat down beside her, until she finally stopped crying and wiped the tears away with the back of her hand.

"Grandma will let me go with you if you ask her to," she whimpered. We sat quiet and still for quite awhile after that, then I helped her to stand up and we went back into the house. Mary Lee started sobbing again.

"Both of you come here," Grandma said.

Grandma was still sitting in her rocking chair, massaging the chew in her lip. We silently walked across the room and stood before her. I was feeling guilty and thinking she was mad because of our behavior when she told us the news. She leaned to the side, spat in her coffee can, and sat upright again. "Your Daddy wants you back, and you're his son....I can't stand in the way," she said. "He doesn't know Mary Lee is here, but he won't care if she goes with you." Then she looked at Mary Lee and asked her if she wanted to go with me. I could feel the tension leave my whole body. I looked at Mary Lee and watched a smile crease her tear-streaked face.

Saturday afternoon, a few days after the letter came, we waved Grandma and Uncle Marvin good-bye, as the train slowly pulled away from the station in Memphis, Texas. Our destination—Rock Springs, Wyoming.

FOURTEEN

When I left the Valliants for my long bus ride back to my dad in March 1946, I wasn't expecting my life to be different living with him. I was terrified at the thought of seeing him again, but just as frightened that he wouldn't show up at all. I wasn't even surprised when he sold my rifle and new clothes for beer money. And I wasn't upset to find him in his same sorry state of being as when he left me on the Valliant ranch six months before. I wasn't surprised at any of this, because I knew my dad like no one else. My only surprise was that he was still in the same town where he had promised to meet me.

As we walked along the hot pavement out of Chillicothe, my mind was busy with only one thought: how to escape.

Maybe it was because I was six months older, or maybe it was because I had seen how other people lived, but, for the first time in my life, I could see Dad for what he really was. I was sure he had some terrible problems that made him that way—problems that even he couldn't do anything about. But, I couldn't help him, and I couldn't think of any reason I should hang around any longer than it would take me to escape.

Even though I felt sorry for him, I didn't want to be near him again, yet here I was, with no place to run or hide. I couldn't stand the sight of him as he walked ahead of me holding his thumb in the air, begging for a ride. His clothes were dirty and reeked with spilled drinks, he had a sour body odor and his whole appearance disgusted me.

Before staying on the Valliant ranch I didn't know who I was (or if I was anybody). I still didn't know *who* I was, but living with the Valliants, I recognized that I was *somebody*. On the ranch, I discovered I could learn and do things—that somebody cared if I was hungry or cold—or if I was sad or happy. Dragging my feet behind Dad, watching his slow, lanky gait, and thinking about all that I had lost, I was totally consumed with sadness and dread.

I was wallowing in self-pity to the point of choking, when I heard a dog barking. The noise was coming from a farmhouse on our right, where a variety of old junk cars were scattered about. Several dirty little kids were playing in the wreckage of the front yard. Suddenly, a large, black, mixed-breed dog came charging at us. Dad picked up a big stone from the roadway and threw at the dog, barely missing. A door opened from the house and the dog retreated from a harsh command. Following the dog's path of retreat with my eyes, I saw a large, fleshy woman standing on the house porch. Her feet were solidly planted, hands on her hips, staring at us menacingly. I glanced back at her scolding, sour face, and wondered if Dad was scared of her, too, because he sort of picked up his pace a little.

It was past noon, and we had walked more than a mile from Chillicothe. My feet were hot, and my throat was so dry I could barely swallow.

Before living at the Valliants I wouldn't think of questioning Dad's judgment, or suggesting alternatives to his actions. Now, I was angry, and thinking how much I wanted to be away from him and I didn't really care what his reactions were. "I'm hungry," I whined. "Let's go back to town and get something to eat." I quickly braced myself for a punch, but there was only a long, thick silence.

When the blow didn't come, I opened my eyes. He had turned around, staring down at me with a strange look about him. "I'm hungry too," he said. "Let's walk back. Maybe we can bum a meal from a restaurant."

I went back to feeling sorry for myself, lagging further behind, dragging and shuffling my feet in the small gravel and dirt on the roadside. I was partially shaken out of my depression when a large truck roared by, pushing me aside with a strong gust of hot, dirty air.

___

It was past noon when we walked back into Chillicothe. The town was quiet, with only a few cars passing on the street, most of them going somewhere else. An orange tractor pulling a large wagon approached. Driving the tractor was a small boy, about my size, wearing a straw hat. "I could do that," I said to myself. The boy waved at a man on the street and continued on his way.

We passed a small restaurant on the street. At the end of the block we turned the corner and then entered an alley. The alley was littered with old boxes, loose papers and broken glass. The smell was a combination of stale grease and dead animals, which seemed to match the yellowish-brown, dirty walls of the buildings. A stray dog was eating from an overturned garbage can. He glanced up at us a split second before returning to his meal.

We stopped. Dad knocked on a greasy screen door. A little Chinese man with a black ponytail peered out, wiping his hands on a dirty apron.

"I'm broke, and my son is hungry," Dad said, laying a hand on my shoulder. "Do you have any left-over food?"

"I see," the Chinese man said, with a little bow, before he darted back into the dark kitchen. The smell of fried food was strong, and I could hear my stomach growl.

We waited maybe five minutes, before a tall man, about Dad's age, appeared in the doorway. He had a look about him that caused me to step back. Dad started to say something, but the man cut in before he could say a word. "The boy can eat now," the tall man said. "You can eat after you mop the kitchen floor." He turned and disappeared into the dark kitchen.

Dad muttered something under his breath, grabbed my arm, and yanked it hard enough to make me wonder if it was still a part of my shoulder. Dad rambled toward the street, cursing under his breath. I stumbled and fell, and now he was dragging me. I felt a slow, hot resentment rising deep down in my chest. I wrenched my arm from his grasp. "You're hurting me," I yelled.

Dad looked at me, and I made my eyes slits and stared back at him. His jaw set, his face turned red, and I recognized that old animal-like fury in his eyes. I braced myself, but I didn't see it coming.

Lying on the ground, it felt like a firecracker had exploded inside my head. All I could see was red stars. I was still dizzy and kind of wobbly in the knees when I tried to stand up. Then the hurt really came and I started to cry. And that's when Dad stared at me with that mad-dog look again, and said, "You better shut your damn mouth or you're gonna get it again…and I mean right now!"

Dad paused in front of the second-hand store where he had sold my rifle. Then, he opened the door and we went inside. My little rifle lay on a shelf with a tag attached. *He's going to buy my rifle back,* I thought. I smiled to myself and forgave him for whacking me on the head not five minutes ago.

"Would you have any use for any of these items?" Dad asked a tall, skinny man behind the counter. I hated him again. I turned my head and watched people passing on the street.

"Well," I overheard the skinny man say, "I guess if the boy can't use them any more….they *are* nice clothes." I heard the cash register open and close, felt Dad's hand on my shoulder, pushing me toward the door.

At a little grocery store, Dad bought a loaf of bread and a package of bologna. From there we walked to a grassy area on the outskirts of town and smoothed a place in the grass to eat. Soon after we started eating, ants came from all directions. I knew all they wanted was something to eat, so I threw some crumbs on the ground and watched as they struggled to move them to a safer location.

There were never any shared emotions, or touching, between my parents and any of us kids. Until the beatings in the hotel room, I never experienced any deep feelings for my parents, good or bad. Now, I was sure I hated him, and I was just as sure that I would never forgive him for all his other bad treatment the past twelve years. Still fresh in my mind was how the Valliants and their neighbors lived, and I knew there was something terribly wrong with him and something terribly wrong with my life when I was with him. He didn't seem like real people to me anymore. I thought about Queenie and Red, and the hotel room, and my resentment for him was so strong I wanted to scream as loud as I could and kick him until he couldn't move. And I knew that was wrong, but I couldn't help it.

Leaning back, supporting myself with my elbows, I closed my eyes and inhaled the musty scent of the hot grass. I was feeling a deep sense of aloneness, mixed with intense hostility toward my Dad. I hated him and feared him at the same time, but all of this seemed to have a calming affect on my mind. I told myself I wasn't afraid of him any more. *If he won't let me return to the Valliants I will walk away in the night while he sleeps off a night of drinking.* Finding Grandma would be simple, I thought. They always returned to Memphis and I could find them any Saturday afternoon. It had been a year since I lived with Grandma; I could still smell her fried chicken, and feel the excitement of hanging out with Uncle Marvin. It would be easy to slip away from Dad, and even though I didn't know how to get to Memphis, I wasn't afraid to try. Dad wouldn't find me for a long time, and if he did, I would be older, and I could always depend on Uncle Marvin for protection.

All these thoughts eased my mind, but, deep down, I knew that wasn't what I really wanted. At Grandma's there would be no learning to read—just picking cotton and stealing chickens. Stealing chickens was fun, but picking cotton was hard work. I wanted to go to school, have friends, nice clothes, a horse, toys to play with and books to read.

Slowly I relaxed and sensed a release of tension, and fear, and some of my hatred for Dad went away. I stared at the ants wrestling with their breadcrumbs and ate my sandwich.

Dad was lying on his back, with his hat shading his face, dozing on the grass. I finished my sandwich and drank some water from a glass milk jug he had bummed from the grocery store. Watching the ants crawl over his shoes, socks and pants, I smiled and waited. I could hear a light snore just before he jumped to his feet, ripped his shoes and pants off, and wildly brushed off feasting ants from his lower body. I yawned and pretended to be coming out of a deep sleep. He gave me a look as if to say it was all my fault the ants were making a meal out of his body. Carrying the water jug in one hand and scratching with the other, he moved off toward town without saying a word.

He started for the road in his usual long-legged stride, which I could never match. I'm huffing and puffing and trying to put a plan of escape together, all the while feeling as if I swallowed my lunch whole. Now, I can feel a sense of urgency about getting away from him. I know it's just a matter of time before he tries to wear me out with his fists again, and I've made a decision to either fight back or run and hide some place that he will never find me. And I know this is dangerous, because if he catches me I'll be a goner for sure.

I can almost read his mind: *He's different from the little kid that I left on the ranch—just a big pain in the ass and getting worse.* I'm sure he's sorry that he sent for me in the first place, and that kind of eases my mind too. But I'm still scared all the time and mostly I'm scared because I may never get the nerve to run away.

We were standing by the roadside near a gas station, Dad thumbing. I still had a headache from his punch, and I guess the hot sun and road dust had something to do with it, too, but I simply didn't care any more. "Dad, I want to go back to the Valliants." I said, without stammering a word, and a lot louder than I intended. I braced my feet and tensed every muscle, ready to duck a big one and run as fast and as far as I could go. He turned and gave me a puzzled look, then turned back to the road. In a minute or two, he looked at me again, but he didn't say anything.

I was twelve-years old now and not the helpless little boy he had left six months ago. He couldn't know what was in my mind, that I wasn't going to take any more of his abuse. But for sure, he had to know that I didn't blame myself any more for all of his bad treatment.

About the time I was wishing I could count all the 'sons-of-bitches and bastards' who plastered road dust in our faces, a rickety old Ford sedan pulled over and stopped. Dad got in the front and I crawled in the back.

"Where you going?" the man asked.

"Wichita Falls," Dad said.

"I'm just going to the next town, but you should be able to get a ride right into Wichita Falls from there."

I laid down in the seat and slept until I felt Dad shaking me, then I heard the man say, "This is Vernon, and it's as far as I go. There are no hotels here, so you best keep going." I wasn't completely awake yet, but the thought crossed my mind that we would be sleeping under a bridge if there were a hotel on every corner in town.

The sun was low in the sky when we got another ride that took us right into Wichita Falls.

Dad was a fast walker and I was barely keeping up. I stared into every alley we passed, just daring myself to make a dash for it, knowing all along that he was stone sober and could catch me without half trying. We entered an area of tumbled-down decaying houses, barking dogs and screaming little kids playing tag on the streets. Two wino-types passed us on the sidewalk, arguing and waving open bottles enclosed in paper sacks. Dad turned into a walkway where a Negro man and a white couple were sitting on a porch. The Negro man was sipping from a bottle wrapped in a brown sack.

"I'm new in town," Dad said, looking down at the white man, "and was just wondering if you folks could tell me where I could buy a bottle."

"This town's dry's dirt," the black man said, without looking up. "And, no suh, we ain't drinking no liquor, but if we wuz I wouldn't tell you where to get none. You go on and look after that little boy now."

The moment the Negro man said it that, I knew he had made a serious mistake. Dad fixed his eyes on the black man, who was still staring at his feet, and Dad's face got red. Then his whole face changed into that crazed, glassy-eyed look that I had seen before—a sign that said someone was gonna get a whipping. There was a long, deadly silence. I had already pictured how the black man would look laying there dead. Just in time, though, the black man slowly rose to his feet, and said, "Ah, hell, we'll sell you some sugah watah if you got sum' money."

"I got money, and I ain't particular about the brand," Dad said. I breathed a sigh of relief. The black man limped into the house and returned with a bottle wrapped in newspaper. Dad counted some change into his hand, stuck the bottle under his arm, and turned away.

Dad opened the bottle and sipped as we walked out of the neighborhood. It was getting dark. I was hungry and worried about where we were going to sleep. But even with my growling stomach and other worries, I was feeling good, thinking about that menacing look I'd given him after he nearly broke my arm. "Where we going? I'm hungry," I managed to say, with a lot of effort.

"Shut up," he said, slurring his words. "we're gonna get something to eat then find a place to sleep." I knew the grocery stores were closed and we didn't have enough money to eat in a café, but I didn't want to push my luck by reminding him of anything so simple.

Dad checked a couple of small stores, grunted, and just kept walking. We had reached the railroad tracks when I panicked. Knowing for sure I was pushing my luck again, I reminded him he hadn't called the Valliants. He swung his bottle in the air as he turned, and I ducked. He didn't come all the way around with his swing, and I stood and looked up at him square on.

"If you want to go back so damn bad we can call *now!*" he said, catching his balance.

I waited for a minute or two, while he held the bottle to his face for another long swig. Finally, I took an extra deep breath, and said, "I wanna go back."

Dad turned and started walking back toward town without saying another word. I breathed another sigh of relief.

We found a bus depot in the main part of town. Dad borrowed a pencil from a short, chunky man behind a counter, staggered over to a pay telephone and dialed a number. I heard him ask for the number of Booth Valliant in Saratoga, Wyoming. I watched him write something on a piece of paper that he'd torn out of the phone book, and I kept watching as he dialed a number. He asked to make a collect call.

I heard him talking to someone, but I didn't want to hear it. I left him and walked to the other side of the station, where I flopped down on a wooden bench near a Mexican couple with three kids, all of them, even the kids, sat quietly and looked straight ahead.

I could see him from where I sat, and studied his face as he talked. I knew Dad had practically made a living at what he was doing, but the longer he talked the more doubtful I became. He was mooching them for extra money, and I was convinced things weren't going his way. I stared at my feet, embarrassed for him. I glanced at the Mexican family (still looking straight ahead) and squirmed on the bench.

Finally, he stopped talking, hung up the phone and walked toward me. "What'd they say?" I stammered.

"They'll send the money tomorrow."

I inhaled a deep breath and my mind started racing, too excited to even try to speak. I followed him to the back of the station where he talked to the chunky man behind the counter again.

As we were leaving the station, I ran up to him, pulled on his sleeve. I looked right at him, and said, "Can I go tomorrow?"

"What's your damn hurry?" he said, loud enough for the Mexican family and everyone else to hear, then he pushed me, hard.

He still had the bottle tucked under his arm and continued sipping as we left the bus depot and walked the dimly lit street. We found the railroad track again and started following it out of town. He finished his drink and pitched the empty bottle between the tracks.

The night became as dark as a cellar. We groped our way along the tracks at a snails pace, until the earth between the wooden ties gave way to thin air, and I knew we were home. We hadn't eaten since sharing our bread and bologna with the ants. By now I'm getting really hungry and my thoughts turn to sharing some hobo stew under the bridge.

We carefully made our way down a steep slope and under the bridge, where my hopes of sharing hobo stew were lost. We had the space all to ourselves. Dad had staggered and fell when he reached the bottom of the slope. I started looking for cardboard boxes for bedding and tried to keep my eyes on Dad as he reeled in the darkness. It wasn't long before he was flat on his back and I could hear his loud snoring.

I kept feeling my way around the damp clay soil for some loose cardboard boxes to cover dad with, but all I came up with were a few loose papers that I instantly threw away. Finally, I lay down on the soft clay, and huddled close to Dad to keep warm. I tried to sleep, thinking I wouldn't notice the cold air so bad, but I couldn't. All I could think about was all the fun I was going to have back on the ranch.

Late the next morning we walked back into town and found a grocery store, where Dad bought a quart of milk, bread and a large chunk of bologna. Dad was in a good mood while we ate our breakfast in a small public park. There were slides, swings and other things for kids to play on. I finished eating first and started playing on one of the slides. Dad got to his feet and walked over to stand under a tree near where I was playing. He leaned against the tree and watched me with a half-smile on his face. I started to feel sorry for him, and the thought crossed my mind that he wouldn't be such a bad guy if he didn't drink, and wear me out with his fists every time he felt like it.

One of the reasons I felt sorry for him was because he looked so pitiful, with several days' growth of whiskers, puffy eyes and dirty, rumpled clothes he'd slept in—for who knows how many nights. He smiled at me and I waved back. A lump came to my throat and I felt like crying, without understanding why. I wondered what would become of him after I left. When I was feeling so bad for him that I wanted to run over and give him a big hug, he called to me, in a slurry voice, "Let's go check Western Union and see if your money is there."

I stared at the Big Ben wall clock in the Western Union store while Dad talked to a man at the desk. I had serious doubts about getting any money, and I had stopped daydreaming about life on the ranch. Not only that, if he did get some money, he could easily as not spend it all on booze. He was smiling when he left the desk. He looked at me, and said, "Let's go get that ticket."

Dad said the bus would be in at two-thirty in the afternoon, which seemed about as long as I'd lived. He said there was lots of time to do some other things, and I knew perfectly well what those other things were. He started off in the direction where he had bought his last bottle. I wondered if the Negro man would be there again and it crossed my mind that Dad might actually kill him this time.

The Negro man wasn't sitting on the porch, and neither was anyone else. Dad had to knock on the door several times before a very large, frizzy-haired white woman appeared behind a screen door. They talked for a few minutes in hushed tones, and I guessed she figured out exactly what Dad wanted. I waited on the porch while he went in and did whatever it was he had to do for a bottle.

We returned to the park, where Dad sat on the grass and drank from a brown paper bag, while I walked in circles around the merry-go-round. I was still lazily walking in circles when he finished the bottle and threw it as far as he could across the park, then he stretched out on the grass and went to sleep.

I listened to his snoring for maybe fifteen minutes before I shook him. "It's time for the bus to leave," I said, "we have to go." He pulled himself up, brushed off, and staggered along beside me. It was after one o'clock when we arrived back at the bus depot. Dad sat on a bench holding his head in his hands; I walked up and down the block in front of the depot, and wondered how to say good-bye to a Dad who was glad to see me go, but probably wouldn't remember it, anyway.

———

The big Greyhound bus braked to a stop. The door slid open and passengers streamed out in a line toward the station. I shook Dad, "It's here, it's here!" He reached in his pants pocket, handed me my ticket and separated two one-dollar bills from several other bills in his hand. He slurred some words that I didn't understand and resumed his slumped position.

I stocked up on candy for the trip and waited by the door of the bus until the driver returned from the depot. I wanted to be the first one on the bus, but the driver told me to wait until the other passengers found their seats. I glanced over at Dad and waved as I stepped onto the bus. He raised his head and nodded. I found an empty seat next to a short fat man who smelled almost as bad as Dad after he'd cleaned all those chicken houses. He was wearing a straw hat, and a dirty white T-shirt under a pair of grimy bib overalls. But I didn't care. I just breathed a big sigh of relief and looked straight ahead as the bus pulled away and gathered speed.

FIFTEEN

I was worn out and tired beyond belief. I felt like just scrunching down in the seat, closing my eyes and shutting out everything. Instead, I sat upright and very still, with my hands between my knees, staring at the seat in front of me. Two days had passed since I stepped off a bus in Chillicothe, Texas—it seemed like two months. With a vacant mind, I tried to recall the events of the past two days and think about my future at the same time. I pictured Dad sitting on the bench with his face in his hands, and a wave of sadness swept over me. I didn't feel anything for him, but I didn't want anything bad to happen to him either, and all of a sudden I felt strangely guilty because he wasn't coming with me.

I was sad and happy all at the same time. Finally, I leaned my head back on the seat and listened to the steady drone of the engine and the sizzle of tires on the pavement. The bus was warm, and my eyelids were heavy. Before dozing off, I had some nervous thoughts about what the Valliants would think of me; my clothes were wrinkled and dirty, and I was returning without my new clothes, my .22 rifle and my suitcase.

When I woke, the bus was stopped and the driver was saying something about a meal stop. Rubbing sleep from my eyes, I stepped off the bus to see the last rays of the sun in the west. I was standing by the driver, near the bus door, watching the passengers file into the little diner. "Better get something to eat, son," the driver said. "It'll be two hours before we stop again."

I spent all of my money but a few pennies on a hamburger, pop, potato chips and more candy. Back on the bus, I was asleep again soon after the little town disappeared into the distance.

At mid-morning, we had a short stop in Laramie, and I knew we weren't far from Rawlins. Squirming in my seat next to the window, I hardly paid any attention as we flew by herds of antelope, and several flocks of sheep, with their herders and dogs not far away.

It was probably about noon when we entered the outskirts of Rawlins. I pressed my face close to the window looking for the Valliants. They were both out of the car and waiting in front of the bus depot when I spotted them. A blast of cold air greeted me as I stepped off the bus. "You didn't give old Red much of a rest," Mr. Valliant said, with a wide grin. "He hasn't even had time to miss you."

"Where's your coat?" Mrs. Valliant asked. "The bus driver will get your suitcase." I had practiced what I would say a thousand times during the bus trip, but all I could do was wet my lips with my tongue, and stare at the hard pavement.

"Well...I'll bet you're hungry," Mr. Valliant said. "But first we better get you some more clothes." Holding my hand, Mrs. Valliant led me down the street and into a clothing store, where I got a jacket, a pair of cowboy boots, two pairs of pants and two new shirts. Mrs. Valliant insisted I change into a clean pair of pants and shirt before leaving the store. During our short walk to the café, I thanked them several times for the new clothes and boots.

I didn't want to tell them that Dad had sold my clothes at a second-hand store, and I didn't want them to think I carelessly lost my suitcase and rifle. I solved my problem by curling up in the back seat and pretending sleep until Mr. Valliant stopped at the ranch gate.

When we entered the house, I could smell cigarette smoke mixed with smoke from burning logs in the fireplace. I followed Mrs. Valliant into the living room. Pete (the sheepherder) was standing with his back to the fireplace, smoke curling from a cigarette between his fingers. He turned and looked our way, smacked his lips, pulled hard on his cigarette and pushed out a huge cloud of smoke. When the smoke cleared, I could see a faint smile behind his thick beard.

Claude Grimes (Mrs. Valliant's bachelor brother) was sitting on a threadbare couch, facing the fireplace and reading a book. He looked up and moved his lips like a fish, without saying anything, then returned to his reading. "Never mind him, Dennis, let me show you to your room," Mrs. Valliant said, casting a cold look toward Grimes.

That was the first time I had ever seen Mrs. Valliant give a bad sign to her younger brother. They had lived together in the same household all of their lives. During the time I lived with them, before my trip to Chillicothe to meet my dad, I had never heard either Grimes or Mrs. Valliant express an out-of-sort word to each other. It was like they were born and raised on separate planets but both were determined to exist in peace. Even with all of her talking (either to herself or someone else), I had never heard her say a bad word to him, or about him.

Without a pressing need, Grimes rarely talked, anyway. Not that he was unfriendly or anything. When I lived with them before I asked Mr. Valliant if there was something wrong with Grimes because he didn't talk much. He said Grimes was a very smart man, but he guessed he didn't talk much because he just didn't believe in jawing about nothing.

The "Upper Room," as it was called by everyone in the household, was south of the main living area, separated by a step and a large wooden door. Through the door was a large room with a musty smell, cluttered with boxes, discarded clothes, old magazines and household items. West of the large room were two bedrooms. I glanced through the open doorway at the first bedroom on my right. It looked like just another storage area for cardboard boxes and old clothes. She led on through a passageway in the disorder and into what was to be my room on the southwest side of the large room.

My room was small, just big enough for a single bed and a dresser. In the corner next to the dresser was the storage area for all the extra rifles, pistols and shotguns that weren't carried in vehicles or scabbards on the ranch saddles. I couldn't count numbers, but I roughly figured there were more rifles and pistols in there than all my fingers and toes, and there were several boxes of ammunition stacked on top of the dresser. Mrs. Valliant looked at the boxes of ammunition scattered about, and sighed.

"I told Grimes to put this ammunition in the dresser drawer so you would have a place to keep your things."

Clacking her teeth and muttering to herself, she opened the bottom dresser drawer and I helped her neatly stack the ammunition. She smiled and turned toward the window located on the south side of my bedroom. "You'll like this bedroom best," she said. "You can see the mountains, there's lots of light, and in the summer you can open your window and get a cool breeze."

I smiled. A good feeling came over me, and I said, "Thanks."

I followed her back through the clutter and into the living room. Mr. Valliant had brought in an armload of wood for the fireplace and was busying himself stoking the fire. She went to the kitchen. Grimes looked up from his book and called out, "What's for supper?"

"There isn't going to be any supper unless someone empties the ashes and builds a fire," she said.

Mr. Valliant turned away from the fireplace. "I was getting ready to do just that."

Grimes wormed his way off the couch, lit two kerosene lanterns and settled himself down again with his book.

There was something about Mr. and Mrs. Valliant that gave me a warm feeling inside. They didn't hug or kiss or anything like that, but you just knew it was all there if they decided to. But they looked and acted so different that I almost laughed when I first saw them together. Mrs. Valliant hardly ever stopped talking, and it was necessary to listen closely to know if she was talking to someone else or to herself; it seemed to make little difference to her. She was a tall, fleshy woman and a little stooped. Her skin was loose and wrinkled, and hung under her arms. She carried her head thrust forward in an attitude of attention, as if she were looking at, or listening to, something far away. She moved with a slow shuffle and always spoke in a very loud tone, as if everyone around her were stone deaf. Her face was fleshy, and somewhat ashen in color. Her laugh was high pitched, and she often laughed at something funny she had said to herself. She nearly always smiled when she looked at me, and I would smile back.

When Mr. Valliant spoke it was usually about things on the ranch, or something he wanted done. He was barrel-chested, with slightly stooped shoulders, wide spaces between his stubby yellow teeth that had probably never seen a dentist, and a little potbelly that touched the saddle horn when he rode. He was at least a head shorter than Mrs. Valliant. He had dark brown, inquiring eyes, set deep in his ruddy, round face. A sunburned hat line ran around his forehead, which contrasted with the thin, gray hairline around his otherwise bald head. He was bow-legged and walked with an old man's limp. He secretly chewed Beechnut tobacco, and aside from Mrs. Valliant, I may have been the only one on the ranch who knew about his tobacco-chewing habit.

Mrs. Valliant was born on the ranch. Mr. Valliant was born in California. They met when Booth came to Wyoming to work as a teamster hauling copper ore from the mines south of the present ranch house to the railroad near Rawlins.

I was told Grimes' and Mrs. Valliants' father homesteaded this land in the late 1800's and built the house where Booth and Anna have lived since their marriage.

Mrs. Valliant said when she was a little girl, she watched as logs were skidded from the mountains, formed by hand and put into place to frame the long, low ceiling log house.

After supper Pete left for the bunkhouse, and the others settled down with a book. The room was silent. I stood with my back to the fireplace, listened to the knots exploding in the red heat and allowed my body to absorb the warmth until I felt limp and my head started to nod. Mr. Valliant stood and removed a lantern from the fireplace mantle and handed it to me. "You've had a long day, Mister Man," he said, "you better hit the hay."

With heavy feet and rubbery knees, I took the lamp and wove my way through the Upper Room. Lying in bed, staring at the dark ceiling, I felt an aching in my chest, as the full weight of what I had done hit me. Even though I had lived with the

Valliants for six months before returning to Dad, I felt I barely knew them. They hadn't told me if they would keep me and send me to school, and I had promised myself I would never return to Dad. I hadn't told them (or anyone else) about my nightmare and I was afraid to go to sleep. I listened to the crickets make their screeching music, and tried to push the thought away.

"Hey, Mister Man." Mr. Valliant whispered, in a friendly, growling-like tone, "You're gonna get bed sores if you sleep any longer."

I pulled the covers off my face and blinked at Mr. Valliant's wide smile. I sat up in bed on one elbow and stared at him, while trying to adjust my eyes to the sunlight coming through the window. All I could think to say was, "What are we gonna do today?"

"If you were me and I were you, what you would have me doing?" he replied. I gave him a sleepy grin, and he turned and walked away.

We were through eating breakfast; Pete was finishing his coffee and his second cigarette. He turned to Mr. Valliant, "Can Dennis help me feed today?" Glancing at Grimes, he continued, "My helper wasn't feeling too good yesterday, and he doesn't look any better today." Grimes didn't look up, or break his practiced rhythm of spooning his soft-boiled eggs and wiping the excess from his mouth with the back of his other hand—almost in one motion.

"Think you can do that Mister Man?" Mr. Valliant asked, looking across the table at me. (He never called me by my real name, Dennis, always, "Mister Man.")

I smiled and nodded.

"You got an extra pair of coveralls?" Mr. Valliant asked Pete. Pete nodded and pushed a cloud of smoke across the table toward me.

I stood up and moved away from Pete's smoke cloud. Watching from a safe distance, I wondered if his smoking so much had anything to do with his frail body and the monstrous warts that protruded through his beard; or his extra large head that looked out of proportion to his string-bean body. Anyone who knew Pete could only guess at his age or where he came from; he could be forty-five or fifty-five and dropped down from the moon, as far as anyone knew—or cared for that matter. He was a born sheepherder and a good hired man, and I guessed that's all anyone needed to know about Pete.

I made up my mind about Pete the very first day I met him, over six months ago. He was a good guy, even though he was about the strangest looking man I had ever seen. He wore thick prescription glasses, tinted dark brown. His dull gray eyes sunk deep into his forehead, almost if they had been sucked in when he was kicked in the head by a horse, which left a half-moon impression in his skull above his left ear. He had worked for the Grimes and Valliant ranch eighteen years and had never told anyone about a family, or where he came from the day he walked onto the place and asked for a job.

SIXTEEN

Time passed. I helped Pete feed hay to the livestock; Grimes calved heifers and watched the older cows drop their newborn. By the middle of May, the cows were through calving, and the green grass was starting to come in the dry pastures. It was time to prepare for lambing operations.

For reasons I never understood, Pete wanted me to know the Valliant outfit was different than the other sheep operations in the country. Or maybe it was because I was there and he didn't have anyone else to talk to, but he told me everything he thought I needed to know (and a lot more than I could remember) about raising sheep and how it was done on the Valliant ranch.

Some things I did remember, though. He said the Grimes and Valliant ranch was located in Carbon County, one of the largest sheep raising areas in Wyoming. Some of the larger bands ranged up to fifty thousand head of sheep. The Valliant ranch had one of the smallest bands of sheep in the county, two thousand head. The breeding, care and lambing operations on the larger ranches were less hands-on and a lot different from the system used by Booth Valliant. The average survival rate of lambs in the larger outfits was seventy-five percent. Survival rate on the Valliant ranch was ninety-eight percent.

The first Valliant lambs were born about the middle of May. Four or five lambs came the first day, then twenty to fifty every day thereafter, until near the end of lambing, then down again to four or five each day.

About an hour before daylight, Mr. Valliant came to my room and repeated his standard wake-up call. Mrs. Valliant insisted I drink a glass of milk and have a hot cup of coffee before I walked down the hill to the corral, where I saddled old Red, and ran the other horses in from the pasture. When the horses were safely in the corral, I caught and saddled Brownie (Mr. Valliant's horse), tied both horses to the hitching rack near the house and fumbled my way to the porch in the semi-darkness.

It was barely daylight when we went to our waiting horses and made ready for the long day. I was tall for my twelve years and, in my mind's eye, Mr. Valliant was short for his age. We were the same height, and both needed to use the hillside for an advantage to mount our horses.

The first few days I learned plenty about delivering lambs. My hands were small, and right away Mr. Valliant showed me how to turn a lamb inside a sheep when it was coming ass-end first, or lose my arm inside her bottom if the lamb's head was too big to come out by itself. It was a gooey mess and it made me a little sick at first, but I didn't let on. Then we'd find a ewe fighting to have a lamb that was just too big to come out, even with Mr. Valliant and me both pulling on it. I'd sit on her head while he sliced her belly open with a pocket knife and pull the lamb out. The lamb usually lived, but the mother didn't have much chance—probably because we just sewed her up with a needle and thread and let her be.

A docking herd was a small band of ewes and lambs (usually about 200) kept separate from the big herd waiting for the castration, de-tailing and ear marking ritual. Every Sunday evening, this new band of 'dockers' was driven into the corral and kept overnight without food or water. Before sunrise the next morning, Grimes and I built a fire in a barrel specially designed to heat docking irons and then we returned to the house for breakfast. About sunrise, Grimes, Mr. Valliant, Pete and I returned to the corral for the docking operation.

Grimes sat on a stool behind a large log, with the top flattened slightly, pocketknife in hand. Mr. Valliant, with docking irons, sat behind another large log flattened on the top, which was situated close to the barrel with the fire. Pete and I were the wranglers.

Pete and I caught each lamb separately for the ritual. The front and back legs were held together, and the lamb was helplessly carried on its back to the operating tables. The male lambs (wethers) were carried to Grimes, and their butts placed on the log. Grimes cut the bottom skin off the pouch, pushed its nuts through the skin with his thumb and forefinger, grabbed both nuts with his teeth, bit down, and pulled them out of the pouch. I couldn't watch as he leaned to the side and spat the bloody mass from his mouth into a heap. With its nuts still cooling on the ground, we carried the lamb a short distance and placed it on the log, butt down, again, in front of Mr. Valliant. With a hot, wedged iron he burned off the tail about one-inch from the base. If it were a ewe lamb, its ears were cropped with a sharp pocketknife to mark the year of birth.

After the docking operation, the small flock was driven to a separate, larger pasture, where they were joined in another week by another docked herd. This herd was eventually built to a number large enough to be herded as a separate unit, and then moved on to a mountain pasture—with Pete as the herder.

By the second week in June, all but a few of the new baby lambs had been born. Pete had herded the sheep to summer pasture in the mountains the week before—the summer was half gone.

School would start in less than two months. I couldn't read or write, not even my name, and I hadn't received any home schooling since returning from Texas. I worried myself to sleep every night, because another year of school would pass, I would be another year older, and still a "dumbhead."

Mr. Valliant and I were returning to the ranch about dark, leading the team we used to move Pete's sheep wagon. Our saddle horses knew their way home and we let them go at a fast walk. Wanting to approach the subject, but not knowing how, I pulled up beside him. "How long does it take to learn enough to go to school?" I asked.

He let out a short laugh that sounded more like a grunt. "I don't know," he said, without looking my way. "Guess you better ask the Missus that question. She was a schoolteacher, and a good one, too. Most of my learning has come from just doing."

Supper was usually a quiet meal. Of course, nobody expected Grimes to say anything. If there was any conversation at all, Mrs. Valliant did most of the talking. She'd say things about her Book Club or tell a funny story about what some "old hen" had said at the last Ladies Aid Society meeting. Mr. Valliant might say a few words about something he wanted done on the ranch. I sat like a deaf mute, except an occasional, "Pass the butter or beans." But that particular meal I wanted to speak; to ask when I could start learning to read—when I could start school. Instead, I pushed my food down as fast as I could, rehearsed my speech to myself and said nothing.

After supper I helped Mrs. Valliant clear the table. She was washing dishes and talking, either to me or to the dishpans. I was drying and putting dishes, silverware, pots and pans in their proper places. "Can I go to school this fall?" I asked in a stammer, not wanting to interrupt her.

"Richard is coming over tomorrow, and we're going to talk about it," she said. Richard was one of five children, and the only boy. The girls were all married and lived in various cities throughout the country. Richard was married and had three boys, Mark, Craig, and Spike. He worked for a neighboring rancher, and his family visited the ranch twice during the six months I lived there before returning to my dad. Mark was fourteen years old, Craig was my age, and Spike was six.

On their other two visits, Mark ignored me, Craig looked at me and laughed. I wasn't looking forward to their visit; mainly because I despised Craig, but it wasn't any fun to be around Mark, either. Mark made me nervous, and he was always there to protect his little brother. The last time I saw Craig, I wanted to punch him out, and probably would have, too, but he made it a purpose to hang on Mark's shirttail.

From first sight, I judged Craig to be a big sissy. He was short and skinny, with long arms, dainty hands, and a chin too small for his face. He struggled to keep his long brown hair out of his face, and away from his darting brown eyes.

In my judgment, Mark looked and acted more like a normal boy. He ignored me as if I were an old sore on a horse's rear end, but I didn't have anything else against him. Mark had brown hair, and dull brown eyes. He was a head taller than me, with a barrel chest and broad shoulders. Although he had never said a word to me, I could tell right off what he was thinking: *a dumbass, skinny kid from Texas who stuttered, and couldn't read or write his own name.* It wasn't just me, though. Mark acted like he was better than anyone in the whole world. That was just the way he was around everybody.

It was Sunday morning. I saddled Red and Brownie, tied them to the hitching rack, washed my hands in the creek and sat down for breakfast. "Don't forget," Mrs. Valliant said, to no one in particular, "Richard and Ellen will be here today." I winced.

After breakfast Mr. Valliant and I rode to the south pasture. We still had about two-hundred head of sheep that hadn't gone to the mountains with the main herd—ewes that were late giving birth, and lambs that weren't old enough to travel. We rode through the herd and found everything satisfactory, which meant I was through for the day.

Riding back to the ranch in silence, I tried to think of some trick to get Craig away from the house, where just he and I could be alone, either to be friends, or settle things some other way.

We were a short distance from the ranch house when I spotted Richard's black, 1934 Ford, which looked exactly like Grandma's car. Spike was throwing rocks at the willows below the hill, and Craig and Mark were huddled with Richard, as if in serious discussion. They looked up as we rode across the little creek south of the house. Mr. Valliant dismounted and handed Brownie's reins to me. I couldn't stomach the thought of sitting at the dinner table, trying to eat, while Mark and Craig grinned at each other, pretending to share a big secret. I wished with all my heart they weren't staying for dinner. Mark gave me blank look as I rode off toward the barn. Craig stared at his feet.

Returning to the house, I grabbed a towel and a bar of soap from the porch and washed my hands in the little creek that trickled through the yard. When I went inside they were all gathered around the table ready to sit down for dinner. Ellen,

Richard's wife, came toward me. "Dennis, you poor little boy; it's so good to see you again," she said, with puckered lips. I shied away when she touched my arm and found an empty chair, across the table from Craig, who was holding his mouth laughing and enjoying it.

Ellen was sitting next to Craig. She flashed me a little smile. Ellen was about thirty, or maybe a little older. She seemed nice enough, but I didn't trust her. After all, she *was* Craig's mother, and I imagined that she agreed with his opinion of me. Throughout the long meal I yearned to get Craig's attention and quietly mouth, "You little son of a bitch," or another curse word that I could safely mutter in one short breath. Instead, I sat quietly and hurried through my meal, excused myself and carried my dishes to the sink.

Mrs. Valliant followed me to the kitchen. "Booth and I need to talk to Richard," she whispered. "Why don't you and Craig go outside and play for a while." I cringed, then nodded. I walked outside and stood on the little bridge over the creek.

I heard the porch door open and close, then footsteps on the bridge. I guessed who it was, but I kept my back to the door and my eyes glued on the area around the barnyard. Suddenly, I heard several quick footsteps and started to turn just as Craig dug his shoulder into the middle of my back. Lying on my backside, with no more serious injury than my pride, I stared up at Craig, who was having himself a good laugh.

I jumped to my feet and grabbed for Craig just as Mark stepped off the porch onto the bridge. I had my hand on part of Craig's shirt when he pulled loose and leaped behind Mark. Chasing Craig, my momentum hadn't slowed when I slammed into Mark. I had a handful of Mark's shirt and was reaching around with my other hand trying to grab a part of Craig. Mark grabbed me with both hands and pushed me backward with such force I landed on my back on the grass.

Looking up at their laughing faces, I really wanted to punch both of them out. But something in me rang a huge warning bell; I could only get one punch off before being mauled by Mark, and the Valliants could be watching from the kitchen. I jumped up, quickly brush myself off, and hurried toward the barn at a fast walk. As I opened the yard gate, I heard Craig giggling like a little girl. He wanted to be sure I could hear him, and his taunting laughter got louder as I made my way down the hill toward the barn. When I got to the corral, the first thing I saw was a pitchfork leaning against the fence. I looked at it a long time before I walked over and talked to Red, cursed, and made threats under my breath.

After cleaning Red with a brush, I wandered around the barn area, throwing rocks, and kicking manure clods against the fence. Grandma's little house and good old Uncle Marvin flashed through my mind, and again my thoughts turned to flight. *I don't belong here,* I thought. I will always be on the outside, unprotected and unwanted. The Valliants will never take my side over Craig's, and they'll throw me out if I fight back or do anything to hurt him. I walked around the corral some more, dragging my feet, until I heard a car rumble past the bunkhouse.

Before going inside, I washed my hands in the creek and splashed water on my face. The house was as quiet as a funeral parlor. Grimes was lying in his bed off the kitchen, fully clothed, reading a book. In the living room, Mr. and Mrs. Valliant were huddled on the couch in quiet conversation. She looked up as I entered and gave me a worried smile. "Sit down, Dennis; we need to talk to you," she said.

I was in no mood to sit, and remained standing, shifting from one foot to the other. After a long moment, I reconsidered, slumped down on the far end of the old couch, lolled my head back and closed my eyes. I was sure they were mad because I'd fought with Craig and I was trying to think of some easy words to say to defend myself.

Mrs. Valliant twisted her way out of the bottomless couch and struggled to her feet. She fumbled with some ornaments on top of the fireplace mantle, then shuffled over and stood before me. After another long pause, the color drained from her face, and she looked straight at me, settled her bridgework, and started to speak: "Dennis, we've had a long talk with Richard and Ellen. As you know, we're getting old, and, after talking to Richard and

Ellen, we realize how foolish it would be for us to try and keep you and send you to school. Richard thinks we can get you into Father Flannigan's Boys Town in Nebraska. You'll like it there. It's like a regular ranch, with horses, and everything we have here."

I didn't say a word. But, all of a sudden I hated Richard Valliant, his wife, Ellen, Mark, Craig, and poor little Spike, who didn't know I existed.

They waited in silence for me to say something. I could feel my skin getting hotter, and I thought: *I won't cry.* I turned my head and focused my eyes on Mr. Valliant, trying to read something in his face. He stared straight ahead, unblinking, and I turned again and fixed my eyes on the smoke-stained wallpaper. I squired and fidgeted, all choked up and wishing I had a place to hide.

I knew they were waiting for me to say something, but my mind was busy and I didn't think I could say anything right then. Not only had Mark and Craig beat the shit out of me, but now I was going to get kicked off the ranch.

When I stopped feeling sorry for myself, I thought about how nice they were for allowing me to return here from Texas, and how probably it wasn't their decision at all for me to go to Boys Town. Deep down I felt they wanted to keep me, and see that I went to school. I didn't know for sure if Richard and Ellen had talked them into sending me away, but I blamed them, anyway.

Sitting there in the stillness, I recalled the joy and relief I had felt the moment I stepped on the bus in Wichita Falls, Texas. During that long bus ride back to Wyoming I convinced myself I wouldn't have to live my life working in the cotton fields and, until now, everything seemed so sure. I banked all my hopes and dreams on living on the ranch, working and earning my keep, going to school, and maybe even finishing high school. Now my world was turned-upside-down again.

The thought of going to Boys Town (wherever exactly that was) reminded me of the spooky, hollow walls of the St. Joseph Orphanage, and how sad my brothers and sisters looked when I waved them good-bye at the locked gate.

Mr. Valliant and I remained seated, each staring at the wall. Mrs. Valliant went back to the fireplace and made a pretense of straightening ornaments on the mantle, again. Grimes had stopped reading in favor of a nap, and I could hear his rhythmic snoring, interrupted occasionally by a gurgling sound. The only other sounds in the room were from crickets, singing their screeching chorus, calling to each other from across the room.

I felt betrayed. I wanted to tell them they couldn't drag me to Boys Town with a team of horses. But I could tell they were really sad about the whole thing, and probably just wanted to get it over with. They had been good to me from the first time I had met them, and it made me think about where I would be if they hadn't taken me in six months ago, then sent for me when everything was going to pieces with Dad.

Mr. Valliant shifted his position and looked at me. "Well, whaddaya think, Mr. Man?"

I numbly got to my feet, shrugged my shoulders, and looked straight at Mrs. Valliant. "Yeah, Boys Town sounds okay," I said quietly.

"I know you'll like it," Mrs. Valliant said. "Richard brought me their address. I'll write the letter tomorrow, and Grimes can take it into town when he goes in to get chicken feed," she concluded at a gallop.

We all waited in a numbing silence until I turned and hurried outside. I stood on the little bridge, watched the thin clouds reflect the orange sunset, breathed deep breaths of cool air and tried to ignore the burning in my eyes.

––––

The sun was setting deeper into the horizon. I was still standing on the bridge when I remembered that Red needed hay, the chickens had to be fed and the eggs gathered. I grabbed a bucket from the porch and hurried down the hill toward the barn. Finished with chores, I started back to the house and saw Grimes, carrying a milk bucket in each hand, carefully measuring each step as he made his way off the steep hill in front of the house. He didn't look right or left, as he shuffled along, dragging his feet, the milk buckets swinging forward and back to match his slow gait. "Hi, Mr. Grimes," I said, as we passed. He nodded, without turning his head, still looking down at his feet. I knew Grimes wasn't being unfriendly or mean. He was just being *Grimes,* and I didn't feel anything bad toward him for not speaking to me.

I was dreading going back to the house, hanging out until supper, and then trying to act as if everything was normal. Walking slowly toward the house with my bucket of eggs, I paused at the bottom of the hill and turned to watch Grimes, still scuffing his heels as he made his way toward the barn.

As I watched Grimes, my mind reflected upon the hopelessness of my own life. At that moment I felt a small kinship with this very old, stooped man, who invited pity. But the comparison stopped short when comparing myself with his physical features. I knew I could never be as old as Grimes, stooped shouldered, with a potbelly that hung over my jeans, or have hair that always looked like a rodent had slept in it. Maybe it was because how the day had gone for me, but for the first time I realized how pathetic, unwanted and alone he looked, and I felt the same pity for him as I was feeling for myself.

One night, while helping Mrs. Valliant do the dishes, she told me Grimes was born on the ranch and had worn the same pair of Levi jeans his entire fifty-two years of life then she chuckled at her own exaggeration. She said after she and Booth got married they encouraged Grimes to court some 'school marms' and get married, but even as a young man he was too bashful to ask anyone for a date. Now, according to her, he was an 'old codger' and still too bashful to speak to a woman.

———

At supper that night Grimes and Mr. Valliant talked about hiring another man to help Grimes irrigate, and who they should ask to help move the cattle to the summer pasture later in the week. And there was fence to be fixed around the Forest Service permit. Mrs. Valliant chipped in with what the Ladies Aid Society planned for their monthly meeting on Wednesday. Any other night I would have eaten quietly, met their glances, smiled, and pretended to be interested in what they were saying. Tonight, what they were saying was just noise, and I wanted to get out of there as fast as I could.

Finished eating, I excused myself, carried my dishes to the wash bench, forced a smile in the general direction of the table and hurried off. I stopped by the fireplace and lit a kerosene lantern to help guide me through the maze of discards in the Upper Room. I did my best thinking just before going to sleep, and I was anxious to start trying to figure out what was going to happen next in my life. I blew out the lantern, and crawled into bed. It felt good just to lay there on my back and be alone, to relive the events of the day and think about all I had been through just to get here. My run-in with Craig and Mark was no big deal—I could handle that. Boys Town was something else. I was sure they expected me to be excited about going there, and were disappointed in me.

Closing my eyes, I pictured the high fences surrounding Boys Town and barren stone buildings—just like at St. Joseph Orphanage. I could feel the rejection, hear the laughter when they learned I couldn't read or write and see them in little groups on the playground, strutting, pointing their fingers and smirking.

On the ranch, if things weren't going well I could saddle Red, ride as far as I could see and be alone to work out my problems. At Boys Town the gates would be locked, and I would be forced to withdraw into my shell again inside those gloomy walls.

My neck muscles were tight and my head ached. I thought some more about my options. Each course of action ran in all directions and eventually led to nothing. There was no simple solution. I couldn't decide upon a plan that was even remotely attractive, and I couldn't settle on a course of action for any of my weak plans.

I tried to snap myself out of it with the thought that I still had some time before a decision could be made about my future. Grimes wouldn't mail the letter until tomorrow, and it would be several days before we received an answer from Boys Town. Lots of things could happen.

SEVENTEEN

I woke early, dressed and sat on my bed thinking. The work had slowed on the ranch. Today I would ask Mrs. Valliant to start teaching me some letters, and numbers. If I worked hard I could maybe learn to read and write, and they'd have to think twice about sending me away.

Mr. Valliant and Grimes were seated at the kitchen table. Mrs. Valliant was frying ham and eggs and humming a little tune when I emerged from the Upper Room. I entered the kitchen and eased myself into my usual place at the table. Grimes continued looking at his empty plate. Mr. Valliant looked at me and smiled. "Well, Mr. Man, did you have a good night's sleep?"

"I slept great." I replied smiling toward Mr. Valliant, relieved the tension had been broken.

Mrs. Valliant looked at me, smiled, smacked her lips and said something that I didn't understand. Grimes had both elbows on the table, holding a knife in one hand and a fork in the other, staring at his plate. "Move your arms or you're going to get burned," Mrs. Valliant demanded, waving a hot skillet in front of him. Grimes jerked backwards and dropped his arms to his side, as if awakened from a deep sleep. Mrs. Valliant shoveled ham and eggs onto his plate from a hot skillet. Chuckling, she continued around the table serving Mr. Valliant and me, then filled her own plate and sat down.

Mrs. Valliant asked Grimes what time he would be going to town and told him she had some mail for the post office. Grimes forked a large piece of ham into his mouth and chewed as he mumbled, "I don't know, after I get through irrigating, I guess."

The "mail" would be a letter to Boys Town. I could have saved them the stamp, but I wasn't ready to reveal the feeble decision I had made before going to sleep last night. I ate in silence while my thoughts turned to when I would be free to ask Mrs. Valliant when she could start teaching me to read.

"Better catch up old Brownie and Red this morning," Mr. Valliant said, as I rose from the breakfast table. "We need to ride the Forest Service fence. Snow probably mashed it down pretty bad. Need to get someone up there and get it patched up before the Moser cattle get down on us—and tie on your jacket. Can you fix Mr. Man and me a lunch?" He asked, looking at Mrs. Valliant.

I hadn't ridden the boundary fence between the Valliant ranch and the U.S. Forest Service, but I knew it was somewhere above Pete's sheep camp. I also knew it was at least five miles from the ranch to the Moser turn-out point, and it would be another five miles from there to the end of the fence; it was going to be a long day. We wouldn't be back to the ranch before dark, and it would be too late to talk to Mrs. Valliant about school. I asked to be excused, grabbed my hat off the peg on the porch and hurried toward the barn.

The Forest Service boundary fence ran east and west around the north side of the mountain. The Mosers, Valliants and several other ranchers had permits to graze cattle on Forest Service land from about the middle of June until the middle of October. Each rancher turned out one bull for every thirty-five cows and calves. The thousand or so head of cattle mixed and mingled as they grazed on the common land until separated and claimed during the roundup in October.

Mr. Valliant waited by the yard gate with our lunches and jackets until I brought the horses up from the barn. We tied our jackets and lunches behind the saddles, led our horses to the hillside, mounted and rode for about an hour without saying anything. When the wagon ruts turned into rolling prairie country, Mr. Valliant finally broke the silence. "Guess the best place to start is over where Moser turns out, and see how far we get from there."

Mr. Valliant rarely said anything at all unless he was talking about sheep, cattle, or the ranch, but I was hoping he would tell me some things about Boys Town. "You ever been to Boys Town?" I asked, knowing all the time he hadn't.

"No, never heard of it until yesterday."

"Do you remember what Richard said about it?"

"He didn't say much. It's just a place for boys who don't have a home."

"You think they'll take me?" There was a long pause, and knowing what his answer would be, I turned in my saddle and watched his face, hoping to read something in his expression.

"I don't know," he finally said.

He said it in a way that made me believe he didn't want to talk about it any more, but that didn't go for me. I wanted to tell him how I felt about Boys Town, how much I liked staying here on the ranch and how badly I wanted to stay and go to school. But now I didn't feel comfortable telling him anything, and so we rode on in silence.

In and out of small sagebrush valleys and over rocky ridges, we rode for about an hour. My stomach was rumbling. I knew it wasn't time for lunch, but I was about to suggest we stop for a snack when I noticed a dust cloud about a mile ahead of us. "Moser is turning in today," Mr. Valliant said. He gave me a look as if I should know what he was talking about, and kicked Brownie into a slow lope.

Ed Moser Hereford ranch was Valliants' nearest neighbor, the ranch houses being about five miles apart. Ed and Margaret Moser had two boys, Clay and Stephen. I had never met the Moser boys, but, since they were close neighbors, I was sure they had to be friends of Mark and Craig. And I was just as sure that Craig had told them about the skinny kid from Texas, who was as dumb as a box of rocks, and could barely talk. I wasn't expecting much from Clay and Stephen.

The cattle were through the gate and onto Forest Service land when we approached the herd. With the Moser cattle were Ed, Clay, Stephen and another rider, whom I guessed to be the hired man. Clay looked about a year younger than me, and Stephen about my age.

Mr. Valliant rode over to talk with Ed and the hired man. I hung back and sat on Red a short distance from the herd. Red was nervous, throwing his head and shifting from one leg to the other, wanting to join the other horses. Clay and Stephen glanced my way and I guessed that they wanted to get a good look at the kid from Texas. I looked their way and smiled. I wanted to ride over and act friendly, but, even at a distance, I could see that trying to be nice would just make me look like a fool.

When I glanced their way again they were riding toward me, side-by-side, then they circled to my right at a slow walk. Completing their circle, without taking their eyes off me, they stopped and glared in my direction. I busied myself at keeping Red under control and ignored them. After what seemed like all day, I glanced up from my fixed position on Red's ears and saw Mr. Valliant turn his horse and ride my direction. Putting Red beside Brownie, I shot a quick glance at the Moser boys and caught a menacing little grin from Stephen and a blank stare from Clay.

Without checking his horse, Mr. Valliant greeted the Moser boys with a wave of his hand and a smile as he rode past them. "We better get moving, Mr. Man," he said, "We got a long ride ahead of us. They're gonna push the cattle farther south. Maybe that'll keep them away from our fence for awhile."

We rode away at a slow trot. I could hear laughter behind us and I wondered if Mr. Valliant suspected it had anything to do with me.

Where the Mosers turned cattle out was an area of treeless sagebrush plain. Calf Creek was over a mile to the east. The Valliant boundary fence stretched from their turn-out point east, across the creek and up a steep hill, then over a much larger wooded hill and on beyond. We had ridden about half a mile and noticed very little repair needed—just a few staples where wires were hanging limp after being pushed down by the winter snows.

It had been at least six hours since breakfast, and the hard knot in my stomach from my encounter with the Moser boys was now replaced with a constant rumble. I was riding behind Mr.

Valliant, making a pretense of watching the fence. Putting Red in a fast trot, I rode up beside him. "You getting hungry?" I asked.

"I was just thinking about that. We'll eat at the beaver ponds, just over this hill."

Mr. Valliant rode on; I followed—deep in thought. I wasn't expecting acceptance or friendliness from the Moser boys, and so I wasn't surprised at how they treated me. They were in their world and I was in mine. In their world they had a mother and a father, friends, a permanent home, and not a care in the world about tomorrow. In my world I had the clothes on my back, old Red to ride, serious doubts about where I would be next week and a lot of bitterness toward the world and everyone in it except Mr. and Mrs. Valliant.

I wanted to believe I wasn't all that shook up about Clay and Stephen's treatment, telling myself they were just a couple of sissies. Smiling to myself, I wondered how they would stand up against my friends in the gang at Reliance. One look at Hector Sanchez, with his yellow teeth that were too big for his mouth and I could just see them running for cover. I fought Hector Sanchez and I couldn't imagine either of them standing toe-to-toe with him. To make myself feel even better, I imagined that they couldn't ride half as good as me, and, besides, their faces were buttermilk pale, as if they hadn't been in the sun much. I was feeling good, even superior to them. For one thing, Pete had taught me the right way to ride, I had some practice, and I knew I was a better rider. To be perfectly honest with myself, I had to judge my fighting and riding skills superior to theirs, which made me feel a little smug. And, I thought of some ways I would prove myself if we ever met again.

But it really didn't matter about the Moser or Valliant boys. I would be gone soon—and I would probably never get the chance to prove my fighting and riding skills to any of them. By now I knew wherever I went there would always be the likes of the Mosers and Valliants to deal with. That's when everything I'd learned with my fight with Hector Sanchez would come in handy, I told myself.

We rode on in silence, and no matter how hard I tried, I couldn't stop feeling a burning sensation in my gut about Clay and Stephen giving me dirty looks. I knew I wasn't like other kids in lots of ways, but I couldn't understand why they didn't like me. I couldn't read or write and I stuttered something terrible, but deep down I knew that wasn't the reason. It was because I didn't have a mother or father or anyone else to back me up. That had to be it. I'd show them all, though, I told myself. I had something that none of them had. I just didn't know what it was, yet.

We stopped at the crest of the hill that sloped down into Calf Creek. I could see for miles up and down the steep valley. The creek bottom and hillsides directly ahead of us were thickly covered with aspen trees. As the creek wound its way to the lower stretches of the valley the aspens gave way to rusty willows and glittering cottonwood trees. To the north the aspens thinned into scattered ponderosa pines, then solid dark green ponderosa and spruce trees. We sat on our horses in silence, awed at the breathtaking sight. I breathed deeply of the cool breeze that nipped my face and rattled the aspen leaves and imagined myself owning a place like this some day. After a few moments, Mr. Valliant looked my way, smiled, and urged his horse over the crest and down the steep hillside.

Stiff kneed, with their rear ends tucked under them, occasionally sliding, or stumbling on a sharp rock, Red and Brownie picked their way down the steep grade toward the creek bottom. These were experienced mountain horses, raised in rugged country. As colts they chased and played on steep rocky slopes. But knowing all of this didn't keep me from being scared enough to pee my pants. Pete had told me stories about horses falling on steep slopes; he even knew about cowboys getting killed that way. And that's why he had taught me how to ride down steep grades—leaning back with the slope, feet lightly in the stirrups—ready to roll off to either side, just in case.

We found a grassy clearing above a large beaver pond, untied our lunches from the saddles, found a fallen tree near the creek and spread our jackets. Leaning against the tree, we ate without saying a word, while listening to the water tumble over the pond, watched birds skim the water and trout rise to the surface to feed on bugs playing on the smooth water.

———

It was almost dark when we finished riding the fence line. In the trees and deep valleys, the fence was in bad shape—posts broken off and wires smashed to the ground from deep snows. I knew I would be one of the hired hands, working long hours and sweating like a horse, repairing the damaged fence. But right now I was more concerned about the constant rumble in my belly from lack of food. As the sun sank lower on the horizon, there was a sudden coolness and a strong smell of earth and pine needles. We exchanged glances, and kicked the horses into an easy lope.

About two hours later, we rode into ranch headquarters. Mr. Valliant dismounted, handed me his reins and, with arthritic slowness, limped into the house. After unsaddling, currying and feeding the horses, I trudged toward the house in the darkness, so tired I had to remember to put one foot in front of the other to keep from falling.

I was too tired to wash my face and hands in the creek, but I did it anyway, because I knew Mrs. Valliant would stare at me until I got myself up from the table and out to the creek. Mr. Valliant was at the table staring at his empty plate, holding his coffee cup in one hand. Mrs. Valliant looked up and smiled as I came in. I could hear Grimes' loud snoring, coming from his room off the kitchen. I didn't even try to understand what Mrs. Valliant was saying, or if she was talking to anyone or to her self. After stuffing myself, I wobbled through the maze of discards in the Upper Room and fell on the unmade bed.

EIGHTEEN

While Mr. Valliant and I were riding the Forest Service fence Grimes was in Saratoga rounding up more ranch help. The new hands were hired to fix fence and work in the hay field later in the summer. Grimes settled them in the bunkhouse, where they spent the night. I met them at breakfast, where Grimes introduced them as Jerry and Clarence Hagen. With their frazzled red hair and identical rooster tails, they could have passed for twin brothers, except they were Cousins—both from the same town in Missouri.

The Cousins were sleepy-eyed and unwashed. I guessed that Grimes hadn't given them a wash basin, soap or towels. They sat looking down at their plates, eating quietly. I glanced at them several times during breakfast, judged them to be about twenty-one-years old and something other than ranch types. They wore almost identical blue, flowered, short-sleeved shirts, brown slacks and low cut shoes. They didn't say anything or even look at me when Grimes pointed to me and said my name, and it was then that I thought they might not be Right, like my Uncle Eugene.

"Dennis, can you catch up old Red and run the team in?" Mr. Valliant said, looking at me from across the table. "We need to start fixing that fence before the Moser cattle get down on us."

I nodded and started for the porch where we hung our coats and hats. I had my hat on and striding toward the door when I overheard Mr. Valliant say, "You guys know how to harness and drive a team, don't you?" I smiled, and could barely keep from laughing as I charged out the door.

I cut out a matched team in the pasture and ran them hard all the way to the corral. This team was grass fat and had been used in harness only once since last summer. Acting like wild mustangs, they circled the corral with tails in the air, snorting snot, farting and throwing their heads. With halters in hand, Jerry and Clarence cringed outside the pole fence. I tied Red outside the corral, turned toward the Cousins and watched. I could see Grimes doing something or other near the wagon.

The new hands were frozen to the pole fence. Now I was sure they had lied to Mr. Valliant about knowing how to harness a team; and sure as day, they would be taking a ride back to town if Grimes found out they had lied. I was disgusted and feeling sorry for them at the same time.

Grimes would be checking on his new hired men within minutes. I had to act soon, or forget it. Suddenly, I thought, "Maybe they aren't like my Uncle Eugene at all, and just need a hand, like me." I jumped over the corral fence. "Throw me the halters and keep out of the way," I said, as best I could. They never moved while I caught and haltered the two horses. I handed a lead rope to each of them. "Come on, I'll show you where the harnesses are," I said.

Grimes was still gathering tools and loading the wagon for the trip when I finished showing them how to harness the team. They smiled and thanked me several times. I had two new friends—whether I wanted them or not.

With lines in hand, I stepped the team over the wagon tongue and Grimes helped me hook the traces, while the rookies looked on, wide-eyed. I wasn't worried about Grimes asking them to drive the team. He knew these horses were ready to run and I was sure he didn't want himself, hired hands, tools, and wire scattered over half of the ranch.

Grimes put his foot on a wagon spoke and struggled to pull his body onto the seat, while I held the lines and kept the team under control. Still holding the lines and keeping the team calm, I put my foot on a spoke, grabbed the seat, and handed the team to Grimes. The new guys jumped on the back, and I had to cringe when they yelled, "Gettum up," in a dude-like tone. The crew was now ready for the five-mile trip to the work site—an arthritic old man, a twelve-year-old kid, and two greenhorns who'd probably never seen a fence before.

It was all Grimes could do keeping the high-strung team under control while climbing the steep hill toward the house. He halted the team in front of the ranch house. "Either of you guys got any gloves?" he asked the two smiling redheads.

They stared at each other as if he were speaking Pig Latin instead of plain English, and slowly shook their heads. "Dennis, go get our lunches and ask Anna to look in my room for some old gloves," Grimes said, while shaking his head in disbelief.

As I entered the kitchen, I heard Mrs. Valliant playing a little tune on the piano. I decided not to bother her and darted into Grimes' room and found several mismatched gloves scattered here and there. I grabbed several gloves, our lunches off the kitchen table, and dashed out the door. Grimes loosened the lines and started his work crew toward the mountains.

It was about a two-hour trip from the ranch house to the Moser turnout gate and the beginning of our fence line. The first half of the trip was on a wagon road and fairly smooth. Grimes had his hands full keeping the fat, sassy team under control for the first hour. I prayed they would be settled down before we turned off the wagon trail and started over the sagebrush for the last half of the trip.

It took a little longer than I'd hoped for, but the horses finally stopped acting like young colts when they were white with sweat around the harness leather and puffing like this was their first time in harness.

There was nothing for me to do during the long trip except watch the old man keep the fresh horses under control, think about how I was going to tell the Valliants that I wasn't going to Boys Town and ponder my other options.

I was earning a hundred dollars a month in wages, and I had only drawn a small amount for pocket money. If they would allow me to work until school started I would have about two hundred and fifty dollars to get on my way. They wouldn't have to know where I was going. If Mrs. Valliant would teach me to read, I could rent a room in Saratoga and go to school until I could find another job to earn my board and room. I decided no matter how late we returned from building fence I was going to ask her to help me learn to read. I already knew my ABC's and could count to one hundred; I couldn't imagine there was much more to it.

Bouncing over the sagebrush and small rocks, I had all I could do to keep my seat. Every now and then I glanced back to see how the Hagens were doing. I caught Clarence looking my way; he smiled, as if he was on his way to a picnic. Grimes held the lines tight and maintained a tight little smirk all the way. I imagined Grimes was just feeling good because he would be spending the day sitting on his ass watching the Missourians and me fix fence.

Clarence and Jerry's fun ended soon enough. As I guessed, they didn't have a clue what to expect when their buggy ride ended at the Moser gate. "You guys unload what you need," Grimes said, pulling the team to a halt. Clarence and Jerry jumped off the wagon, ran to the back, then stood just looking at each other, until I started unloading cans of staples, shovels, small rolls of used barbed wire, hammers and wire pliers. When the tools were unloaded, Grimes mumbled something that I didn't understand and started the team toward Calf Creek.

We all just looked at each other for quite awhile, the Cousins staring at the pile of tools and materials. I shoved a pair of pliers in my pocket, placed a hammer in a bucket of staples, grabbed a role of wire and carried all of this to the fence where I saw the first broken wires. They copied my actions exactly, then followed me to the fence and stood watching like helpless children.

I glanced toward the creek and saw Grimes unhooking the team. He would tie the team to the wagon wheels, then walk back and stand around watching. I didn't feel the same excitement about saving their hide as I did this morning, but I had to consider what would happen if Grimes fired them. They would have a long walk back to the ranch house, and I would be fixing fence with Grimes all summer. I had never worked with Grimes, one-on-one, and I wasn't excited about the chance. I grabbed a loose wire and started making a loop to splice two wires together. "You guys know how to stretch wire?" I asked, knowing the answer. They shook their heads like identical twins, and made a clumsy effort to hand the other end of the wire to me. "Okay, just stay close to me and I'll show you," I said. They danced around making extra motions and movements, physically and mentally struggling to learn how to splice wires, nail staples, dig post holes and set new posts; all the while keeping a sharp eye out for Grimes, who was walking toward us at a snails pace.

By noon we had repaired the fence to the hill overlooking Calf Creek. We had used all of our new posts, and I was so tired I could hardly walk. My helpers didn't look at all tired. I was eating my sandwich when I glanced at Grimes. He caught my look and widened his painful, pursed-lip, little grin. "You boys will get some exercise this afternoon", he said. "We're out of posts. There's some nice aspens about half-way down the hill to the creek." I glanced at the Hagens. They were staring at Grimes with blank expressions.

This was my first work trip up here, and it took me a minute or two before I understood what Grimes was talking about. "He can't really mean it," I said to myself, knowing all along that he meant exactly what he said; he was going to kill us. I groaned and laid back on a clump of sagebrush. After they had eaten, Clarence and Jerry got up and wrestled each other around like a couple of small boys. I lay on my back with my eyes closed, groaned, and cursed Grimes under my breath.

After the short lunch break, Grimes motioned us to the wagon. The Hagen cousins were yet to figure out what was going on. I found three axes in the wagon, and gave one to each of them, keeping one for myself. Grimes pointed to the aspens, midway between us and the creek. "There they are, boys," he said, pointing toward the aspens. "Cut as many as you can before quitting time, and pack them back to the wagon."

Clarence and Jerry didn't move, and Grimes could see they were confused. "You're gonna cut some fence posts," Grimes said, in a grumbling tone of voice, "and carry them back up the hill and put them in the wagon! Understand?" They nodded, as if to say they understood, but I was sure they didn't.

We picked our way down the long hill to the first grove of aspens. Grimes could have just as well whistled *Dixie* for all they knew about what he'd told them to do. I was tired of playing teacher, but mostly I was just tired. I wasn't an expert with an ax, but I had cut my share of firewood for the fireplace last winter and figured I could do my part. I moved to my first tree and started chopping.

Grimes couldn't see us from the wagon. I didn't look at them, but I knew they were following me, and watching what I was doing, until I had my first eight-foot fence post cut. I balanced the post on my shoulder and started for the wagon, without looking back. When I was out of the trees and starting up the hill, I could hear some faint chopping noises.

Grimes was sitting in the wagon seat picking his teeth and grinning when I topped the hill. On my return trip I met the sweating pair coming out of the aspen groves, staggering under their load.

All afternoon we cut and carried posts up the steep hill. As nearly as I could tell, Grimes never moved from the wagon seat, always wearing the same grin as he watched me unload my posts. I was disgusted with the Missourians and purposely arranged my cutting and carrying posts to avoid them. Sometimes I would pass them on the climb to the wagon, resting, out of Grimes' view.

It was almost sundown. The wagon was full of posts, and all three of us were nearly dead. Grimes said the posts we'd cut were needed to repair some fences closer to the ranch. We would unload them in the morning. Starved, weary and boned tired, we rode the wagon back to the ranch in dead silence. Several times during our trip back to the ranch house, I glanced at the new hands, trying to sleep while lying on their backs bouncing around on the load of posts.

Grimes halted the team at the ranch house, and we both turned and looked at the two still figures sprawled over the posts. "Hey boys, you gonna sleep all day?" Grimes shouted, in a laughing way. When they didn't answer right away, I thought they might be dead, and I was relieved when one of them groaned.

———

I couldn't quit, and, for one reason or another, the Hagen cousins didn't quit. By the third day of fixing fence I had forgiven them of their lying ways and we became good friends. They were eager to learn, and, while playing teacher to them, I learned I wasn't as smart as I thought I was. I soon taught them all I knew about fixing fence, and, together, we struggled to learn the rest.

We had been fixing fence four days, and Grimes was wearing down from observing our work from his wagon seat. Arriving back at the ranch just before dark, Grimes stopped at the house. "You guys can unhook and put the team away," he said with a tired voice. The chance to teach the Cousins a new skill made me feel like a teacher again, but I didn't have to say or do much, as I watched them unhook the wagon, remove the harnesses and lead the team to the pasture gate.

Walking back to the bunkhouse I promised to let them catch the team the next day and teach them how to drive the horses before we hitched to the wagon. They slapped me on the back and thanked me several times before we stepped into the bunkhouse. I waited for them to wash up, and I could see they were on a new high. Our aching bones and tired muscles forgotten, we laughed, pushed and shoved each other on the way to the ranch house.

The next morning, after having my coffee and milk, I went directly to the bunkhouse instead of going to the corral to catch Red. The guys were dressed and waiting for me. They looked worn and tired. I caught Red, Jerry boosted me up on his bare back, and I tore off to the end of the pasture to fetch the team. After cutting the pair off from the other horses, I was careful not to run them too hard.

Jerry and Clarence each grabbed a halter and cautiously approached the horses. They haltered both horses and walked them to the barn, smiling all the way. After they harnessed the horses I hooked the horses together in the large corral, and they had their first lesson on driving a team. Now they were real ranch hands, showing off a little, giving voice commands to the horses, and stepping a little too high.

Early on, Grimes told us about the annual carnival and rodeo in Saratoga. He said if we could finish the fence by the Fourth of July he'd take us to town for the celebration.

Grimes seemed to enjoy himself the most when we were near death, but since he seldom changed facial expressions, it was hard to tell for sure. By the beginning of the second week, Clarence and Jerry became experienced hands at fence repair, and what time we weren't complaining about our sore muscles, we laughed, joked and poked fun at Grimes. We finished the last section of fence July third, just about sundown.

NINETEEN

July Fourth. I did the chores in record time, then I hurried over to the bunkhouse to get Clarence and Jerry. They were up and dressed in their best polyester slacks, flowered shirts, low-cut shoes, and grinning all over themselves. I wore a new pair of Levi's, green and red stripped snap-button shirt, new cowboy boots and my work straw hat.

Mrs. Valliant had been to town the day before and cashed our paychecks. Clarence and Jerry had fifteen-dollars each. I told them I had five-dollars and I expected to spend it all. We slowly walked to the house, laughing, pushing and shoving like three little kids.

The Cousins and I finished breakfast in a hurry. Grimes slowly spooned his eggs as if he had all day just to do that one thing. I couldn't take it any more, and when I left the table the Cousins followed right behind me. Just for something to do, we were throwing rocks at Magpies settling on a dead sheep carcass not far from Grimes' old Ford, when Jerry piped up. "Hey, look at the Dude." Grimes was almost strutting in his new clothes, a clean pair of jeans, a dark blue shirt, new boots and a new gray felt hat.

"Are you sure you boys want to go in and spend all your hard-earned money?" Grimes said.

"Hell yes, let's go," we said, all together.

The little town had come alive. The two cafes were full, the bars were overflowing and the streets packed with cowboy-types, kids of all ages wearing western hats and boots, and mothers carrying messy little kids with cotton candy. There was hardly a place to stand on the streets.

Grimes drove the one block length of the business district without finding a parking place. He slowly drove across the bridge over the Platte River, which divided the town, turned around and crawled through town again. He stopped in front of the drug store, and without looking at any of us, he said, "Okay, you guys, get out. Stay out of trouble and meet me tonight at the Fireman's Hall by ten o'clock. If you're not there I'll leave you."

"Okay," I said, and we piled out of the car.

We joined the milling crowd and soon found our way into Donelan's Drug Store. After waiting in an endless line, I bought a banana split. It cost thirty-five cents, but I didn't care; I would've paid more for it. I'd never had a banana split, and I ordered it by pointing to a picture hanging behind the counter, that showed two halves of a banana on a dish, three dips of ice cream between the banana halves, and topped with fruits, nuts and chocolate. Clarence and Jerry settled for fifteen-cent double-decker ice cream cones.

I had never been to a carnival or a rodeo and I had never felt this much excitement about anything. Bouncing along on the dirt road, on the way to Saratoga, Clarence had told me a carnival came to their town every year. He described the Ferris wheel, merry-go-round and two or three other rides that ran cold chills up my spine. He said some carnivals had midgets, people with six fingers, three-legged men and fat women weighing six-hundred pounds or more. When Clarence was finished with his story, Jerry leaned toward me, cupped his hand around my ear, and whispered, "All carnivals have a naked girly tent, and we've seen her more than once."

About ten o'clock excitement started to build, with people all over the street, and we soon learned what the excitement was all about. There was going to be a parade.

There was a roll of drums in the distance, music from the band, thunder of hooves, and I knew the parade had started. A very old fire truck led the parade, creaking and wailing so loud it was hard to hear the music.

The parade started somewhere near the grade school, about four blocks west of town, and passed Donelan's Drug Store. From all the excitement generated by the crowd, I expected more. The fire truck came first, then the high school band with baton twirlers, then about twenty cowboys and cowgirls of all ages and a shiny Model-T Ford, with an uncertain sounding motor, bringing up the rear.

The band disappeared across the bridge, and the music stopped. Several horseback riders returned to town, rode the streets, and visited with friends or family.

The rodeo would start at one o'clock, and people were already starting to walk, or drive, the one-mile distance to the rodeo grounds. From the corner of my eye, I noticed Grimes coming our way. He stopped closest to Clarence, and asked, "You guys want a ride to the rodeo grounds?"

The small dirt road was crowded for the short trip, people walking on both sides of the road, and horseback riders giving way to cars and pickups slowly crawling to the high ground. Near the top of the hill, Grimes stopped, and we quickly crawled out, waving him away without a word from any of us.

The rodeo grounds stood on a flat plain overlooking the Platte River. The carnival had set up a short walking distance from the rodeo. We could see the Ferris wheel before we reached the rodeo and my heart quickened. I had seen carnivals at a distance while traveling with Dad, but never dreamed I would actually be doing any of the rides.

There were horseback riders in the arena, and other riders moving Brahma bulls around in small pens. We could tell the rodeo wouldn't start for some time yet—the carnival was the place to be.

We strolled around the carnival for a while, enjoying the noise and excitement. I walked up to a trailer selling huge balls of cotton candy. It cost a dime, but I didn't care, it looked like it should cost a lot more. We watched some older boys shooting air guns at small ducks swimming in a pond. They weren't hitting anything; it didn't look that hard and I wondered if they were city kids dressed like cowboys.

In the midway there were tents to throw balls at milk jugs, basketball hoops set up with rims that looked smaller than the balls, darts to throw at bottle necks, and tents with small bearded guys out front barking the fortune telling powers of the secret women hidden inside.

Clarence heard some teenagers talking about a naked lady tent, hidden somewhere in back. Jerry looked at me and whispered (as if he was afraid the whole world would hear him), "I told you, Dennis, I told you."

We found the tent and stood around watching some grown men, wearing cowboy hats, smoking cigarettes and looking over their shoulders. Strange music drifted out of the tent, which was tightly guarded by a man with a funny little dude hat, who let people in and out through a little canvas flap. A piece of paper nailed to a board between two posts showed the price to be one dollar. Jerry said, "We're going. Come on, Dennis."

I'd never seen a naked girl, and I really wanted to go in there with Clarence and Jerry and have my excitement. I thought about my small allowance for the day—but mostly I was just scared, thinking that Grimes might be there because chances were he'd never seen a naked girl, either. I motioned for them to go without me, and whispered to Clarence that I would meet them over by the Ferris wheel.

———

I bought another cotton candy, and watched some kids shoot baskets and throw balls at milk jugs. I wandered over and stood near some other rides that squeaked and rattled, listened to the screams from little kids, and watched nervous mothers waiting to lead their dirty little kids off the noisy rides.

I was standing near the Ferris wheel, wondering what was taking Jerry and Clarence so long in the girly tent, when I spotted Craig and Stephen waiting in line for tickets. The sight of Craig brought back the burning humiliation from the time he rammed me off the little bridge on the ranch. I searched the area with my eyes, thinking Mark might be nearby. When I saw they were alone, my anger and frustration got the best of me. I really wanted to kick the shit out of Craig, just to even the score, and since I would be leaving the ranch soon, I figured this would be my last chance. I could even see myself kicking Stephen's ass, if he wanted some.

The Ferris wheel was creaking and groaning, as if trying to drown out the loud music. Craig and Stephen were standing in a long line, waiting to buy tickets, laughing and having fun, without a care in the world. I approached from their backside, and then angled to the right, for just the right shot at Craig's back. When I was about ten feet away, I started running, lowered my shoulder and aimed at Craig's ribs. My aim was perfect. He landed on his side in the dirt, with me on top, flailing my fists.

Craig was dazed, and I was having at him with both fists, until Stephen started kicking me. I let go of Craig and grabbed Stephen by the leg and bit down as hard as I had ever chewed on a piece of meat. He ran off through the crowd, screaming like a little girl with ants in her bloomers. While I was off guard, Craig jumped on top of me and whacked me a few good ones on the head.

About that time I felt a weight lifted off of me and looked up to see Jerry and Clarence holding Craig in the air by his shirt collar. They released Craig and he quickly disappeared into the crowd that had gathered to see the fight. I was gasping for breath and filthy dirty. Overall, I was pretty beat up, but I could feel myself smiling. My legs were still trembling when Clarence and Jerry got around to asking me what happened. I said, "I'll tell you later."

I was brushing the carnival dirt off my pants when I remembered the naked lady show. "Hey, did you see her?"

"Man, you missed a great show," Clarence said, shaking his head as in disbelief. "You should have seen her; she took it all off." He drew an hourglass in the air with his hands.

"Let's ride the Ferris wheel," I said.

I rode the wheel once with Jerry, while Clarence rode in a seat alone. Clarence bought two more tickets, and I rode the Ferris wheel again while Jerry watched on the ground.

Clarence suggested we walk into town and look for some different excitement. At that, we joined a hoard of other fairgoers leaving the rodeo, choking on the dusty road that led back into town.

We wandered back and forth along the one block length of Main Street and watched a group of women setting up some long tables and putting out lemonade, large platters of sliced meat, ketchup and hamburger buns. A line formed and someone said the Ladies Aid Society was selling a roast beef dinner for sixty-five cents, which included lemonade. We filled our plates and found a place on the street curb to sit down and eat.

Craig and Stephen walked across the street to my left and headed for the food table. They didn't see me. I stopped eating and just watched while they piled their plates with food. Craig still hadn't seen me when they sat down on the curb about ten feet to my left. I smiled to myself. He didn't look as clean and fresh as before I rolled him in the dirt at the carnival. His face was covered with carnival dust and a large tear down the seam of his shirt brightened my mood even more. While they sat chewing their food, I pointed in Craig's direction and whispered to the Cousins, "Those are the guys I was fighting with."

Clarence and Jerry leaned to the side and stared at Craig and Stephen. "Geez, they're big, you want us to whup 'em?" Jerry said.

I said, "No. They're related to Mr. Valliant." Truth is, I didn't think they could whip anybody, not even skinny old Craig, and I didn't care any more, anyway. I was starting to get a bellyache, thinking about my future on the ranch and having a hard time swallowing the last bites of my roast beef.

At first I felt good about getting my revenge on Craig, but now I was feeling guilty about how it all happened, like I had done something really awful and had forgotten most of the details. It was bad enough before Jerry looked at me as if this was the most fun he'd ever had, which made me feel even worse.

All the fun had gone out of it. I just wanted to load up and go home. But that didn't happen. It was early in the evening, the dance wouldn't start at the Fireman's Hall until nine o'clock, and Clarence and Jerry were just getting wound up. The Richard Valliants would be at the dance—and the Mosers. There was nothing for me to do but tag along, hide my fears and pretend to be enjoying myself—and watch my back.

We walked around town some, then strolled across the bridge over the Platte River—just killing time. The Cousins seemed relaxed, without a care in the world, but that didn't go for my state of mind. The Valliant and Moser boys would be stalking me all night. I tried to pull myself together. Grimes would be at the dance, and probably even the town cop. Anyway, I could whip old Craig any day of the week, if it were just he and I.

I wanted to tell Clarence and Jerry the truth about how I felt, but I still didn't. They were my only two friends in the world, and I didn't want them to think I was a chicken. Anyway, I didn't think they would be much help in a fight. Maybe later in the evening I would tell them. I decided to wait and let the evening play itself out, take my chances of not running into serious trouble—and try to keep from throwing up from my nervous stomach.

We bought our tickets early and stood around listening to the three-piece band play some warm-up music. The hall was soon full of adults, teenagers, and little kids pushing each other across the dance floor. I couldn't dance, and Clarence and Jerry either couldn't dance, or didn't try. There was nothing much we could do except stand with our backs to the wall, and sip on soda pop purchased from the concession stand.

I watched Grimes dance three times to slow music with an old, prune-faced little woman. She smiled, raised her heels in the air, and clung to his shoulders, as he slowly swung her in circles. Grimes never changed his expression from his slit of a smile (if in fact, that what it was), although, one time I thought I saw a flicker of white between his lips.

I stayed close to Jerry and Clarence, and much to my surprise and relief, serious trouble didn't come. All the Valliant and Moser clan attended the dance. None of them looked at me, not even once. Toward the end of the evening I got to thinking they (all of them) had something really ugly planned for me—things they couldn't do to me with so many people around. I also imagined that Craig had cried to his parents, and they wouldn't waste any time telling Mr. and Mrs. Valliant about my cowardly attack on him.

It was exactly ten o'clock by the Fireman's Hall clock on the wall when I spotted Grimes coming our way across the dance floor. He motioned for us to follow, and we walked out of the dance hall in a group of four. I breathed a sigh of relief, and again after I climbed into the back seat of Grimes' Ford.

TWENTY

Quietly sitting in the back seat between Jerry and Clarence, headed home, I should have felt safe and secure. But after everything that had happened, the ranch didn't seem like a safe place to be any more. And I couldn't stop feeling I had no one to blame but myself. I relived the fight over and over, and then I pictured Richard's black Ford sitting in front of the house as we arrived back at the ranch. I could see Mrs. Valliant in her faded, rose-colored, chenille robe standing in the driveway with a protective arm around Craig, him sniffling and clinging to her waist. She would glare at me with angry, accusing looks, and tell me to gather my clothes and sleep in the bunkhouse. They would deal with me come morning.

My head jerked forward and I nearly fell on the floor when Grimes made a quick stop at the ranch gate. I quickly awoke and glanced toward the ranch house for any signs of the black Ford. It was a moonlit night. The driveway was empty, and I couldn't help the big sigh of relief. The tension drained from my body and I whined a sleepy goodnight to Clarence and Jerry when Grimes stopped at the bunkhouse. Grimes crept on toward the ranch house, where he let me out of the car at the gate. I quietly tiptoed through the Upper Room, into my small bedroom, and flopped faced down on the bed with my clothes on.

Grimes opened the yard gate near my window and I heard his feet shuffling on the path beside the house. I climbed out of bed, yanked my clothes off, and piled them in the corner where I always put them—all the while thinking about where my thoughts should be traveling.

My life would be different from now on; nothing would be the same on the ranch again, I thought—and my relationship with Mr. and Mrs. Valliant would never be the same. I felt cold and empty, wishing I could be in Memphis, stealing chickens and picking cotton with my Uncle Marvin.

Through a sleepy haze, I found myself thinking about my relationship with the Valliants, if they liked me at all, or just felt sorry for me. I had been doing hired man's work. Did they think of me as just another ranch hand? I slept in the same house with them, but that could be because the bunkhouse was small and needed for the extra help. Why did they have me return to the ranch from Texas? Would they try to find Dad and send me back when they learned about my attack on Craig? My head was spinning with questions, and I couldn't answer any of them.

I hadn't told the Valliants about Craig shoving me off the little porch in front of the house. Should I tell them when they questioned me about my actions toward Craig at the carnival? They always spoke so highly of Craig and Mark. What good boys they were. No, I couldn't tell them, I decided. I'd never seen either Mark or Craig get a whipping or scolding and Mrs. Valliant just might think I caused the whole thing. Then I thought about the dripping version that Ellen would relate to the Valliants, how I attacked Craig unprovoked, and how battered and bruised his body was, and how it was lucky for everyone Craig wasn't killed or something.

All this so disgusted me that I sat on the edge of my bed and thought some more. I reminded myself that there were other places I could live. I could find Grandma again in Memphis, and, even though there would be no school, there would still be love, protection, and Uncle Marvin to hang out with. Also, just before the Hagens and I finished the Forest Service fence they told me I could return to Missouri with them. They said their mother wouldn't care, and, anyway, they were going to get a job and find a place of their own and I could live with them.

I had learned to do a man's work on a ranch, and there were other ranches around that needed hired hands. All of these things I had already considered after the Valliants mentioned Boys Town, but I felt a real need to review them again in my mind to prepare myself for a showdown in a very few hours. Overall, I felt lucky that this wasn't the only place in the world that was safe from my dad.

Tomorrow would be Friday, July fifth, another work day. My eyelids were heavy. I decided to lie down and try to get a few hours of sleep. There was no way I was going to resolve anything tonight.

Since returning to the Valliants, I'd been experiencing my nightmare at least once a week. Usually I could feel it coming on, either just before, or just after, going to bed. The sensation would come from somewhere within me—a gloom, or a sickening feeling in my gut, that would make me shudder and want to run away. I would feel somewhere between the world I was in and the world the nightmare was about to take me into—a feeling I had no control over. There was nothing to hold on to and no place to hide. Sometimes the Blob would dart in, and then dash out again, causing my chest to hurt with a rush of fear. I was feeling like this as I glanced at the Big Ben wind-up clock standing on the ammunition dresser. It was late, well past midnight. I shuddered with the thought of my approaching nightmare, facing the new workday, and the showdown with the Valliants at the breakfast table. I finally decided there was no avoiding any of these unpleasant things to come and carefully laid down in bed, where I soon curled into a squirming knot of pain and fear.

I sat straight up in bed, blinking and rubbing my eyes. The sun was high in the sky, shining directly through the window and onto my bed. I panicked. It was late and something just didn't feel right. What it was is there had been no wake-up call from Mr. Valliant. I took this to mean I no longer had a job, either. I glanced around my tiny jail-cell room, looking for an empty box in which to pack my few belongings. Finding nothing and hearing faint voices from the lower part of the house, I decided to brave up and face my punishment. What else could I do? They had me dead to rights.

I could see the kitchen table from the doorway as I stepped out of the Upper Room. Mr. Valliant was at the table staring into a cup of coffee. Mrs. Valliant was standing over the stove, banging pots and rattling pans. She was saying something to herself, or to Mr. Valliant. I walked into the kitchen and was startled to see Mr. Valliant turn and look at me with an amused grin. Mrs. Valliant looked at me without changing her expression and continued smacking her lips, dispersed with, "hmm, hmm, hmm," and muttering other words which I couldn't understand.

I sat down in my usual place across the table from Mr. Valliant and stared at my empty plate. Mrs. Valliant placed a steaming cup of coffee in front of me and went back to the stove. I helped myself to the sugar and cream. The suspense was mounting and I wanted to get it over with. When it seemed I could wait no longer, Mr. Valliant raised his head and looked straight at me. "We gotta move Pete's sheep wagon today, Mr. Man," and then he winked. "You better eat and catch Brownie and Red and get the team. The boys will be up pretty soon; Grimes has something planned for them." His grin widened. I returned his grin, but my spirits were not lifted much; I was still waiting for the hammer to fall.

"Ellen called this morning," Mrs. Valliant said, standing directly behind me, chewing on a piece of bacon. Her hot breath, mixed with spittle, rattled the hairs on top of my head. "She said you and Craig had some trouble at the carnival."

"Yes Ma'am," I replied in a low voice, and raised my eyes slightly to see Mr. Valliant still grinning.

"You two have to learn to get along. He's a good boy and you can't be fighting with him. But you're a good boy, too, Dennis. Now, when you see Craig again I want you to apologize to him. Ellen is very upset."

"Yes Ma'am," I murmured, again, but with no intentions of keeping my word.

I finished cramming down the last of my breakfast and scurried down the hill toward the barn, in high spirits. I met Clarence and Jerry as I led Red from the corral. They looked anxious and worried. I had told them at the dance that I might get fired because of my fight with Craig. "Mr. Valliant doesn't give a damn," I said, "and Mrs. Valliant is mad as hell, but I didn't get fired." They grinned, slapped me on the back, and we had a good laugh.

———

Grimes yelled at me as I was turning Red toward the pasture. "Run in the bay team with the others, Jerry and Clarence are going to clean corrals today."

Cleaning corrals meant sitting the manure spreader in the corrals, unhooking the team, and allowing them to stand two or three hours, while wet manure, mixed with hay, was pried from the corral floor with a manure fork and thrown into the wagon. When the wagon was full, the team was again hitched up, and the manure was taken to the field and spread. A chain in the bottom of the spreader moved the manure to the back which was caught with a paddle that threw the wet manure high into the air and spread it evenly on the meadow—and, depending on the direction of the wind, just as evenly on the driver's back and head. *Poor guys,* I snickered to myself.

Mr. Valliant was ready with our lunches and a large canvas bag of supplies for Pete when I returned to the ranch house, leading Brownie and the team. Mrs. Valliant walked beside him to the yard gate. She smiled at me and touched my shoulder. I returned her smile, sighed, and took a deep breath. I helped Mr. Valliant tie the supplies across the back of one of the horses, and held the team while he led Brownie to the hillside to mount.

It was a beautiful, sunny day. I'd slept very little during the night, but, at the moment, I couldn't remember when I had felt better about life. I cursed myself for being so upset about my troubles with Craig, relived the fight in my mind several times, and I could feel myself riding a little taller in the saddle. In my mind, the score was even, and I stretched my imagination to the point of visualizing Craig and I being friends.

TWENTY-ONE

The sheep were scattered like a thousand little cotton balls over the hillsides. Pete was standing in front of the wagon rinsing his false teeth in a bucket of water and holding a cigarette in his toothless face like a cigar. Pete shoved his teeth between his hollow cheeks, smiled and seemed pleased about seeing us. His beard had grown and I could only see a hump of hair covering the largest wart on his left cheek. Pete said two ewes had been lost to coyotes during the night and we would have some bum lambs to take back on our next camp move. I knew what he meant by that. We couldn't take them back today because it would be impossible to identify the bums for at least a week, when their heads would be blackened with dung from stealing milk from the backside of unsuspecting mothers.

The sun was settling in the west when we finished moving the wagon and leveling it the best we could. Pete was bringing the sheep to their new bed ground when we finished our job and started the two-hour trip back to the ranch.

I had not spoken to Mrs. Valliant about teaching me to read since returning to the ranch, but the subject was never far from my mind. I imagined the Valliants thought I would soon be leaving, and their obligations to me fulfilled. As the days wore on my situation seemed more hopeless, and I could only be sure of two things: there was no way I could start to school in September, and I was *not* going to Boys Town.

We arrived back at the ranch just as the sun disappeared below the horizon. Stopping at the ranch house, Mr. Valliant handed Brownie's reins to me and I led the horses to the barn, before stopping by the bunkhouse. Jerry and Clarence were lying on their bunks, looking like part of the barnyard, and smelling the same. I stood looking at them, while they pretended to be dead. "Hey guys, let's go eat." I said, in a cheerful tone. They groaned, got to their feet without a word, and we walked to the house in silence.

———

The letter arrived. Not long after I started living with the Valliants I learned to read the mood of the household by listening to a few lines of Mrs. Valliant's monotone chatter (even though I couldn't understand many of the words), and I could tell something was different as I entered the kitchen. The Cousins were still on their hands and knees, bending over the little stream, scrubbing manure stink from their faces and bodies. I walked to the table and sat down. Mrs. Valliant touched my shoulder from behind. "We got a letter from Boys Town today," she said, then walked back to the stove.

I could feel my face get warm. I followed her with my eyes as she left the kitchen and walked into the living room and shuffled some papers on the roll-top desk. She returned with a single piece of paper outstretched in her hand, handed it to me, and resumed her conversation with the cook stove. I put the letter in front of my face and stared at it for a moment, confused. It was no secret to either of them that I couldn't read one single word in the letter.

Grimes was reading a book in the living room, waiting to be called for supper. The Cousins were still scrubbing themselves in the creek. Puzzled and anxious to know what was in the letter, I looked at Mrs. Valliant and stammered, "*I* can't read it."

Mrs. Valliant said something that I didn't understand. "I'm sorry, I can't hear you," I said.

"Boys Town said they can't take you," Mr. Valliant said. There was an edge to his voice.

"It's okay, Dennis," Mrs. Valliant said. "I'll read it to you later."

Clarence and Jerry came to the table and plopped down in their manure-soaked clothes, smelling like the barnyard after a heavy rain.

I went to bed immediately after supper and lay awake for a long time, staring at the dark ceiling and listening to the crickets sing their scratchy tunes. School would start September ninth, just two months away. I could read no better than the day I returned from Texas, which was not at all, and I couldn't count past one hundred. I couldn't write letters or numbers, and I knew there was no way I could start school in September. Everything was going wrong. I felt the only thing I had to be thankful for was the letter from Boys Town, relieving my anxious thoughts about how I would tell the Valliants about my decision not to go there.

When I left the ranch and returned to my father all I could think about was returning to the ranch. But now I'm here, the dreams are gone, and it's not what I expected at all.

I didn't want to return to Grandma; there would be no school, ever—just picking and hoeing cotton, and stealing chickens the rest of my life. I didn't have enough money saved to live in town without a job, and I had no prospects for a job. Mosers were the only neighboring ranchers I had met, and, for sure, I couldn't ask them for a job. In desperation, I decided I would talk to Jerry and Clarence again about returning to Missouri with them after the hay harvest. If things didn't turn out living with the Hagens I could always go back to Grandma.

After making my decision to leave the ranch with the Cousins, I slept well. Mr. Valliant woke me at dawn with his standard greeting. At breakfast, Mr. Valliant and Grimes discussed the necessary preparations for the hay harvest, which they hoped to start in one week. A full crew required seven men and the ranch was two men short. They decided Grimes should go to Saratoga and spread the word about their need to hire, and Mrs. Valliant was to call the county agent in Rawlins for his help in hiring a crew.

At breakfast, Mrs. Valliant had said she needed to hire a local girl from town to help her with the cooking and housekeeping chores during the hay harvest.

The Cousins and I were cleaning harnesses before starting to repair some of the horse-drawn hay equipment, when I saw Grimes and Mrs. Valliant leave the ranch in separate cars. We were still in the shop working on the sulky rakes when they returned in the late afternoon—not five minutes apart.

Grimes stopped at the bunkhouse and two young cowboy-types got out of his car, each carrying a canvas bag. Grimes drove off in the direction of the ranch house. Mrs. Valliant drove by a short time later. A young girl was sitting in the seat beside her. The girl looked to be about eighteen-years old. Jerry and Clarence looked at each other with raised eyebrows. Jerry smiled broadly and punched Clarence on the shoulder. "Hot *damn!* Jerry shouted, now we're cooking, man!"

The Cousins and I went to the bunkhouse to meet their new roommates. One looked to be about twenty-five-years old and the other man, wearing a sour face, looked about thirty. The sour-faced man was short and stout, with a thick neck, jutting jaw and several days growth of whiskers. He wore dirty Levi jeans, a straw hat, black snap-button shirt and a worn-out pair of low-heel work boots. His breath smelled of whiskey. "My name is Jack...Jack Mitchum," he said, slurring his words. "but you damn well better call me Blackjack."

The Cousins and I said, "Okay," in unison, nodded as fast as we could and managed a weak group smile.

The younger hired hand was tall, maybe over six feet. He wore a straw hat, faded Levi jeans, blue snap-shirt and cowboy boots with slits worn through, or cut through, at the sides. He had a few days growth of beard under his friendly, sunburned face. "I'm David Morgan," he said. "You can call me Dave, as long as you don't forget to call me for supper." He let out a little chuckle.

We washed our hands and faces in the creek, went into the kitchen and Mrs. Valliant introduced us to her new help. Her name was Dana Dix. She was a shy, tall, rather slim girl, with a sweet smile, crooked front teeth and dull red hair that hung shoulder-length. She wore loose, green, cotton pants over her long legs. When her back was turned, the hired hands looked her over and exchanged grins. My interests focused on the way she always grabbed the cloth on her pants, above the knee, with her left hand and lifted her leg before taking a step—then the sudden clumping noise of her left foot when it hit the kitchen floor.

At the supper table, Mr. Valliant and Grimes questioned the new hands about their riding and teamster skills. Mr. Valliant seemed to be satisfied that the new hands could handle themselves around horses, because he said they would go with Grimes and me to bring in the teams for the hay harvest.

"Dennis," Mrs. Valliant whispered, as I scraped my plate, "when Dana and I finish the dishes, I want to read you the letter from Boys Town."

I said, "Okay," but I didn't understand why. Mr. Valliant had already told me that Boys Town wouldn't take me. I walked outside and watched the guys amble down the hill toward the bunkhouse.

It wasn't long until Mrs. Valliant joined me on the little bridge in front of the house, carrying the single sheet of paper in her hand. She didn't say anything before putting the letter to her face and started reading in a quiet voice. When she finished she dropped the letter to her side and looked at me with a sad, tormented expression.

The contents of the letter held no surprises for me. Father Flanigan thanked her for inquiring about Boys Town. I would not be a good candidate for his school, he said. The other boys would take exception to my lack of reading and other skills and make my life uncomfortable. He suggested she look into some special schools in other states that may consider admitting a boy of my slower learning abilities.

She was still looking at me with a sorrowful expression, when she said, "I don't know what we're going to do, Dennis. I told Richard about the letter and he said not to worry about anything. He'll come over soon as possible to talk about it."

I wanted to tell her how sorry I was for how she felt, but my eyes started to burn and I had to turn away. I desperately wanted to tell her the truth, that I never intended to go to Boys Town, and, anyway, I would be leaving with Clarence and Jerry. I didn't tell her all of this because I was afraid she would send me back to Dad.

The next morning I saddled Red and corralled the other horses. For the new guys I cut out a sleek steel gray mare and a fat, round belly, roan gelding, neither of which had been ridden for over a year. The gray and the gelding were both twelve-years old, or more, were reliable saddle horses, but would prove to be a challenge for the first hour or so for the new hands. Grimes' old horse, Billy, tagged along and corralled with the others.

There were two teams in the small pasture. The extra workhorses needed for hay harvest were pastured on the open range part of the ranch. It would require four good horsemen to drive them the five miles back to ranch headquarters. The teams were together with a few mares and some wild geldings.

Grimes said it would be an all day trip to find the horses, pressure them across gullies, hills, and creek bottoms, until they were finally driven into some smaller pastures, where the job would get easier. We had ridden only a short distance from the barn when Blackjack noticed the strange way Grimes rode in his saddle.

Grimes never rode old Billy straight up, like other cowboys. He rode with his ass sticking out to the left side, leaning the rest of his body to the right side to balance himself. I could see Blackjack noticed this right off, because he kept staring at Grimes. Anyway, we're all just riding along, not saying anything, until Blackjack pipes up in his brackish tongue, "Hey Grimes, what's the matter with your ass? You got piles or something?" Everyone laughed. I laughed too, although I didn't know what the word piles meant until Jerry told me later that day. Grimes either didn't hear Blackjack's remark, or didn't care, and he didn't say a word.

We found the horses bunched on a hilltop, violently switching their tails—fighting deer flies. They ran toward us and circled in a curious manner, then high-tailed it toward more open country. Luckily for us, their path of travel was toward the ranch headquarters. Grimes motioned to the rest of us to let them go, and I knew it was because it would be too much of a job for our small crew to cut the teams out of thirty or more wild horses. They ran until they were snorting and white with sweat, before we slowly rode upon them. It wasn't long before they were munching on fresh grass in a smaller pasture. From there, it was a cinch to trail them further into the corrals, where we cut the strays and turned the workhorses out into the small horse pasture with the other ranch horses.

Blackjack, Dave and I drove the strays back to the open range on a high run. Our horse roundup had taken much less time than we had expected, and by early afternoon we were back to repairing harnesses and talking about how much fun the roundup had been.

TWENTY-TWO

Most outfits in the Platte Valley had started to use tractors and converted, stripped-down, Model-A Ford cars for the hay harvest. The Valliant ranch used horses. Booth Valliant scoffed at using motorized hay equipment by saying he could pay for the whole hay harvest for what his neighbors paid for gasoline. Anyway, what was he going to do with the teams?

I'd never worked in hay harvest. But I could harness and drive a team and I was excited to get started. I had a vague idea what it was all about from what Mr. Valliant had told me—and I had helped repair all of the equipment. Mr. Valliant said knowing how to handle a team was most important; the rest would come with experience on each piece of equipment.

My first job was driving a sulky rake. It was a greenhorn, boring, disgusting job and I hated it from the first day. The sulky rake had two large metal wheels on each end, which supported a row of metal teeth spaced about four inches apart. The rake itself was ten-feet wide, with a wooden tongue attached to the front where two horses were hitched. On top of the contraption was a metal seat for the operator. I drove around and around the field until the teeth were full of hay, raised the teeth at the same place each time, dumping the hay in a windrow. The teeth were raised by the use of a foot-operated trip mechanism. My rake had a dog-clutch in the wheel hubs. When I activated the foot pedal, the rod to which the teeth were attached, would catch in the wheel hub and lift up the teeth until the hay dropped free, then the teeth would drop again. Day after day, I fought sleep, sometimes dragging completely through a windrow. Clarence was assigned to a similar fate.

The most dangerous and prestigious job was mowing hay. Grimes and Blackjack got the two mowers because they were considered the best teamsters. A run-away team pulling a mower could kill the driver, the team, and destroy everything else in its path. It didn't look dangerous, and every day I dreamed about sitting behind the most powerful team on the ranch and watching the hay fall into a perfect path. After riding the sulky rake for two weeks, I begged Mr. Valliant to put Blackjack on the rake and let me operate the mower. It was another week before he consented, and a disgruntled Blackjack and I changed jobs.

The mower was a simple looking machine. The six-foot mower, or sickle blade, was off-set to the right, slightly in front of the driver, who sat in the middle of the machine on a metal seat that hung behind the two metal wheels on each side of the mower. As the horses pulled the machine, gears under the seat turned the sickle back and forth and laid the hay out in a smooth surface. Only the youngest, biggest, and strongest horses were used to pull the mowers. Mowers were extremely hard to pull and the horses had to be rested, or allowed to "blow", about every fifteen minutes. At noon, the team that worked in the morning was taken to the barn and a new team was used in the afternoon. The only danger of a run-away team was during the first hour of mowing.

Throughout the haying season, I was allowed to change jobs and I succeeded in learning to operate the other two types of machines used in haying, which were the Pusher—used to push the hay over the wooden stacker, and the Sweep, which gathered the hay in the windrows and moved it to the stacker.

We were into hay harvest about a week when I started hanging out with the other hired men in the bunkhouse after supper, learning their ways, and watching their pastime play. Their games were rough: boxing matches with real gloves, arm wrestling, or shooting sheep turds off each others heads at ten paces. Of course, the sheep turd was placed on top of a hat, which sat loosely on top of their head. Blackjack was the only one who could hit the turd dead center every time.

They didn't let me join in any of the games, which I understood completely. But I never thought for a minute that anyone would ever get seriously hurt, until they all started picking on my friend, Pete. It was almost dark when I decided to leave the house and see what the guys were doing. I could hear angry voices long before I got to the bunkhouse. They were all calling Pete names and pushing him around. I yelled, "Hey, you bastards, stop it!"

They all looked at me with menacing stares, and someone said, "Stay outa this kid." I froze. Pete ran for the outhouse. When they turned away from me, they—all four of them—raised their pistols or rifles and fired into the outhouse, not once, but more times than I could count. They were all jumping around and laughing. All I could say was, "You killed him, you killed him! Oh *shit!*"

I was in shock, unable to cry, with the sure knowledge that I would never, ever, see my friend, Pete, again. For a minute or two I just stared at the outhouse, picturing Pete riddled with bullets, his body all crumpled, his head dangling lifelessly in one of the holes. Then I tried to get straight in my mind why anyone would shoot poor old Pete, then stand around and laugh about it.

When I couldn't stand their crazy laughter and my grief any longer, I turned and started walking slowly toward the house. That's when I heard Pete call my name. I turned and Pete was crawling out the outhouse door on his hands and knees, laughing his fool head off. I never asked him, and he never said where he was when all the shooting was going on, but I never completely forgave him.

When it was too dark for outdoor games, the men all gathered in the bunkhouse to play poker and tell dirty jokes. There were some cruel jokes, mostly by Blackjack, about Dana and what should be done with the wooden leg while they were doing it. He bragged that she constantly kept her eyes on him and boasted she would be a sure thing for him at some time in the near future.

Meanwhile, Dana and I had become good friends. I felt sorry for her, and I didn't laugh at the bunkhouse jokes. Dana told me herself how she had lost her leg from an innocent insect bite when she was only six years old. She said the bite became infected and they had to amputate her leg above the knee to save her life.

Sometimes Dana and I took short walks together after supper. Her grabbing her left leg, placing it in front, limping, then dragging the wooden leg behind, then bending to the right and slightly forward to allow the leg to catch up for another lift ahead. Me slowly scuffling along beside her, trying not to watch what her wooden leg was doing. She told me her family was very poor. She had several brothers and sisters, with her being the oldest, and she had to quit school during her sophomore year to help her mother look after the household. I told her some things about my life, leaving off the troubles with my dad, and confided to her about my plans to leave with Clarence and Jerry.

At mealtimes I took particular notice, and always repaid Dana with a big grin, when she regularly saw to it that I got the extra large piece of pie. I smiled to myself every time Blackjack ended up with the smallest portions of everything. She told me she hated the way Blackjack looked at her and despised him in every way.

———

Every Saturday night Grimes drove all the hired men to town. I was never allowed to go—Mrs. Valliant saying they were just going to get drunk and raise 'cain' and I would likely get thrown in jail with them. Some Saturday nights, the Valliants would take Dana and me into town for a picture show. They rarely went to the picture show with us, though. While waiting for us, they visited with people on the street, or drove to the cemetery and walked about the graves.

It disappointed me to see them parked in front of the theater when the show was over. I wanted to run past the bar, just one block away, and see what the guys were doing. Dana would tell them all about the picture show on the way home. I'd sit quietly and imagine all the excitement the hired men were having. Grimes and his crew wouldn't be home when we arrived, because he allowed them a ten o'clock curfew. At exactly ten they were expected to meet him at Donelan's Drugstore, those who were waiting came back to the ranch—the others were left.

Blackjack never, ever, made the curfew. Grimes would go back into town on Sunday afternoon to get him out of jail, or off the street—always broke, dirty and hung-over, with part of his paycheck still souring on the front of his shirt. I immediately went to the bunkhouse when Grimes brought Blackjack home. He'd been in a fight and he looked so bad I wondered how he had survived at all. He'd describe the fight in detail and we'd all shake our heads. I pictured some poor cowboy still lying and bleeding on the street, with all his teeth gone and his nose smashed flat. He once told us he had a price on his head in some other state, and I stopped to wonder why anyone would pay a price for such a sorry head as his. After listening to his weekend adventures, we would slowly walk with him to the ranch house for supper, with him still feeling the drink, pulling his hat down over his eyes, dancing around in front of us, reliving his weekend battles.

TWENTY-THREE

It was early on in August; we were less than half through haying. Richard had been to the ranch two times since we received the letter from Boys Town. Because I suspected he had something to do with the letter, I was suspicious of him and immediately left the house when he came. I would walk to the barn, all puffed up, kicking stones on the road, resenting Richard and everybody else in the whole world. I didn't care what they talked about, I'd tell myself. I didn't belong to them, or anybody else. After hay harvest I would show them all.

It was Saturday. School would start on Monday. I felt like standing up and shouting this simple fact to everyone at the breakfast table. No mention was made about me starting to school or teaching me to read since the letter came from Boys Town. My rage and frustration steadily built to the point that I was constantly in a state of bad humor—all my energies given to resentment, despising myself for being such a dummy and blaming the Valliants for all of it. My chest hurt, and I heard very little of the conversation around the table until Mr. Valliant remarked that it would take about another two weeks to finish putting up the hay crop.

I was in a towering rage all day, yelling at the team pulling the heavy mower, cursing them when they needed a breather. I had been mowing hay for several days, and I was glad today was one of those days, because I could be alone and not have to talk to anyone. After supper, I would tell them about my plans to leave the ranch. I wanted the day to end, to get on with it. Maybe they would fire me and I could leave now—tonight.

Clarence had written to his mother about my coming and he said she was looking forward to seeing me. I felt okay about going away with the Hagens. But, deep down inside, my soul was crushed; I would be leaving the ranch forever.

I reasoned that Clarence's mother could teach me to read and do math, and maybe I could even start to school next year, but that wasn't what I really wanted. I loved the ranch, the Valliants, the daily chores, the routine. I wanted the Valliants to care about me, to want me to stay and live with them. I wanted to be a part of their family.

Now, I realized that none of that was going to happen. I was just another hired man that came and went. I would go with Clarence and Jerry. If Clarence's mother didn't want me I would catch a bus and return to Grandma. Grandma would be leaving Memphis in November. I knew they went to Dallas from Memphis, but I also knew Dallas was a big city and they would be hard to find. I eased my mind with the thought that Missouri couldn't be that far from Memphis, and I would have plenty of time to catch Grandma before she left.

Monday came and went. It was just another day of mowing, raking, sweeping and stacking hay for everyone except me. I couldn't get it out of my mind, what it would be like to be in school, playing football, baseball, and making new friends. I didn't speak to anyone all day.

———

Two more days and hay harvest would end and I still hadn't told the Valliants about my plans to leave the ranch with Clarence and Jerry. For several days I went into my poor little fella mood, and didn't speak to anyone except Dana.

Every night before falling asleep I resolved to tell the Valliants about my plans, but I always found some excuse not to say anything. I could tell Mr. Valliant noticed the change in me and he did his best to cheer me up with one-liners at mealtime, but, unlike the past, I failed to find humor in his small talk. I kept my face down, ate as fast as I could, quietly excused myself and walked alone to the bunkhouse.

During this time I was deep into feeling myself unworthy, somehow at fault for something I couldn't identify. The feeling never went away after I saw the expression on Mrs. Valliant's face when she told me about the letter from Boys Town. I always felt that somehow she saw through me and didn't like what she saw. I had a feeling that much of the Valliants' time was given to talking about how bad I was and what a sad thing it was that I had become a burden to them. My feelings of unworthiness increased after I heard Mrs. Valliant remark to Mr. Valliant: 'Poor Dennis, he will always have to do the hardest kind of work because he will always stutter.'

During the last two weeks of haying, I drew emotionally farther away from the Valliants. Aside from the time I was with Dana on our short walks after supper, I spent most of my waking hours either working, wandering around the barns and corrals in a trance, or hanging out with the guys at the bunkhouse. Some nights I would go directly to my room, lie on my bed, and think about Mary Lee. It bothered me not knowing what had become of my sister after we left Reliance. She was the only true friend I ever had, and I spent a lot of time wondering if I would ever see her again. Sometimes I imagined finding her again. We walk down a little road toward a beautiful ranch house where we are welcomed by a friendly old couple. The old couple insists we attend school, where all the kids become our friends. After school we join other kids laughing and playing games. Sleep overcomes me, and sometimes I dream about her, but my dreams are more like nightmares: Mollie marries a cruel man who beats Mary Lee, and she runs away into the darkness.

The house shook from thunder and lighting. Sheets of rain swept my window. I dressed and went down for breakfast, dreading a long day with nothing to do except think about leaving the ranch. None of the hired men had raincoats. Their wet shirts stuck to them, as they quietly ate their breakfast.

Everyone seemed to know, but no one spoke the words: today was the last day of work. There was only one small field of hay left to stack, and the hay was already in the windrow. We all silently understood that Mr. Valliant wouldn't keep a full crew on the ranch two or three days waiting to harvest a few windrows of hay.

I could picture the ride into town, all of us cramped into Grimes' little Ford. Everyone was through eating, just staring at their plates. "That hay in the windrows is going to be several days drying," Mr. Valliant said. "The Missus will get you guys a check and Grimes can take you into town. If you ask around, there'll be some other ranchers looking for help."

Mrs. Valliant bent low and put her face to my ear. "Dennis, wait until it stops raining to milk the cow," she whispered, "Booth and I want to talk to you."

At that moment I was sure Dana had told the Valliants about my plans to leave. I was both relieved and disappointed. Dana was my friend. She knew I wanted to stay on the ranch and she had told them, hoping they would change their mind about keeping me. Now that the word was out, I didn't need to explain anything. Maybe they wanted to apologize, or wish me good luck, but I didn't want any of that. I would get my paycheck and walk out the door—and I didn't need to explain where I was going.

Mrs. Valliant sat at the roll-top desk to figure time and write paychecks. I went to my room and packed my things into a cardboard box. I carried the box through the house and sat it down near the door of the porch. When I straightened up, Mrs. Valliant was standing there, just waiting to speak. She asked me to come with her to the living room, and then she asked me to sit down.

"Dana told us about your plans to go with Clarence and Jerry," she began slowly, measuring her words. "We're sorry to hear that you're leaving. Booth and I have been talking and we're worried about what might happen to you if you leave the ranch."

"But what about school?"

"We can talk about that later," she said, putting an arm around me, pulling me close.

I was afraid to say any more. I smiled at her for a fleeting moment, turned and hurried through the kitchen and onto the porch and grabbed my box. Coming back through the kitchen, Dana stepped in front of me, clutched my shoulders with an iron grip and hugged me, causing me to drop my box. She was crying. I didn't want Dana to see my face, and I wriggled free and ran through the house.

The rain stopped, and the hired men came back to the house for their paychecks. Dave was first to get his check. "Good luck, Dennis," he said, smiling.

Blackjack walked out the door without a word. Jerry and Clarence were last. Clarence and Jerry turned to leave and I followed them outside. "They asked me to stay," I said. "I won't be going with you."

"If you change your mind you're welcome any time," Clarence said.

Clarence walked back into the house, returned with a piece of paper, folded it several times and stuffed it into my pants pocket. "That's our address," he said.

———

Maybe part of it was just a temporary swaggering show of courage, but I definitely felt better about everything than the scared-rabbit little boy who timidly stepped off the bus from Texas back in March. I had worked as hard as any of the hired men and learned more than most of them. I'd faced rejection (imagined or otherwise) from the people I most depended upon, and planned other ways to live my life. No one is going to push me around again, I decided, not my dad, not Craig, not Mark. I wasn't afraid of being kicked off the ranch any more. Anyway, I knew how to work on a ranch, and I could find another job if things got tough again. I had Clarence and Jerry's address, and, as a last resort, I knew where to find Grandma.

At last I was going to learn to read and go to school—and be just like other kids. I didn't feel loved, but I didn't feel unloved. I knew I wasn't wanted, but I didn't feel particularly unwanted, and I sensed there was a difference.

With the hay crew gone, there was no more work for Dana. She would return home and look for another job, cleaning house and cooking for another ranch. That night we took our walk along the road on top of the hill. She apologized for telling the Valliants about my plans to leave. I told her it was okay; I was glad she had told them, it worked out better for me.

When I returned from my walk with Dana, Mrs. Valliant said she and Booth needed to talk to me. Mr. Valliant and I sat on the lumpy couch and Mrs. Valliant paced the floor in front of the fireplace. Dana went to her room with a book. "We don't know what we are going to do with you, Dennis," she started, "but we didn't think going with Clarence and Jerry was the right thing. We've talked to Richard. He likes you and he isn't happy that you can't start to school this fall. We've spoken to Pauline and Bob Ware. They can't have kids and they may want to adopt you. You can't start to school now, but if I can teach you to read, you can start to school next fall. You can help Booth on the ranch and I'll give you lessons every day. Maybe you can learn to read and count numbers and do some simple math. We'll just have to wait and see."

I smiled, thanked them for letting me stay and hurried off to my room. I knew Pauline and Bob Ware. Bob was a Presbyterian minister in Saratoga, and Pauline taught piano lessons.

It was just another one of my secrets, but I had sooner walked to Missouri than be adopted by Pauline and Bob Ware, or anyone, for that matter. I didn't want anyone owning me again, telling me what to do and wearing out my bottom with a switch whenever they felt like it. Whatever needed to be done in my life I could do it—with maybe a little help from the Valliants.

Waiting for sleep, and still feeling good about not having to leave the ranch, I reflected on what Mrs. Valliant had said. I felt she had made a study of me, but with all the wrong conclusions—she didn't know me, not at all. She had me figured as a dumb little cotton-picker, who stuttered, and she figured because I was slow with my speech, I must be slow in my head. But that's not how I judged myself at all, not any more. I knew I was energetic, aggressive, and smart enough to learn to read. Learning to do things on the ranch came easy and I figured I was at least as smart as Craig and Mark. I could learn to read, count numbers and do math—she would see—they would all see. I would go to school, and some day I'd even learn to talk as good as anyone.

TWENTY-FOUR

Ranch life went on and I pulled my share of the weight, like any hired man. The only difference was, after the last of the hay was stacked, I no longer received a man's pay. I was given board and room and five dollars a week, and was schooled by Mrs. Valliant when time permitted, which seemed more than fair to me.

Schooling was always secondary to ranch work, though. On days that I couldn't spend time with Mrs. Valliant on new lessons, I carried slips of paper in my pocket and learned to spell words while doing ranch chores on horseback, or cleaning the chicken house, or shoveling manure from the barn.

I was in a hurry to prove to myself I could learn, to show the Valliants I wasn't a dummy, to make them proud of me—all the time thinking about the day I would start regular school. There wasn't a moment in my waking day that I wasn't learning new skills, or rehearsing something I had learned the day before. On days that Pete taught me to spell new words, I rehearsed them all day and surprised everyone at the supper table. Everyone encouraged me except Grimes. But I never once figured it was because he didn't like me or anything. Grimes was just being Grimes.

In early October we brought the sheep home from the mountains, separated the lambs from their mothers, and culled the old ewes. Ewes were culled at age six, regardless of physical condition. The old culled ewes and weaning lambs were placed in a feedlot corral and fed alfalfa hay and grain for two weeks, or until the lambs felt comfortable being weaned.

The second week in October, we drove the old ewes and wether lambs to the rail head (a distance of ten miles), located at Tie Siding. They would be shipped to Denver by rail where the old ewes were sold as "canners," and the lambs bought by feeders to be fattened for the eastern lamb meat market.

It was the middle of October, cattle roundup time. Snow and blizzards were expected any time after the end of October and losses could be high—it had happened before. During roundup, we saddled our horses early and rode the five miles to the Forest Service boundary, then separated before riding into the golden Aspen meadows to search for cows and calves.

Riding alone throughout the day, each cowboy gathered as many cows as he could find and drove them out of the trees toward the ranch boundary. By late afternoon we threw our small herds together, cut out the stray cows and calves and drove the Valliant cattle through the boundary fence. Within a few days, the cows would trail themselves to the ranch headquarters and be let into meadow pastures with the sheep.

Roundup lasted for two weeks, and during this time I had no schooling from Mrs. Valliant—but I always had scraps of paper stuffed in my pockets. The first day we sat at the kitchen table after roundup, she was amazed at how much I had learned on my own, and showed a different attitude toward my learning abilities. I could now read in a second-grade reader book, add and subtract single digit numbers with ease, and Mrs. Valliant said my spelling ability was far beyond anything she had imagined. Because I had had little time for printing my letters, and no skills in cursive writing, we decided to concentrate the next few weeks on writing skills.

Steer calves were over-wintered, summered on lush foothills pasture and sold as yearlings. Cold, snow and blizzards could roll in any day now and it was time to round up the yearlings and drive them to the railhead, known as Tie Siding, for shipping to buyers in Denver.

The long cattle drive to Tie Siding was scheduled for Saturday. Mr. Valliant asked Craig and Mark to help. Although I hadn't seen them, I was sure they still resented me for not leaving after hay harvest.

The day I had looked forward to the most turned crappy almost from the beginning. Early on in the drive, I was feeling good, like I had won something or had one over on them. The feeling didn't last long. And if I could judge from the looks on their faces, Craig and Mark weren't enjoying the day much either. We kept our distance, when possible, with them riding one side of the herd, me the other. When it was necessary for our horses to be close, to keep the herd moving, I glanced at Mark, and we exchanged blank looks. Craig never acknowledged my glances, staring straight ahead, as if I didn't exist.

The first hour of the cattle drive, I tried to be friendly with Craig by riding past him with a friendly, "Hi." The first time I thought maybe he didn't hear me. The second time I rode so close that our horses' shoulders touched, then I looked directly at him and repeated my greeting. Both my tries at friendliness ended with him turning his horse off at an angle and riding away from me.

I didn't want to finish the drive with feelings I couldn't pull myself out of, with Craig riding off feeling smug, bragging to Mark and his friends how he had frustrated and made a fool out of me. I could picture myself lying in bed that night beating up on myself because I had stuck my neck out and let him chop it off. No way was I going to let that happen. I had to do something to wipe that proud, bullshit little smile off his face.

We corralled the steers at Tie Siding, watered them, and loaded them into railroad cars for the trip to Denver. Mrs. Valliant had gone ahead of us in the car with a hot meal. We finished off roast beef sandwiches in the shade of the corral before starting the long ride back to the ranch.

My feelings were hurt to the point that I wanted to crawl into a badger hole; I needed to make my move. But before I tried to level the playing field I wanted to make one more gesture of friendliness. I wracked my brain half of the way home trying to figure out how to show an act of friendliness, but mostly I thought about how to get even when that didn't work.

I was riding to the left, then came Grimes, Mr. Valliant, Pete, Craig and Mark. Pulling back, I put Red into a trot behind the other horses and moved between Pete and Craig. With a cigarette dangling from his mouth, Pete turned and flashed me a smile. Craig continued staring straight ahead.

What to say--how to say it? I pondered. The sentence had to be short. "Hey Craig, you play football?" I asked. No answer. Not even a look. I'd had it. He was going to pay.

I couldn't just drag him off his horse and beat the crap out of him in front of everybody, nothing like I pictured doing. I rode close enough for our horses to touch shoulders. "Craig—I heard that you're a cheerleader," I said, in a sissy-like tone of voice.

Everything about him changed. His face suddenly became red and awful. It took him a minute to get all puffy and red, before he looked at me. "You son of a bitch," he sputtered. I pulled on the reins, and moved to the back of the other horses, feeling good all over.

Supper was a slow, silent meal. The food was good and there was lots of it, but everyone was saddle-worn and bone tired. Each of us, engrossed in our own private world, ate, excused ourselves, and wearily shuffled off to bed, or to be alone: Pete to the bunkhouse, Grimes to his bed, the Valliants to the threadbare couch, and I to the Upper Room.

For the first time in weeks, I was utterly downcast; wondering if I had made a serious mistake not going with the Cousins or returning to Grandma's. Lying in bed, I relived the events of the day and thought of a dozen ways I could have acted differently, which I imagined would have caused a different outcome. I viewed Craig as a sissy and a spoiled mamma's boy. His feelings and pride had been hurt and there was no way I would ever be able to get along with him. I thrashed in bed and worried. *When I start to school, Craig will turn all the kids against me.* I convinced myself that my dream of making friends and being like the rest of the kids in school just wasn't in the cards.

If the Valliants knew about the hard feelings between Craig and me they didn't let on. Several times during the past few weeks I thought about opening up and telling them how much it hurt me to be rejected by Craig and shunned by Mark. But I reasoned that, after all, they were their grandparents, and it wasn't likely they would sympathize with my needs. To make matters worse, they never missed a chance to brag about what wonderful grandsons they had. I'd come a long ways since returning from Texas; if I could just hang tough a little longer, until I could learn to read better and get some more experience with ranch work, I could get a job most anywhere—far away from all the Craigs in the world.

I thought again about running away before winter came on full blast, and the weather got too cold to hitchhike. If I ran away, I would be all alone in the world unless I could find Grandma or the Hagen cousins, and it scared me to think about it. But how much worse would that be than being ignored, pushed from behind, and laughed at, with a lot more to come? Now half asleep, I figured that sooner or later I would have to admit that life on the Valliant ranch would never be right for me. I just didn't fit.

The next morning, with the ugly experience of the cattle drive pushed into the back of my mind, I was eager to face the new day. Every day seemed to hold a new adventure, and I was ready. At breakfast, I heard Mr. Valliant say: "Work is going to be kind of slow around here until we start feeding cattle. You guys want to flex your muscles on some colts?"

I glanced at Pete, who wasn't saying a word, and wondered if flexing his muscles on a colt was how he received his half-moon-shaped head. "Yeah, I guess Dennis and I could run in some of those long yearlings and take a look at them," Pete said, after a long silence. "I don't think we got muscles enough, or corral enough, to handle those ol' stout two-year-olds."

I was almost light-headed. I could feel myself smiling while I finished breakfast. I looked at Mr. Valliant and he broke with a little mischievous grin. Mrs. Valliant mumbled something to herself about broken arms and broken legs. Pete finished his breakfast in silence.

When chores were done, Pete, Grimes and I saddled and rode the five miles to the flat prairie, west of the headquarters, where the extra horses grazed year-around—no matter what the weather or condition of the grass. The only time these horses saw a human was during the early summer, when it was necessary to gather the draft teams for haying. Aside from the draft horses, and two or three saddle horses that were seldom ridden, none of them had ever been inside a corral or had a rope on them. They were unbranded wild horses.

There were about thirty horses in the herd, and it was necessary to drive them all to the corrals. The colts couldn't be driven without the mares, and the mares wouldn't separate from the draft horses. The draft horses knew the way and once they started toward the ranch, the wild horses followed.

I sized up all the colts from the first sighting of the herd. They were wild as coyote pups. My favorite was a steel gray that was always near the lead of the pack. He was too small to be a two-year old; I guessed him to be a long yearling, or about sixteen-months old. When the herd was safely corralled, we put our saddle horses in the barn and sat on the fence for quite awhile, watching the horses mill around the corral, kicking and biting at each other; some of them trying to escape by jumping the high fence.

"I'm going to take the little black with the one stocking foot," Pete said. "Which one catches your fancy?"

"I want the steel gray," I said. "I'll call him Sonny Boy."

We cut our two picks from the herd and trailed the others back to the wild horse pasture.

I didn't know how to break a colt; I would be taking all my lessons from Pete. "We'll keep those two colts in the round corral for a few days," Pete said, shifting in his saddle. "They'll settle down and get used to the notion of being confined in a few days. If we put them in the pasture they'll tear down every damn fence on the ranch until they get back to the open range."

The weather stayed good until the middle of December, with frosty mornings, and short, crispy cold days. During the morning hours Pete fixed fence, cleaned barns and prepared the hay wagons in preparation for feeding at the first snow. After helping

Mrs. Valliant wash breakfast dishes, I'd take my place at the kitchen table with my books, pencils and papers. But concentrating on school work was hard; my mind was on Sonny Boy.

The colts were allowed to settle down in the round corral two days before starting the gentling and breaking routine. We introduced ourselves to the colts by standing in the middle of the pen and watching them run in circles, snorting and trying to jump the fence. After about half an hour of running in circles, they were ready to give us their attention. Pete roped Sonny Boy with his lariat, snubbed one end to the snubbing post, located in the middle of the arena, and that's when the rodeo started.

Sonny Boy kicked, reared, snorted and raised some general hell until he decided to break loose with a steady pull against the rope, braced all four legs and pulled backwards. The rope tightened around his neck, shutting off his breathing. It took about three minutes of this before Sonny Boy slowly slumped to the ground and rolled over on his side.

When Sonny Boy hit the ground, Pete ran down the rope and sat on his head while I loosened the rope from the snubbing post. The three feed sacks that we had tied together were nearby. I used the sacks to flog him about the rear and shoulders, sat on him, and rubbed the sacks all over his body. After catching his breath, he wanted up. Pete held him as long as he could while I continued rubbing his backside with the sacks.

Wild-eyed, Sonny Boy propped himself upright on wobbly legs, his breath coming quick and heavy. I held the rope snug while Pete slowly worked his way up the rope. He was within touching distance when Sonny Boy reared, and the whole performance was repeated.

Pete haltered Sonny Boy on the ground and removed the lariat from his neck. I tied the halter rope to the snubbing post, and we walked away. Soon he was on his rubbery legs again, his whole body as unsteady as a bowl of Jell-O pudding. It was a full fifteen minutes before he regained his composure. We left him standing, with the halter rope tied to the snubbing post. Pete was cursing because he had lost his cigarettes in the dirt during the excitement. We walked to the bunkhouse for a fresh pack of Chesterfields and left the colt standing, tethered to the snubbing post.

Sonny Boy was still dazed and wild-eyed when we returned to the corral. Pete removed his halter and we watched him for a while before catching the black colt and going through the same choking down and sacking process. The black colt wasn't much of a horse. One sacking was all he needed before we approached him and rubbed his neck.

"I'm gonna name that old black colt Short Chance," Pete said, as we left the corral. "He don't have a lot of life." I was secretly wishing Sonny Boy didn't have quite as much life and would have gladly traded him, but I didn't say so.

The next day we saddled both horses, tied the reins to the saddle horn and left them in the corral, while we fixed a break in the horse pasture fence. Returning to the corral about an hour before sunset, we galloped both colts, riderless, around the corral for fifteen minutes before unsaddling them for the day.

At supper that night, Mr. Valliant asked Pete if we had started riding the colts yet. I could see Pete's crooked smile in the corner of my eye. "Tomorrow's the big rodeo," Pete said. "We've done about as much as we can do without getting in the saddle and kicking the hell out of them."

My breath quickened, and I stopped eating. Mr. Valliant looked at me with a grin. "If you break a leg we'll have to shoot you," he said. Grimes broke into a wide smile, and for the first time I saw the yellow stubs of his teeth.

———

Grimes leaned on the corral fence, grinning, as Pete and I prepared the colts for their first rider. We saddled the colts and led them around the corral several times. They acted like old saddle horses, and my breathing returned to normal. Pete said I would be first and led Short Chance to an adjoining corral.

With weak legs, heart pounding with fear, I mounted the big colt while Pete held onto the halter under the bridle. I sat upright, one hand on the saddle horn, desperately holding the bridle reins with my other hand.

"I'll lead him for a while," Pete said.

Sonny Boy and I circled the corral several times behind Pete. Without a word, Pete unsnapped the lead rope and stepped to the side. Sonny Boy stopped. I let him stand for a long time before nervously urging him on with gentle nudges with my heels. For over an hour the steel gray and I became as one, circling the corral one way, me urging him into a turn with the reins, then circling the other way.

From that day until the first blizzard, the second week in December, I rode Sonny Boy from supper until dark. After the first week, Pete allowed me to ride him outside the round corral, then a larger corral. Then the big day with Pete riding Short Chance and me riding Sonny Boy, we rode to the Forest Service boundary fence and back.

———

I awoke to a howling blizzard. It was the morning after our long ride on the colts. Snow was hitting my bedroom window and sticking to the pane, blocking my vision of how really bad the weather was. I yanked all the quilts over me, covered my head and went back to sleep.

At breakfast Mr. Valliant said I would need to start helping Pete feed the cattle and sheep. I looked across the table at Mrs. Valliant. "Don't worry, you'll have plenty of time for your lessons in the afternoons," she said.

I put on all the clothes I could find, cap with earmuffs, scarf and mittens. The wind was howling, pushing snow with such force it was a struggle to keep my balance. Pete had the team in the barn and harnessed when I staggered through the barn door. He laughed. "Are you going to Alaska...or what?"

It felt good to be standing with my back to the blizzard as we rode the wagon toward the first haystack. The hay was stacked in a mound about twenty-feet high, surrounded by a pole fence eight-feet high, forming a square twenty-feet by twenty-feet. I thought back to last summer, when I was one of the crew stacking this huge mound of hay, and tried to remember what machine I was operating that day.

Pete maneuvered the team and wagon close to the haystack, downwind from the blizzard, and secured the lines. I grabbed my pitchfork, scrambled onto the stack, handed the end of my fork to Pete and helped him with the steep climb onto the stack.

Pete had modified the hay wagon to allow for a hay catch barrier on one side of the wagon, always positioned downwind from the blizzard. The barrier was simply a tall fence made of four-by-four lumbers, with double strands of chicken wire stretched across it.

When the wagon was loaded, I drove the team in wide circles around the meadow. Pete forked and pushed hay off the side. We fed one load to the cows and a load to the sheep. After dinner, we hauled two more loads of hay into the feedlot corrals, one for the weaning heifers, and one for the weaning ewe lambs.

That same day, we caught Sonny Boy and Short Chance and turned them loose with the other ranch saddle horses.

TWENTY-FIVE

Winter came on with fury. When it wasn't snowing it was blowing, with temperatures subzero much of the time. Before bridling the draft horses we always dipped the bridle bits in the creek, which caused a coating of ice to form on the metal. This prevented the steel bits from searing the lips and tongues of the horses. My problem was, no matter how many layers of clothes I put on, I still couldn't keep warm. While Pete drove the team toward the haystack, I danced, jumped and swung my arms to keep blood circulating in my feet and hands.

Usually, my schooling started immediately after our noon meal and lasted until three in the afternoon. In the evening I read, or did homework by lamplight, pulling my chair as close to the fireplace as I could.

The Upper Room had no heat. During a blizzard, snow sifted through cracks in the window, sometimes accumulating six inches deep at the foot of my bed. I slept in my long underwear and socks, under six quilts, my head covered up, allowing only a tiny crack for breathing. Mr. Valliant would call me in the morning after he had the fireplace going. I'd pull my clothes on in less than a minute, dash through the Upper Room and back up to the fireplace.

Mrs. Valliant had coffee perking in the kitchen. She insisted I drink a full glass of milk, then a cup of coffee with cream and sugar, before I bundled up and doggedly made my way to the barn to milk the cow and slop the hogs. Chores completed, I returned to the house, and turned the hand crank about a thousand times to separate the milk from the cream.

A few days before Christmas Mr. Valiant and I saddled the horses and rode to timberline to cut a tree. When we found the perfect one, I tied onto the base with my lariat and dragged it out of the deep snow, where Pete was waiting with the team and wagon for the trip back to the ranch.

It was nearly dark when we arrived back at the ranch. Pete and I brushed all the snow from the tree, nailed on the wooden stand, and brought it into the house. It was nearly as tall as the ceiling. Mrs. Valliant had already dragged the several cardboard boxes filled with decorations out of the Upper Room. Grimes had done my chores and Mrs. Valliant said she would start supper while I unloaded the decorations.

After a quick meal of canned oyster stew, we all went back into the living room, Grimes with a book, Mr. Valliant with the new *Saturday Evening Post,* and Mrs. Valliant and I at the tree. When we were done I stood back and looked at a ton of tinsel, a thousand round ornaments, and a shiny tinfoil angel perched on top of the tree.

The Valliants, Pete, and even Grimes, said there was a Santa Claus. I knew they were just putting me on, because they said that last year, when I believed every word of it, until I recognized Mrs. Valliant's scribbling on the tags, and the rumpled paper that looked as if it had been used for several years. But I wasn't taking any chances. I marked up several pages of the Sears-Roebuck and Montgomery Ward catalogs, and asked Mrs. Valliant to put all these things in a letter to Santa for me.

Christmas morning I awoke to see Mr. Valliant staring at me from the foot of my bed with his short, yellow teeth showing—his biggest grin ever. "Santa Claus damned near knocked the chimney down and I had to let him out the door when he left," he said.

"Did he leave some presents?" I asked, rubbing sleep out of my eyes.

"Come and see," he said, as he turned and left my room.

It was still dark outside when I pulled my pants on, grabbed my shirt, and ran as fast as I could through the Upper Room.

The kerosene lamps were lit and the battery operated tree lights were blinking for the first time since we hung them. Presents were stacked knee-high under the tree and my stockings under the mantle were stuffed with candy canes and other things I couldn't imagine. Everybody was up and dressed by now.

Outside the wind was howling, causing a ground blizzard from recent snows. But I hardly paid any attention as I hurried to the barn and milked the cow in record time, not neglecting to give the barn cats a few extra squirts in the mouth—all the while dreaming about the things I had circled in the catalogs.

Under the tree I found a real store-bought sled, several new pairs of socks, a flannel shirt, a new pair of boots (I had outgrown my old pair), a new pair of overshoes that fit the new boots, and two new pair of long-handled underwear. I didn't get anything that I had circled in the catalog, but I wasn't disappointed. What I really wanted was a bow and arrow, though. I remembered it cost three dollars, which I knew was way out of line.

Pete received a carton of Chesterfield cigarettes and a pair of red and white wool socks. "Santa Claus should be concerned about the growth in your lungs," Mrs. Valliant said, handing Pete his Christmas wrapped Chesterfields, "which you claim isn't cancer...and your ulcers, but I guess he knows you'd buy the foul-smelling things, anyway." I knew she said that because it had been less than two weeks ago that Pete returned from a doctor appointment and announced to all at the supper table that the grapefruit-sized lump in his chest was nothing to worry about. It wasn't cancer and it would probably go away in time.

After opening presents, Pete and I fed two loads of hay to the sheep and cattle. The Richard Valliant family drove past the barnyard as we were taking the harnesses off the team. I guess Pete read the disappointment in my face. "Hey, pardner, why the long face? Maybe you'll get a pair of boxing gloves for Christmas." He chuckled.

I laughed and my mood changed. Even though I had never mentioned my troubles to Pete, he had to know that something wasn't right with my attitude when Craig was around.

Before the Christmas dinner feast, it was customary for the men and boys to all pile into the old stripped-down Model-A Ford and drive through the meadows shooting jackrabbits. The rabbits were Christmas treats for the four sheep dogs on the ranch. Mr. Valliant had given me another rifle to replace the one Dad sold in Texas. Craig and Mark went hunting last Christmas. I wasn't invited, but I reasoned it was because I wasn't old enough to be trusted with a firearm. I hadn't asked to go hunting this year; I just assumed that I would be part of it, now that I was a year older and had my own rifle. I grabbed my rifle, dressed for the cold and waited for the others by the yard gate.

Richard pulled the Ford out of the garage. I waited for everyone to take their positions, thinking I would find a place on the tailgate—after everyone was loaded.

I was still standing by the gate when the old Ford eased off the hill. I unloaded my rifle and trudged to the bunkhouse, kicking rocks along the way. Pete had a fire going in his little potbelly stove and was sitting on his bunk tapping out a Chesterfield on his lighter. He looked up without saying a word, lit his cigarette and stretched out on the bunk. I watched as he puckered his mouth like a fish and blew several smoke rings.

"Are cigarettes bad for you?" I asked.

"Yeah, they cause you to lose your teeth."

I could see that he was telling the truth, but I didn't care.

"Can I have a cigarette?"

"No. Booth will fire me, and, anyway, it will make you sick and you won't be able to eat any Christmas dinner."

I didn't care if I ate any dinner, and I didn't think Mr. Valliant would fire him for giving me a cigarette. I told him if I *stole* a cigarette from him he wouldn't get fired. I reached over and removed a cigarette from an opened package on a little table next to his bed.

Pete grinned and handed me his lighter. I lit the cigarette and imitated Pete when he was trying to get the last goodness out of a Chesterfield, pulling as hard as I could and dragging it all the way down. I went into a coughing fit. After choking, and coughing until I was too dizzy to stand, I flopped down beside Pete on the bunk.

"Don't worry about Craig," Pete said, as we slowly walked toward the house. "He just gets his rocks off by teasing you, that's all. Anyway, you're bigger than him, and he knows you can kick his ass any time you take a good notion."

"I ain't worried," I said, between several loud, pretend coughs. "And thanks for letting me smoke the cigarette...I guess."

———

Throughout the long, cold winter, I balanced school work with livestock feeding, trapping muskrats, sledding on the iced-over meadow with my new sled, making leather harnesses for my dog sled team, and building go-carts in the ranch machine shop. If the weather was good, Mr. and Mrs. Valliant would attend the Farm Bureau dance held on the last Saturday of each month. I'd ride to town with them, go to a picture show, then find them at the dance afterwards. I hated waiting for them until their dance party ended, where all the old ladies fussed over me and insisted I dance with them. It was disgusting, but I was afraid to refuse. I was scared the whole time, and stared straight ahead at their boobs, moved when their feet moved, turned when they turned—all the while feeling like I had a steel rod stuck up the seat of my pants.

I was always the only kid at the dances, which I considered a small blessing. I was shy around kids my own age. I was afraid I would have nothing to say, or I would try to say something and stutter my fool head off.

———

Spring came slowly, with warm, sunny days, then a raging blizzard, and the constant wind. I turned thirteen March 24th. Mrs. Valliant made me a birthday cake and I finally got the store-bought bow and arrow I had wished for all winter. Pete gave me a box of .22 shells and reminded me to stop shooting skunks near the bunkhouse. I was now reading on a sixth-grade level and doing arithmetic with double-digit figures. When reading, I spelled every word before pronouncing it to myself. Mrs. Valliant said I could spell as well as any eighth-grader she had ever taught.

It was the middle of May. Grimes had hired two new hands (Ray and Bob) to help with calving, cleaning corrals, and irrigating. Pete and I were busy fixing fence and preparing for lambing. The lambs started to come on schedule, May 20th. Three days later, my horse, Red, stepped on a rock, and came up lame. May 24th; lambing was in full swing and I was afoot. At breakfast, Mr. Valliant looked right at me and said, "Dennis, Red is going to be out of commission for a week or two, reckon you can handle Sonny Boy for awhile?" I nodded, with a big grin.

Ray and I rode Brownie and Billie to the winter horse pasture and found Sonny Boy with about thirty wild horses. We trailed them to a smaller pasture and into a round corral, about a mile from the ranch house. I noticed right off that Sonny Boy wasn't acting like the gentle horse I had turned out to pasture in December. We separated the other horses, leaving Sonny Boy in the corral. The steel gray ran around the corral, snorting, kicking and acting like a wild mustang until he was white with sweat. I told Ray to put Brownie in the corral until we trailed the other horses back to the big pasture; I would ride Sonny Boy.

I led Sonny Boy out of the corral, mounted and turned him toward the other horses. Sonny Boy walked about four steps before he sprang forward with one giant cat-like leap, lowered his head, dug his forepaws into the ground and exploded like dynamite. I felt my body coming apart in all directions. I grabbed the saddle horn, and about four jumps later I was on the ground, still sitting in the saddle. The fall knocked me unconscious. When I woke up, Ray was kneeling in front of me. "The damn cinch broke," Ray said, in a croak.

Ray helped me to sit up straight. I was still sitting in the saddle, trying to get my bearing and staring at my right leg, which was stretched out in front of me. I looked for my other leg, and could only see part of it above the knee. For a moment I thought my left leg had been cut off below my hip. Ray pulled my missing leg out from under the saddle and straightened it full length. I was relieved, thinking it was just a little bent out of shape. Ray put his hands under my armpits, lifted me up and away from the saddle, then he let go his grip on me. I screamed and crumpled to the ground. I had two left knees. My eyes saw it, but it took my mind awhile to catch up, like when you take a picture in your mind and get it developed later. Still dazed, I leaned back on by hands, and stared at my leg. I could see it was bent, maybe even broken, but I couldn't understand why it didn't hurt.

"Your leg is broken," Ray said in a whisper. I told him he was full of shit, because it didn't hurt. "It's damned sure broken," he said again, in a solemn voice. I told him he'd better get a gun and shoot me then. Maybe I was even smiling, watching Ray go to pieces right in front of me. Without another word, Ray bolted to his horse and raced off toward the ranch house, his legs flailing and kicking, as if he were near the finish line of a great horse race.

The hoof-beats from Ray's horse had barely quit pounding in my ears when it hit me. It was hard to think about anything, except the pain, but in a tiny corner of my mind, I wondered if he really was going after a gun. About the time I thought I would die, one way or the other, Ray returned with Grimes. I was choked up, but not crying, as I stared at Ray's worried face and Grimes' tight-lip smile and wished they *had* brought a gun.

They loaded me into the back seat, and we returned to the house. Mr. and Mrs. Valliant came to the car and conferred with Grimes. I heard Mrs. Valliant say something about Grimes taking me to town, and she would call Dr. Barrett. Grimes eased himself behind the wheel and we rolled off the hill toward town. Every little bump was cause for terrific pain. I couldn't help it, screaming at every little bump on the road—Grimes winching and ducking as if dodging bullets from a posse.

Grimes parked the car in front of Dr. Barrett's office, and left without saying a word. The doctor came to the car, looked at me, and asked if it hurt, which I thought was a stupid question, seeing as how my face was so twisted with the pain that I could barely whisper. When I didn't answer, he felt in his pocket for a sharp instrument that he used to cut my pants off, leaving me lying in my shorts. The doctor left without another word, and it wasn't long before a rancher happened by on the street and helped Grimes carry me into a waiting room full of people.

Mr. and Mrs. Valliant arrived within minutes after Grimes and Dr. Barrett helped me onto a metal table. I was still lying on the cold, metal slab when I heard Dr. Barrett tell the Valliants the femur bone in my leg was broken. The doctor gave me a shot that made me sleepy and took the pain away. Leaving his patients in the waiting room, Dr. Barrett helped me into the back seat of his Cadillac and drove me the forty miles to the hospital in Rawlins.

Lying on my back, I watched while two nurses attached a harness to my ankle and connected it to a pulley at the foot of the bed. The doctor gave the nurses some instructions, and said he would see me again in a few days. The nurses fussed over me and I started to enjoy all the attention—until the hurt came back.

The next day Mrs. Valliant came to see me. She looked at me and started to cry. I thought something bad had happened at the ranch; maybe Mr. Valliant was sick, or some other terrible thing. "Look at you," she kept saying.

Finally, I thought I understood why she was crying. Now, I was jolted with some serious guilt: I'd caused everyone a lot of trouble. "My leg feels good....it's okay," I murmured several times, hoping it would make her feel better.

Dr. Barrett visited me twice a week. About the third or fourth time he came around, he pulled down the sheets, twisted and turned my leg until it hurt, and asked the nurse some questions that I didn't understand. Then, talking to my leg, he said, "It's healing crooked, I'll have to break it." I heard him plainly enough, but I didn't understand what he meant.

Another nurse arrived, stood near my head, and I watched as she poured something out of a bottle onto a cloth swab. "Breathe deeply," she said, slapping the swab over my face.

I'd never smelled anything that terrible before. I didn't know what was going on and I didn't breathe at all. I watched as the doctor quickly put his knee against my leg, and pulled on both sides of the break with his hands. I heard the bone snap, felt the pain, and screamed with all the breath I had left in me. "More chloroform," I heard the doctor say. This time, I breathed deeply with the awful pain, and awoke later with a single nurse standing over me.

Two more weeks passed. The doctor poked, twisted, pulled, and motioned for a nurse, who smothered me with more chloroform. I awoke with a straight leg, again. He left me with the pain, and another two weeks passed. My leg was now looking like a dog's hind leg. Standing by my bed he looked right at me, for the first time since being in the hospital: "Your leg is a little crooked," he said, "but you have a lot of growing to do; in time it will straighten out on its own."

"Thanks," I said, with a big sigh of relief.

I stayed in the hospital six weeks. The last two weeks I was allowed to use a wheel chair, move about the hospital and terrorize other wheel-chair patients and others making their way through the corridors on crutches. Fortunately, my recklessness didn't cause any serious injuries. I figured out from almost the first day that I was special with the nurses and other hospital workers, when I overheard a couple of nurses saying how awful it was that I was an orphan boy and all, and how sorry they felt for me. Right off the bat I started using their affection and sympathies to my advantage, pushing my luck to the breaking point.

From the first day, I learned to maneuver my wheel chair as skillfully as any professional race car driver. Cruising the hallways, I quickly learned who it was safe to antagonize, and who would just as soon whop me up beside the head as look at me. Eventually, I singled out one old voiceless, and otherwise defenseless man to torment. Old "Birch" had been found in an alleyway, drunk and half-frozen. When he was finally thawed out, and fed, they learned that Birch could not walk, read, write, or speak. He had no identification, and after weeks at the hospital, no one had laid claim to him. For lack of a name, they called him "Birch," because that was the name of the street in front of the alley where they found him. He was able to use his arms and shoulders and he could grunt, and I suppose that is how they learned that he smoked a pipe and used Prince Albert tobacco.

Anyway, old Birch and I didn't hit it off from the start. At first I tried to talk to him, just feeling him out for the chase. When he grunted and wheeled his chair away from me, I gave chase, scraping the side of his chair as I cannonballed past him. Birch's can of Prince Albert whizzed past my wheelchair, barely missing my head. I didn't feel even a pinch of guilt about harassing old Birch. I excused off my bad behavior with the thought that he secretly looked forward to our wheelchair games, because he kept coming back day after day.

I returned to the ranch on crutches. At first, there wasn't much I could do except school work and dream about the day I could ride Red again, which seemed about as far away as Christmas. When I was tired of reading, writing and doing numbers, I'd grab my crutches and take short walks into the pasture near the house.

I was glad to be back on the ranch, where I could finish learning whatever it was I needed to know, and dream about starting school in September. Mrs. Valliant reminded me (as she did nearly every day of my life on the ranch), that something good comes of everything. She said the broken leg and my stay at the hospital was all worth it because I had been cured of stuttering. *My awful damn stuttering was gone.* She didn't say it in exactly those words, but I got the gist of it.

My stuttering had gone away so slowly that I hadn't even noticed that I wasn't getting red in the face and puffing up like a poisoned toad with every word I tried to speak. She was so excited that I could talk like a normal boy that she couldn't help herself with questions like, "what happened, Dennis? Did they give you a shot or something?" I couldn't tell her, because I didn't know. But I can tell you that after she reminded me of how normal I was, every night I lay in bed worrying that I would return to my old stuttering self again. But for the time being, I could read, write, do arithmetic, I could talk normal, and I could hardly wait until school started.

There wasn't a book or magazine in the house that I didn't read that summer—and I was doing sixth-grade math. I wasn't allowed to help with any cow punching, or haying, but it wasn't long before I was riding my horse, Red, for an hour or two every day.

In July, Booth and Anna Valliant bought a neighboring ranch, adding several thousand acres of dry pasture and two-hundred acres of irrigated meadow land to their already large spread. According to Pete (who seemed to know everything), the purchase price was $20,000.

The Richard Valliant family moved into the ranch house on the new place, just four miles away. I had plenty of time to think about this new development. The tension was there, and I felt betrayed. But I also recognized that I was growing up, with a different attitude about most everything. For one, I was determined nothing was going to take away my excitement about starting to school. And for another, it had been awhile since I had seen Craig. Maybe he had changed his mind about me and would want to be friends.

The day before school started, Mrs. Valliant and I met with Mrs. Seymour, principal of the Saratoga grade school. The principal (Mrs. Valliant said) wanted to test my skills before deciding what grade would be best for me. We went to Mrs. Seymour's homeroom, where she immediately pointed to a school desk. "Sit," was the first word she said to me. I decided right then that Mrs. Seymour was the most unfriendly person I had ever met.

She tested my reading, writing and arithmetic skills for about an hour. "He can read and write on a seventh-grade level," Mrs. Seymour said, looking at Mrs. Valliant, as if I didn't exist. "But he doesn't know fractions, and he hasn't had American history, or geography. He will need to start in the sixth-grade." Mrs. Seymour went on to say that my attending her school would be conditional. The kids would surely make fun of me because of my size, and if I caused any trouble, or created too much distraction for the other kids, I would have to find some other place to go to school. "Anyway," she continued, "This boy needs to be in a special school." I had to assume by her words and tone of voice that her school wasn't special. And at that moment I wasn't at all sure I wanted any part of her school, anyway.

I didn't like Mrs. Seymour, and I didn't care about history or geography. If I went to her school at all, I wanted to start in the seventh grade.

Part of me wanted to take Mrs. Valliant by the hand and slink toward the door and never, ever, think about school again. It was all a big mistake. The other part of me wanted to find the mop that had left the greasy chemical smell on the floor and wrap it around the principal's beastly head. I didn't do any of these things. Instead, I stood looking at my feet and listened while Mrs. Seymour finished telling Mrs. Valliant all the rules of attendance. Rules that I thought were all fairly ridiculous, and could only be intended for me. I pretty much tuned out on the last part of her instructions, as I was just about convinced that none of this was going to work for me.

TWENTY-SIX

The night before my first day of school, I put the washtub in the pantry, scrubbed my whole body and washed my hair, then went to bed and stared at the dark ceiling for hours before falling asleep. I kept hearing Mrs. Seymour's words over and over, "special school," as if she were talking about my Uncle Eugene.

At breakfast, I couldn't remember my trip to the barn to do chores. With new pants, new plaid shirt, new boots, and my hair slicked back with Vitalis, I should have felt good. I didn't. My clothes, my hair, everything just felt wrong, and I had a knot in my throat that was keeping me from swallowing.

My dreams of being welcomed as the new kid in school, and becoming just like other kids, weren't even close to the nightmare that I now feared was awaiting me. At this moment, what I really felt like doing was just start wailing, like the idiot Mrs. Seymour made me out to be, and tell the Valliants to buy me a bus ticket back to Memphis. And if Mrs. Valliant believed a shred of what that loudmouth principal had said, she would not be surprised.

I was still picking at my eggs and toast when Mrs. Valliant looked down at me and smiled. I tried to return her smile, but it wasn't in me. But I knew she was seeing right through me and I had to say something. "I'll try," I said, "I don't know if I can make it. But I really will try," I said again. Even though I said all of this without an ounce of energy, I could feel her caring smile bearing down on me, and it gave me a good feeling.

"You'll do just fine, Dennis. You can do it. Just hold your head up, and if someone teases you, just pretend you don't hear them."

Three school buses served the Platte Valley school system. Our bus traveled an egg-shape pattern around the southern part of the county, picking up kids on the Spring Creek road first, circled north to Calf Creek, on to Cow Creek, then back to Saratoga—a total traveling distance of about forty miles. The Valliant boys and I were the last to get on the bus from the Calf Creek route. The school bus stop was seven miles from where I lived, and three miles from Richard Valliant's. Richard and Mr. and Mrs. Valliant had everything all planned. I would drive the 1929, Model-A Ford to Richard Valliant's, then ride with the Valliant boys to the bus stop. This sounded like a good arrangement, except the old Ford was stripped-down, with no top or doors, and no one said a word about cold weather and snow.

It was at least fifteen minutes after I arrived at the Richard Valliant house before the three boys charged out the door. I used the time to curse myself for even trying such a stupid thing as this. About the time I was ready to turn the old Ford around and head back to the ranch, someone shouted, "Come on, we're late."

Mark jumped behind the wheel, Craig crawled in beside him, and Spike and I sat in the back. Everyone looked straight ahead, and we rode the three miles in silence.

The Valliant boys seated themselves close to the Mosers in the back of the school bus. I sat in an empty seat near the middle. The taunting began almost immediately after the bus started. For reasons I didn't understand then, Clay sat quietly, somber-faced, looking straight ahead, while Craig and Stephen threw paper wads, hissed "shithead, dumbass," and laughed out of control. Mark sat quietly with an approving smile, and Spike worried himself making spit wads for Craig and Stephen. I looked straight ahead, quiet as a deaf mute. The bus driver, an old, balding man, pretended deafness.

The elementary and junior high grades were both located in one square, dirty brick building, with the gym in the middle. Kindergarten through eighth-grade classrooms were located side-by-side around the outside of the gym floor. Since I didn't know where my classroom was located, I went to Mrs. Seymour's room first. She was standing by the door, staring at me through slits in her eyelids. "Your classroom is at the end of the hall with a sign on the door," she said.

Since there was no "hall", I continued pushing my way through other kids until I found a room with a sign that read, "6th grade—Mr. Young."

I cautiously walked through the door and was immediately spotted by a tall, blonde haired, kindly-faced man of about thirty. Mr. Young turned from writing something on the blackboard. He was smiling. "You're Dennis, Aren't you?" He said. "Mrs. Seymour has told me about you."

Mr. Young seemed to sense my nervousness. "Don't worry," he said, "I'm your homeroom teacher and you're going to do just fine. There's no seating arrangement, but I want you to sit near the front of the room so I can give you some special attention."

I put my pencils and Big Chief tablet on a desk near the front, and glanced around the room. I asked Mr. Young if I could go to the lavatory, which was the word Mrs. Valliant told me to use for toilet.

"Sure, it's on the other side of the gym. But, Dennis, here at school we use the word bathroom. Take a left, then the first door to your right."

I could feel the stares from all the kids as I wormed my way through the narrow passageway, to and from the bathroom. I was taller than any of the kids, even the mature looking ones, whom I judged to be eighth-graders. When the bell rang I went to my seat and scrunched down as low as I could, trying not to attract attention. But my attempt to go unnoticed was wasted during the first five minutes of class.

Mr. Young introduced himself and welcomed the class, then he paused and looked at me. "Class, we have a special student this year, his name is Dennis Boykin. Dennis is thirteen-years old and has never, ever, been to school. Dennis has some speech problems too. Now, I want all of you to be especially kind to Dennis and help him as much as you can."

All eyes were on me. I moved further down in my seat, sweat escaping from every pore of my body. Mr. Young, who I thought was going to be my friend, had just killed any chance I had of fitting in. I wanted to disappear and never step foot into a classroom again.

During recess and noon-hour break I stood out even worse. I hadn't made any friends, some of my speech difficulties had returned, and I felt like I was really in over my head. During recess I watched the other kids play marbles, handball, and tag. I kept to myself and wandered around the schoolyard in a daze, counting the minutes until recess would end and I could sit at my desk and feel comfortable staring at Mr. Young's friendly face.

For several days, the only thing I could really count on was the constant harassment on the school bus. Morning and night I sat in silence while they laughed, hissed, threw spit wads and other things. Sitting in the seat directly behind the bus driver didn't help. He seemed oblivious to anything but his driving and the stupid tune he always whistled. I sat quietly and looked straight ahead because Mrs. Seymour said I was on probation. But on the way home one Friday afternoon I had had enough, and I no longer gave a damn about Mrs. Seymour's probation threats. Near the Moser destination, I turned in my seat and shouted, "Hey, how about I kick all your asses tonight?"

There was a roar of laughter, then I could hear them talking in low tones, and I noted that Stephen Moser didn't get off the bus with his little brother, Clay, at their regular stop.

Suddenly, I realized I would have to make good my threat. I stepped off the bus first, and walked a few steps toward the car, debating whether to stand there or run as fast as my shaky knees could carry me. I knew that I hadn't decided quickly enough when I heard Craig shout, "Hey, shithead, aren't you gonna whip our ass?"

I could hear a rush of feet behind me. I turned just as Stephen dug into my back and took me to the ground. Craig piled on. All my pent-up emotions and hatred came to the surface. I was in a towering rage—a wild animal. I kicked, scratched, punched, bit and clawed at any part of their bodies that I could touch. Their laughter was replaced with, "Ouch, hell, damn, shit, hold that crazy son-of-a-bitch." I glanced toward Mark and little Spike during the fracas, expecting them to join in. They were dancing around, pointing, and laughing.

They backed off, nursing their bruises, and we all piled into the car. I didn't receive a scratch from the fight. Packed in the little Ford, the five of us rode home in silence.

TWENTY-SEVEN

The first big snow came in early November, making it impossible for me to drive the stripped-down Ford to the school bus. Mrs. Valliant said she had found me a place to live and work—closer to town, and just a short walk to the school bus stop. The next day I told the bus driver I needed to get off at the Boris Klein place. I walked the short distance from the bus stop to the Klein Dairy, where I met Boris and Geli and their two preschool girls.

Boris was a short, thin, dark-haired man. He spoke with some strange accent, but rarely said anything at all, except to scold his mousey little wife and two scrawny little kids. Boris' word was law. I learned that from the start. And it wasn't what he said, but how he said it that told me I had better watch my step.

The first day, I cautiously handed Boris Klein a note from Mrs. Valliant. The note said that I was to receive board and room on weekdays, and two dollars for helping to feed cattle on weekends. He grunted and shoved the note in his pocket. Two weeks passed without receiving any pay. I figured he forgot about the note, and I wasn't about to remind him and risk getting worn out with his razor strap.

From the first day, Boris treated me like a boy-servant, someone not quite good enough to live in the house with his family, but slightly too valuable as a servant to be allowed to freeze to death sleeping in the barn. I was too scared to speak to Boris. I didn't talk to Geli, either. She was a cowed little woman who looked like she could jump right out of her skin at any moment.

My room at the Klein's was no bigger than a two-holer outhouse, unheated, with a dirty mattress placed on a set of worn-out springs that sagged in the middle. I didn't have quilts enough to ward off the bitter cold, and I lay in bed shivering, praying for my wake-up call. At exactly four o'clock each morning, Boris banged loudly on my door. By seven o'clock, we milked thirty cows by hand, strained the milk into five-gallon jugs, and placed the jugs in the creek to cool before being picked up by the milk truck.

By seven-thirty in the morning I had finished breakfast and was ready to walk the short one-half mile to the bus stop. There were no showering or bathing facilities at the Kleins', and I wore the same pair of unwashed shirt and jeans day after day. I didn't notice the manure on my boots and clothes, or the particular way I smelled. But the kids in school noticed. Some of the bigger boys held their noses and pointed as I went to and from classes The girls giggled. One day Mr. Young asked me to stay during recess; he wanted to talk to me. I was afraid I had done something wrong until he gently explained that I needed to be more careful about my appearance, "And don't forget to clean the manure from your boots before coming to school." I promised him I would do better.

Meanwhile my grades were exceptional—all A's and B's with the exception of arithmetic. I was having trouble understanding fractions. It was the day after the class had taken six-week tests and I knew I had done well on everything— history in particular. Mr. Young held our history test papers in his hand as he spoke. He went on about how poorly the class had performed on the test—except for one student, Dennis Boykin, who had a test score of 98. "Dennis, who has never gone to school before, has received the highest grade in the class. Now why is that students? Did any of you study, or is Dennis just smarter than the rest of you?"

Mr. Young had just delivered me another deathblow. I slouched in my seat and looked straight ahead. All the kids in front of me turned and gave me dirty looks. I couldn't win. Mr. Young, who was my best friend, was also my worst enemy.

The whole world around me seemed hopeless. I didn't want to quit school, but, most of the time, I didn't know how I could continue on. I couldn't decide what to do, or if I could do anything. All I was really sure of was that I didn't fit in, and, no one, except Mr. Young, wanted me around. I was so unhappy living at the Kleins I felt like crying most of the time, and I couldn't tell anyone. My classmates barely tolerated me, and I didn't feel as if I belonged in school, or anywhere else for that matter. I was stuttering again when I got nervous, which was practically all the time, and my grades were starting to suffer.

The nights were bitter cold in my unheated room, I didn't get enough sleep, and during the day my eyes burned with fatigue and sleeplessness. I hadn't heard from the Valliants since moving to the Kleins, and I was terrified at being all alone in the world.

About this time I met James Caldwell. James, like me, stuck out—for some of the same reasons. He was a long, skinny kid with a shock of blonde hair, pimples all over his face, dirty clothes, and his hands and face appeared not to have touched a bar of soap and water for a long time.

James moved with a natural slouch, his eyes on the ground. I figured if he ever stood up straight he'd be the tallest kid in school. At the same time I couldn't help but wonder how many grades he'd flunked. During the noon break he would be walking by himself, always off the school grounds, with a cigarette between his fingers, head down, squinting, as he glanced from side-to-side, as if he was doing something wrong and at any moment he would be caught and whipped.

I particularly noticed that no one ever picked on James. And, for that one reason, I wanted to meet him. One day I made it a point to circle around in front of him before I walked across the road, then I walked directly toward him, all the while looking at him and studying his walk. As I approached, I said, "Hi".

He stopped, and squinted at me, with red-rimmed, watery eyes. I squinted back, thinking that was probably what I should be doing. I guess he knew who I was, though, because he didn't seem frightened or anything. Finally, he reached into his pants pocket and shoved a crumpled pack of Camels toward me. "Want a cigarette?" he mumbled.

"Yeah," I said, taking the squashed package from his hand. We both lit up. I puffed and pretended to inhale while we walked and said nothing.

The school bell rang. "My name is James Caldwell, and don't you ever call me Jim. Wanna meet me here tomorrow?"

"Yeah, my name is Dennis."

The next day some big boys were teasing me while I waited on the school grounds for James to return home from lunch. When I saw James coming I turned away from them and ran across the road to meet him.

"Bastards," James muttered. "You don't hafta take that crap. Want me to take care of 'em for you?"

I told James I would let him know, but deep down I knew I wouldn't—it just didn't seem right for me not to do my own fighting.

"They used to pick on me until I beat the crap out of a few of them. Just let me know," James repeated.

We talked while we slowly strolled down the sidewalk and puffed on our cigarettes. James told me about his father, who was a drunk, and his poor mother, who had to work all the time to support the family. I felt sad for him and told him so, but I didn't tell him anything about my own sorry father. I told him that I was an orphan working for my board and room for some stupid German guy, whom I hated. He suggested that we run away together.

James and I met every day during the noon break, smoked cigarettes and talked about running away. We were both anxious to leave, but neither of us could figure out how to get any money or where to go. I suggested we try to find my grandma in Dallas, telling him she would let us hoe and pick cotton to earn money to do whatever we wanted. James didn't like my idea; he'd heard that Texas was "hot as hell," and there were snakes everywhere. Anyway, he didn't know how to pick cotton. We never developed any serious plans, or set any dates for leaving, but, as my life became more unbearable living with the Kleins, I thought more and more about leaving, with or without James.

Then, one bitter cold morning, something happened that changed my whole outlook on life. It was the middle of December. The thermometer hanging on the barn door read twenty below zero. Boris and I were milking side-by-side. I finished milking my cow and was removing her hobbles when she kicked with her left foot, hitting Boris' milk stool. The stool went out from under him, with him landing on his rear—the whole bucket of milk spilling over his chest and face. Boris went into a rage.

I kept repeating over and over, "I am sorry, I'm sorry."

Boris' milk bucket flew into the air. The bucket hit me in the chest, knocking me to the ground. The bucket bounced off my chest and hit the cow I had been milking. The cow started bucking and kicking in place, with Boris still lying under her belly. The cow's feet landed in his face and he let out a shrill scream. Now, I decided it was time to move. I raced to the house as fast I could, grabbed my schoolbooks and ran as fast as I could to the bus stop. I hid in some willows until I saw the school bus lumbering toward me. When it stopped, I scurried out of my hiding place and ran toward the door, all the time imagining Boris was only two feet behind me.

After school I went to the Sisson Hotel, called Mrs. Valliant and told her I couldn't work for the Kleins anymore. She asked me to keep working for a few more days and she would find me another place to live. I told her some bad things had happened and I couldn't go back.

I thanked the aging woman clerk for the use of her phone and told her I needed a room for the night. She rested her large body across the counter on her elbows and stared at me for a long moment. "Are you running away from home or something, sonny?"

"No Ma'am," I replied, "I just want a room for the night".

"Well....do you have any money?" she said, without changing her position.

"No, but I can pay you tomorrow."

"I'm sorry," she said, her tone of voice final, "we can't rent rooms unless you pay first. Anyway, you better go home to your momma—if you got one."

It was too cold to sleep under the bridge like we did in Texas, and I didn't know anyone in town. I asked the old woman if I could use her phone again. She watched me while I dialed the number. I listened while the four long rings and one short ring (which was the phone code for the ranch) buzzed in the headset. When Mrs. Valliant answered I told her what the woman said about not renting me a room because I had no money.

Mrs. Valliant asked to speak to "Ethel", whom I guessed was the old fat woman who wouldn't give me a room. After they spoke for a few minutes, the woman called Ethel gave me a hard look. "Well, son, why didn't you tell me you were friends of the Valliants; why you could have been any kind of a common criminal. Sure I have a room for you. Come on up and you can have the nice one with the dresser and mirror—and the bathroom is just down the hall."

I stayed at the hotel two nights without hearing a word from Mrs. Valliant. On the third day she was waiting for me in the hotel lobby when I returned from school. We sat on a wooden bench in the lobby and I told her about my experiences while living with the Kleins. I didn't tell her about getting hit with the milk bucket, but I didn't spare any other details, and I didn't make up anything. About halfway through my story, she started crying. "Dennis, why didn't you tell us before now?"

"I didn't want to bother you," I said.

"We found a nice home for you. And you don't have to work on a dairy anymore," she said, while wiping her face with a tissue. "Pauline and Bob Ware want you to live with them." She had stopped crying now. "Let's go meet the Wares, you'll like them."

We parked in the dirt driveway of a big white house. I had seen it before, because it was built on the same lot as the Presbyterian Church. I could tell she knew I was nervous by the way she smiled at me after she turned off the motor and looked my way. "Dennis," she said quietly, "They're expecting us and they know all about you. Bob and Pauline are wonderful people. You're going to be just fine."

I had seen Bob Ware twice, both times when Mrs. Valliant insisted I attend church with her. That's how I remembered the white house. Later, I learned it was called a parsonage. We were let into a warm house and I was greeted with genuine smiles and hugs. The Wares and Mrs. Valliant visited for a short time. Mrs. Valliant was barely out of the driveway when Pauline insisted upon showing me the house and my room.

My room was the largest bedroom I had ever seen, with a huge bed, complete with a real dresser and mirror, and a study table with a straight-back chair. I couldn't even imagine living in such a fancy house, with everything looking so clean...and breakable. There was a flower-patterned spread over the mattress, a matted rug covering part of the floor, and two little hourglass flower vases sitting on top of white doilies on the wooden dresser. Mrs. Ware smiled down at me and I exhaled. I hadn't even realized I'd been holding my breath. But I wasn't fooled by all of this—the nice house, warm bed, everything— and I wasn't about to build my hopes very high that it would last very long.

———

We're eating supper, the second day I lived with them. "Dennis, I went to the school today and talked with Mr. Young about your school work," Bob Ware said. "Mr. Young said you're doing great on everything, but you're having some trouble with fractions. How would you like some help with those tricky numbers?"

"Yeah, that sounds great," I said.

I was pulling D's and C's in arithmetic, all because I didn't understand fractions.

Every night Bob and I sat at the kitchen table and worked fraction problems. The last test before Christmas break I received a grade of ninety-two on an arithmetic test, with more than half of it being on fractions. Mr. Young announced my grade score to the class, and I wasn't embarrassed anymore; I deserved the grade. They could stuff their smirks for all I cared.

After moving to the Wares, I had less desire to meet James Caldwell off the school ground. I told him I didn't want to smoke any more of his cigarettes, and I had changed my mind about running away. For two days I stayed on the other side of the school building to avoid seeing him. The next time I saw him he pushed me, hard, as we were going into the school building. He asked me what was wrong. I didn't want to tell him that something just didn't seem right. "I've been busy," is all I could think to say to him. The next day James threatened to whip me, saying I acted like I was too good for him.

In the days that followed, I developed an intense dislike for James Caldwell. Suddenly I was thinking that he had cotton where his brains should be—forgetting that he had been my idol just two weeks before. I avoided him whenever possible, because he was a lot bigger than me, and I knew he wouldn't have much problem whipping me good. James dropped out of school before the end of the semester, and I never saw him again.

It was at the Wares that I had my last nightmare. I had probably been living with them a month by then. After it was all over I laid in bed and tried to remember how long it had been since the Blob had visited me, probably not since that Fourth of July night after I blind-sided Craig. Always before it had happened after a bad scene, or if I was particularly worried about something. But I couldn't think of anything that had happened that day to bring it on, and I didn't even feel it coming this time. At breakfast the next morning Bob and Pauline were laughing while they told me all about it.

Bob said he heard me coming down the stairs, something I never did at night, and he got out of bed and met me in the hallway. He asked me if everything was all right, and when I didn't answer, he knew I was sleepwalking. "It was when you opened the door and started running toward town that I realized we were both in trouble."

All I remember about the whole thing is thinking the Blob had me for sure, until I'm awake enough to realize it's Bob who's got his arms wrapped tightly around me. I'm so relieved, then suddenly, I get cold all over. I look down and realize that we're both standing in our bare feet in six inches of fresh snow.

I never told Bob or Pauline, or anyone else, for that matter, about the Blob. But, for years after that last nightmare, I worried it might come back, and it did, partially. It would start, then, all of a sudden, just go away, but never a full-blown attack.

I returned to the Valliants for Christmas break. A good feeling had come over me the short time I had lived with the Wares. Mrs. Valliant noticed the change in me right away. She wanted to know what had happened, and I didn't know how to answer her. All I knew for sure was, for the first time since I could remember I felt things were really going my way. My friend, Pete, was there. I helped him feed hay to the sheep and cattle every day. He said I had grown up and he was looking forward to working with me when school was out.

The Richard Valliant family was at the house for Christmas dinner. Craig and I didn't speak or acknowledge each other, but, for the first time, I didn't feel out of sorts with him.

Three days after Christmas a big storm blew in, leaving two feet of snow—the next day a ground blizzard—then two more feet of snow. The day school was to start all roads around Saratoga were closed. A week later, the main highway south of Saratoga was opened with snow plows, but we couldn't get to the highway—ten miles from the ranch. Snow was two and three feet deep on the level, with snowdrifts reaching eight-feet high. I was still stranded at home a week after school opened for kids in town.

Another week passed. Mr. Valliant said it was hard telling how long it would be before the county could open our roads, but I could ride out horseback if I was willing to try it. I told him I would. I could ride Brownie, turn him loose at the highway and he could find his own way back to the ranch. Brownie was the horse selected because he had long legs and could make his way across the deep snow better than Red. Mr. Valliant said I should cut across the prairie, which would take a few miles off my trip to the highway.

The temperature was two below zero when I left the ranch the next morning. On the back of my saddle I carried a sleeping bag, some small twigs, matches and a two day supply of dried food. Three hours later I met Bob and Pauline Ware at the highway, unsaddled Brownie, and slapped him on the rump to start him home at a dead run.

Sixth-grade basketball practice was held during the noon hour. Mr. Young was the coach. Our class was small and had very few boys to call on for sports. After I started living with the Wares, Mr. Young insisted I start practicing with the team. I had no friends on the team, or the whole school for that matter, and I was afraid of how they would treat me. Two days of sitting with my back to the wall watching the practice and I told Mr. Young I would try. I had never handled a basketball, but, after watching for a while, it didn't look that hard.

When Bob Ware learned I was going to start practicing basketball, he borrowed a ball from the school and started giving me pointers in the gravel driveway outside the church. Bob said he had played basketball in high school and he could teach me a lot. He showed me how to dribble, feint, pass and shoot. He said I looked pretty good. I squeezed in all the knowledge I could—hoping to impress Mr. Young enough to make the team.

I was a head taller than any of the other boys, twice as clumsy, and not very popular with the other team members. But, because of my height, it wasn't long before I was on the starting five. I had found my calling, and I lived and breathed basketball.

Our team played Encampment, Baggs, Elk Mountain and Rawlins sixth-grade, winning every game. Toward the end of the season, I had dreams about being a great basketball player. The opposing teams didn't know I was two years older than anyone else, and treated me as an outright oddity. I enjoyed the notoriety—especially when I would get a pass, stumble my way all the way down the court and score a winning basket. Before basketball season ended, I developed a lasting friendship with Clay Moser, Boomer Davis and Rusty Harrison.

The last day of the school year Mr. Young asked me to stay inside during recess; he needed to talk to me. We were alone in the room. He scrunched into a school desk next to me and looked me square in the face. "My contract hasn't been renewed for next year," he said, "and I don't know if I will be teaching here again. I want you to know it's been my pleasure watching you learn and come alive." He paused for a long moment. "I was an orphan...so I know what you're going through."

Feeling proud and astonished at the same time, I didn't know what to say. Proud that I had done so well and astonished that a grown man, a kind and important man like Mr. Young, had been an orphan. I turned my head and looked out the window, hoping my eyes would quit burning. "I hope you come back next year," was all I could think to say.

TWENTY-EIGHT

Some time after my fourteenth birthday, before the end of the school year, Mr. Young secretly told me that I would be promoted to the seventh grade. Not only would I be promoted, he said, but I was reading and comprehending on an eighth-grade level and he was going to recommend to Mrs. Seymour that I skip a grade and be promoted to the eighth-grade. I could scarcely comprehend that I had survived the school year, played basketball, gained a measure of respect from the other students, and won the friendship of some classmates. Being promoted two grades, which would put me only one year behind my age group, was beyond my wildest dreams.

And it didn't happen. The Platte Valley School System was more like *The Seymour School System*. With an iron hand and fist, the Seymours controlled the curriculum, recreation and athletic programs, promotions, and the general mood of the whole school.

Mrs. Seymour was principal of the grade school and Mr. Seymour was superintendent of the high school. Mr. Seymour was a short, stocky, meaty-faced, balding man, with short stubby fingers, sharp, ugly eyes, blotchy discolored skin and a large sagging belly that hung over his belt. His nose was purple and bulbous, and he tried to swagger when he walked.

Mrs. Seymour was a tall, meaty, giant of a woman. She had an odd growth on her face from which a long solitary hair protruded, and her flesh went every which way when she walked. When standing beside his wife, Mr. Seymour looked like a little fat dwarf. Someone told me that they hadn't been married very long. The first time I heard this, I remember thinking that it was a good thing they were too old to have children. Just picturing a little fat dwarf kid with hairy warts and a big purple nose made me shudder. Of course, I never heard anyone say anything about it, but I know they must have been thinking it, too.

Neither of the Seymours ever showed a friendly smile to a student unless the kid happened to belong to a school board member or other important person in the community. Routinely, Mr. Seymour would leave his duties at the high school and slowly walk through our classroom. If you were not a favored child he would thump you on the head with a meaty finger, which reminded me of how my dad tested a watermelon for ripeness. Other students received lumps on their heads, but I was sure I held the record. I always felt a tinge of guilt after his thumps, like I'd done something to deserve it, but couldn't remember exactly what.

It wasn't long after my first conversation with Mr. Young about a promotion to the eighth-grade that he told me his recommendation had been denied. I wasn't surprised. By his tone of voice, I could tell Mr. Young didn't like the Seymours, but he didn't come right out and said so.

I was disappointed, but thanked Mr. Young for trying and told him I appreciated his efforts. He told me not to worry, "The Seymours won't always be here—you'll get your chance."

I started feeling the high a month before summer vacation, anxious to get away from the Seymours. Thinking about the school year, though, I felt good that I had accomplished something that I felt from the first day that I was licked before I started, but I didn't have much to lose by seeing it through. There were some good times and some bad times, but I tried to remember all the good things, when my mind wasn't busy hating the Seymours.

The one disappointment that left me with a sour attitude about the whole school thing was not being recognized by Mrs. Seymour for my spelling abilities. Every Friday there was a spelldown in the sixth, seventh, and eighth grades. The top three spellers then challenged each other for a junior high spelldown. The object was to pick a top speller to represent the school at the county spelldown in April. From almost the beginning, I was one of the top three best spellers in the sixth grade, and represented my grade in the junior high spelldown.

On several occasions I placed second in the final spelldown. Mrs. Seymour always dismissed my accomplishments as just luck at getting the easiest words. I knew I was good and I had visions of winning the county spelling contest, then the state contest. But I was aware that Mrs. Seymour had other visions; she had obligations to the school board members and to other prominent citizens of the community.

But I had put the school year behind me, and was feeling good during the car trip back to the ranch. I hadn't seen the Valliants for several weeks, and I wanted them to congratulate me and tell me how great it was that I had been promoted to the seventh grade. I knew they were proud of me, but I wanted to hear them say it. I leaned over the seat, with a wide grin. "Did Mr. Ware tell you I was almost promoted to the eighth grade?"

"Yes, we heard, Dennis," Mrs. Valliant replied. "It's such a shame because I know you can do the work. But look at the good side, if you keep going to school you will be sixteen when you graduate from the eighth-grade and you can legally quit school and go to work if you want to." She'd said it as if it would make me feel better, but that wasn't what I wanted to hear.

We rode in silence until Mrs. Valliant turned in her seat and smiled. "I've hired a new girl to help in the kitchen, Dennis. Her name is Helen Myers." I stared straight ahead for a moment, disappointed because Dana wasn't coming back. But my disappointment quickly turned to excitement when Mrs. Valliant described the new girl, already living on the ranch. Helen was tall, (Mrs. Valliant said) with long red hair, a beautiful smile, very friendly, and she knows how to work, very neat and clean, too.

I immediately forgot about Dana, sat back in the seat and went into my own fantasy world—all the while secretly aware that my excitement would be noticed by Mrs. Valliant if she turned around to talk to me. This gorgeous new girl wouldn't know who I was, not like the girls in school, who wouldn't give me a second look. I wouldn't be the gawky, clumsy classmate, with no parents and no home. No sir. I would be someone just like her; a kid earning my summer's wage. I imagined, after I helped her do the supper dishes, we would take long walks along the creek. We'd find a soft grassy area and sit and listen to the ripple of the stream, hold hands, kiss, and perhaps even more. By the time Mr. Valliant stopped the car in front of the ranch house I was trembling with excitement.

I was out of the car, and halfway to the house before my fantasy spell broke. My excitement was gone and I formed a new mental picture of Helen because I didn't want to be disappointed—a more accurate one as it turned out. Yes, Helen was nice—anyone could see that—with a pretty smile, and long waist-length, dull red hair. She was taller than any girl I had ever seen, and skinny as a bed slat, with spindly, twig-like legs. Helen was a real beanpole, but at the moment, she was the only girl on the planet and I wasn't giving up that easily.

I imagined from the start that Helen was attracted to me, because she always smiled when she looked my way. I wanted her to feel that way, because I had a deep-down aching feeling when I looked at her, and I wasn't sure what I could do about it. I had never as much as smiled at a girl in school, and I couldn't look Helen straight in the face and say good morning without my cheeks getting red hot.

Helen was seventeen, and even though I was sure she liked me, I was just as sure she was seeing right through me and having herself a good laugh. I imagined she knew about all the dreams I had been having about her and could only look at me with disgust. This wasn't anything like my fantasy in the car, or how I felt about her when she wasn't around, and my life had become secretly miserable.

Supper was over. I walked to the barn with Fred Harrison (our new hired man), jumped on Red and rode him around the corral without saddle or bridle—just for something to do-- burning off nervous energy. It was nearly dark when I walked toward the house and met Helen halfway. When I saw her I developed a case of weak knees. We both stopped and said hi. "Wanna walk with me?" She said, as I started to leave.

"Yeah," I said.

That was all I needed. We walked and talked until long past my bedtime. Helen's dad had been out of work for years. Her mother worked odd jobs to keep the family going. This was her third summer working on a ranch as a kitchen helper. She talked some about enrolling in Casper Junior College after graduating high school next spring. At first I didn't want to tell her anything about my own sorry life before living with the Valliants, but I didn't want her to think me unfriendly. When I did tell her about myself I just told her that I was an orphan, leaving out all the bad parts about my dad drinking so much and how he had beat the tar out of me all the time. I wanted Helen to like me, and so I told her how I planned to finish high school, then maybe I'd become a doctor or a lawyer—things I made up right on the spot.

Because the Richard Valliant family was on the same ranch now, only one new man was hired for the summer. Fred Harrison was the father of a classmate of mine. He was a nice guy who worked hard and kept to himself when not on the job. He had his own car, went home on weekends and returned to work early Monday mornings. His son Rusty and I had become friends in school.

Craig and Mark helped with the lambing, but we didn't become great friends or anything. I imagined that Craig wanted me to come crawling to him on my hands and knees, cringing like an old dog begging to be petted. I didn't do any of that, and we pretty much maintained our sour attitudes when we were forced together on a job, with neither of us giving an inch.

Lambs were born, sheep driven to the mountains, Forest Service fence repaired, hay cut and stacked, and the summer passed without major incident—almost. Because of my accident with Sonny Boy, and my crooked leg, Mr. Valliant wouldn't allow me to ride a new colt—but I persisted. Between lambing and haying season he said I could start a little two-year-old palomino gelding. Fred Harrison offered to help, and we used the same breaking techniques I had learned from Pete. It wasn't too many days until I was riding Pal in the round corral. Helen was there on my evening rides. I could feel her admiration as she leaned over the corral, smiling and waving. Within a week I was riding in the large corral, and taking short rides through the meadows.

It was Sunday. The Valliants had gone to church. Helen had gone with them, and Grimes was snoring on the couch. I decided to ride Pal to the Forest Service boundary, something Mr. Valliant hard warned me never to do alone. *But who would know?* I reasoned.

I felt a new sense of freedom, just Pal and I with the wind at our faces and the snow-capped peaks to guide us. Not a care in the world, that's how I felt.

On the return trip, I was sitting loose in the saddle, still feeling good, relaxed. I glanced at my watch. Time was running short. The trip to the boundary fence had taken longer than I'd planned. Grimes would be coming out of his nap, and the Valliants were due back at the ranch about now.

I kicked Pal into a slow, easy lope. Suddenly my whole body jerked backward. I struggled to regain my balance in the saddle, while Pal went into a runaway mode. Worse yet, I had lost my reins with Pal's first burst of power, and he had his own head, without that nagging pressure on his bit. I was helpless, on a runaway mustang. I could see a barbed wire fence looming ahead of us, and the last thing I wanted to do was become a part of that fence. At the last moment, I bailed off to the side. On my way to the ground I noticed a long piece of loose barbed wire attached to his tail.

The fall nearly knocked me unconscious. When I regained my senses, I didn't know where I was or what I was doing there. When everything came to light, I checked for broken bones, cuts and bruises. Physically I was in good shape, but I was worried sick about Pal. He was nowhere in sight, and I wasn't close enough to the fence to see if he was tangled in the barbed wire and bleeding to death.

I had a splitting headache but that didn't stop me from running all the way to the fence. I breathed a sigh of relief when Pal wasn't tangled in the broken wire, and again when I could find no traces of blood anywhere. I started walking toward the house. I couldn't see it, but I knew it was somewhere over two hills and across a sagebrush valley. I saw Pal just as I topped the first hill, grazing contentedly on a green spot near a gulley. I was afraid to look at him; I had seen wire cuts on horses. I approached him cautiously, and prepared myself for the worst. Little by little, I checked him over. With disbelief, I found several very small scratches and one minor cut on his chest area, but no major gashes.

I tried to think up a good story to explain the broken fence and Pal's slight wire cuts. Mr. Valliant would be disappointed with me if I told him the complete truth about my adventure. But I had to say something; Pal had some scratches, then there was the matter of the fence, which had to be fixed. So I told a half-truth. I had taken a little ride to the south pasture, and then the wire got caught on Pal's tail. Mr. Valliant raised an eyebrow, but, otherwise, seemed to be satisfied. Mr. Valliant and I spent the rest of the afternoon repairing the fence.

We finished haying earlier than usual. Helen left a week before school started, a sad day for me. But after all, we were only forty miles apart; she promised to write.

TWENTY-NINE

A day or two before school started I saw Richard Valliant pull into the driveway in his black Ford. I went to the Upper Room and sat by the door that adjoined the living room. I listened quietly while Richard and Mrs. Valliant discussed how I would get to the bus stop. I felt bad hearing them talk, and taking their time to worry about me, especially since I hadn't told them that I had made arrangements with Fred Harrison to live with him and go to school. Fred owned a small farm west of Saratoga and he said I could make some extra money on weekends by helping him clean barns and chicken houses. I could use the extra money, but what excited me the most was thinking about playing sports after school, hanging out in the pool hall with Rusty, and his circle of friends.

The Valliants acted pleased when I finally told them about my plans to live with the Harrisons, but I suspected they really wanted me to ride the bus until the weather got bad, then live with Bob and Pauline Ware.

Other than the Valliants, I liked Bob and Pauline Ware better than anyone in the whole world. But, I'm fourteen now, practically a grown man, and, for sure, too old to be adopted by anyone. Besides, I'd decided that I didn't want any more piano lessons, and going to Sunday school and church really wasn't for me.

I peeked into my old classroom, just for old times' sake, or maybe it was because I was already missing Mr. Young. But, there he was, his back to me, writing something on the blackboard. I didn't know what to say, but I finally managed, "Hey, I thought you weren't coming back."

He turned, and smiled. "Well...are you disappointed?"

"No. No…but, you know, you said your contract wouldn't be renewed and all."

"A change of heart, that's all. Anyway, you didn't think you could get rid of me that easy, did you?"

I finally found my real voice, and I couldn't help it any more. I ran right up to him and blurted out, "Hey, you're really back!"

Mr. Young wouldn't be my homeroom teacher, but it felt great knowing that I still had a friend in the school building—and I could count on him in math class.

My homeroom teacher for the seventh grade was Mrs. Glascow. She was a skinny little thing—no curves whatsoever, flat-chested as all get out—tight little frizzy brown curls, shoulder-length. She wore glasses so thick it was a wonder she could see through them at all. This was her first year of teaching. She was jumpy and afraid of everything, especially the kids. The only reason there was any discipline at all was the threat of her sending us to Mrs. Seymour's office.

School lunches cost twenty-cents. A sure sign of poverty was carrying a sack lunch to school, and I had made sure I saved enough from my summer wages to afford lunchroom money throughout the school year. I was standing in the lunchroom line, waiting to hand my two dimes over at the door, when I felt a hand on my shoulder. It was Mrs. Thompson. I knew she was the school music teacher, but I had never been in one of her classes, so I was surprised when she started talking to me. "Mr. Young said you practiced piano while staying at the Wares," she said. "How would you like to play in the school band?" She smiled. I guess she could see I was confused.

"Playing in the band sounds like fun," I said, "but I don't have an instrument, and, anyway, I don't think I could play a horn."

"Believe me," she said, "playing a band instrument is a lot easier than the piano. If you're interested, I have a used trombone I can sell you for twenty dollars. And I can start giving you lessons this afternoon."

"I don't have twenty dollars."

"That's okay; you can pay me when you get it."

My brain went into high gear. I figured if I didn't like the band I could always give the trombone back. *Imagine me in the band.* I almost laughed. But why not, I asked myself. I could read piano music a little. Playing a trombone couldn't be *that* hard. I knew the band took several trips a year with the high school basketball and football team, better than going to Fred's farm on Friday night to clean corrals or chicken houses, I reasoned. I looked at Mrs. Thompson, smiled, and it was settled right there.

After a month of one-hour private lessons each day, she said I was ready to join the band. I felt a sense of pride being named second trombonist, until I learned there was only one other trombonist, Gary Morris. Gary was first trombonist and he welcomed me to the band. "Now the old bag won't know who to yell at from the sour notes in the trombone section," Gary said.

Seventh-grade school work was easier than I expected. I had no problems with any of the classes, including math, thanks to Bob Ware. And it was a good thing, classes being easy and all, because Rusty and I did little or no studying after school. Our life revolved around baseball, basketball, hanging out in the pool hall, and sneaking off to the "Hobo Pool" at night, smoking cigarettes. On weekends we went with Fred to his little ranch, built fence, or helped with whatever work needed done and hunted rabbits.

Fred didn't see the wild streak in me. I remember his words to Mrs. Valliant, as I was leaving the ranch with him the day before school started: 'Dennis will be a good influence on Rusty. He's getting a little hard for his mom to handle when I'm working out of town.'

Rusty's mother was a large, dark-skinned woman, crippled in one leg, and the sweetest woman I had ever known. She bounded around the house cooking, cleaning, and doing everything else that I thought her three teenage daughters should be doing. The daughters, Claire, Susan, and Sandy were all in high school.

Sandy was a freshman, Susan was a sophomore and 'Wild as a March Hare,' as the saying went, and Claire was a senior.

A few days after school started, I borrowed Rusty's bike during the noon hour. I didn't own a bike. Rusty usually rode his bike to school, with me walking beside him or riding on the handlebars. I was speeding by a group of eighth-grade boys hanging out near the sidewalk. Suddenly, an arm flew out, striking me in the face, knocking me off the bike.

They all roared with laughter. Mike Sweeney stepped forward with his big round-face smile and claimed the victory. Mike Sweeney was the school bully, but, until now, I had managed to stay my distance from him and he hadn't bothered me. My nose was bleeding, and, even though I didn't turn to look, the pain told me that my elbow was banged up pretty bad.

I got to my feet and charged head-first, grabbing Sweeney around the waist, my blood wetting his shirt, him pounding me on the head and back with his fists. Mr. Seymour, the high school superintendent, saw the whole thing and immediately came over and yanked me away from Mike. Seymour was furious with me for getting blood all over Mike's shirt. "There's going to be a boxing match tonight," he said.

I knew what that meant—a grudge fight. It was another Seymour rule. When two boys were caught fighting on school grounds they were forced to put the gloves on after school and have at each other. This was a rule adopted by the Seymours to settle playground disputes, and there were few exceptions. It didn't matter how mismatched the two boys were; the more mismatched, the more blood.

Seymour was an ex-marine, and this is how they settled things in the marines. There were no rules and no bells or whistles to signal the end of a round; just standing toe-to-toe, slugging it out until exhaustion or a blood bath overtook the underdog. If they fell on the floor and started wrestling they were pulled apart and forced to stand and keep slugging. The school gym was used for these fights, and students were encouraged to stay after school and watch. On occasion, the buses were held up to allow the bus kids some entertainment—such was the case for our fight.

I knew I was going to get the crap beat out of me, and, at first, I didn't care; I was mad. As the afternoon wore on I started to care. My nose and face hurt from getting knocked off the bike, and my arms ached. Mike was a lot taller and heavier than me and he had a reputation of showing no mercy in a fist fight. Given a chance, I would have said or done almost anything to get out of the fight.

As everyone expected (including me) Mike gave me the worst whipping of my life. I couldn't get up fast enough for him to knock me back down. My nose started bleeding again; I wanted to cry, and my legs were wobbly and weak. When I wasn't getting knocked down, I was begging with my eyes to Mr. Seymour to stop the fight, but when I looked at him all I could see was a mouth full of yellow teeth, surrounded by his pudgy discolored face, and hear a whole gym full of kids laughing and shouting, "Hey, chicken, fight back."

I couldn't count the times I was knocked to the floor, and the fight didn't end until I couldn't, or wouldn't, stand up again. The fight was over and Mike left smiling and untouched, with Mr. Seymour's arm draped around his shoulders.

The whipping Mike Sweeney gave me seemed to satisfy his thirst for my blood, and he never bothered me again—not that year, anyway. Mike Sweeney, and Mr. Seymour couldn't possibly know it, but I didn't consider the fight over. It didn't help my nose feel any better, but I soothed my feelings by vowing that some day we would meet again—under different circumstances.

That year, I made the first string junior high basketball team. I was the tallest boy on the team and I had acquired considerable skill in handling the ball and shooting. Rusty was the shortest kid and the best outside shot. We won all of our games during the season. Because I was a good basketball player, I won a degree of acceptance from some of my classmates and my confidence soared.

After basketball season, Rusty and I stopped studying or doing homework, and my grades dropped to C's and B's. I could see the disappointment in Mr. Young's face, but it didn't bother me enough to do anything about it. We'd skip school and hunt rabbits, or swim in the hobo pool, hurry to the pool hall after four o'clock and smoke cigarettes, shoot pool, talk dirty about girls and act grown-up with the older guys until late in the evening. Rusty's older sister, Claire, wrote our excuses for us. We had colds, the flu, and several mysterious ailments that caused us to be sick at our stomachs or downright bedridden.

It never occurred to me that Mrs. Seymour would think twice about Rusty and me both always being sick on the same days. But she did. She thought so much about it that one day she took it upon herself to check on the two ailing students. That same day, Rusty and I had remembered to wear our swim shorts under our pants and were taking a swim in the town Hobo Pool. Mrs. Harrison was surprised to learn of our failing health and the gig was up.

Mrs. Harrison didn't tell us about the visit from Mrs. Seymour. We were planning our next escape to freedom as we walked to school the next morning. At the beginning of the first class period, Mrs. Seymour and Mrs. Glascow were both standing at the front of the room. Something wasn't right. I was nervous and antsy without knowing exactly why. But what I did know was that Rusty and I were the only two trouble-makers in the seventh-grade, and if anyone was going to be dragged to Seymour's office it would be us. Waiting for the last bell to ring, Mrs. Seymour glanced from Rusty to me with cold, menacing stares. I looked at Rusty out of the corner of my eye, and the look on his face told me he had the same hollow feeling in his stomach.

"Dennis and Rusty, come with me," were the first words out of Mrs. Seymour's mouth.

She ordered us to sit, admonishing us not to say one word, not even a whisper, and left, slamming the door behind her. She returned about fifteen minutes later, followed by Mr. Young and Mr. Seymour. I was sure she had Mr. Young there to prove to him that she was right about me all along, and I was just as certain Mr. Seymour was there to swing the paddle.

For fifteen minutes, Mrs. Seymour ranted on about how unappreciative I was of all the nice folks who had sacrificed so much to help an orphan boy become a decent person—*an orphan who has turned out to be a liar, a thief; a boy who smokes and drinks beer, and plays pool all day when he's supposed to be in school. A boy who has laughed in the faces of all these good people. This is what we get for all of our kindness.* "With that kind of appreciation, maybe you've been on county welfare long enough," she concluded.

I knew I was none of these—not all of them, anyway. But I was worried that Mr. Young believed what she was saying. She passed her final judgment on me by saying it was bad enough that I had turned out to be no good, but my bad influence on Rusty was inexcusable. Mr. Seymour chipped in, saying I was the biggest sissy in school and he was sick of my whining and crying, too.

Did I have anything to say for myself? I could have apologized, promised to do better, and begged for another chance. I looked at Mr. Young. He was sitting with his hands in his lap, staring at the floor. Not that I expected him to defend me—what was there to defend? And so I suffered in silence. I couldn't even defend myself, because I didn't want to do better, and I didn't intend to do better—not in her school, anyway. I was sick of her and her whole damn school, and, once I was out of the building, I didn't intend to ever return. I didn't need any more of this; I was almost fifteen-years old and I would go somewhere else and go to school. Some place far away from the Seymours.

Rusty and I both got the paddle from Seymour, ten swats each, and a week suspension from school. I didn't need to (I wouldn't be back), but I went along with the paddling mostly because I didn't want Rusty to think of me as a chicken.

———

Mrs. Seymour wasn't wrong when she called me a liar and a thief. I *had* lied to Mrs. Harrison about where I spent my days when I was excused for being sick, and I had stolen candy bars from off the drug store shelves, but she didn't know that, because I hadn't been caught. But she was dead wrong about me not appreciating what some folks had done for me. The charges that really hurt were being called a thief and a sissy; I didn't see myself that way at all. She didn't have any proof that I had stolen, and they couldn't say I was a sissy because I had stood up as long as I could while the biggest bully in school made goulash out of my face.

Mrs. Seymour succeeded, but not in the way she thought. She won in that I was quitting school, but she didn't succeed in convincing me that I was low enough to crawl under a snake's belly. From my first day of school I knew she was a witch, and, holding to that opinion, I was convinced she couldn't possibly know who I was. But even with all her wickedness, I didn't understand why she didn't like me or wouldn't give me a fair shake. It entered my mind once or twice that she might have problems of her own (not that I cared for one second). I just wrote it off that some people are bad and some aren't and she wasn't going to ruin my life just because she happened to be one of the bad people.

Rusty cried during the paddling. My eyes burned, but I didn't cry. I guess this didn't set well with old Seymour, because he kept hitting me harder and harder. I can't even remember the last time I cried and I had sooner died than give old Pudge-face the honor. He was all out of breath when he finally stopped hitting me and shouted for us to get the hell out of his school.

We walked home without saying a word, each in our own world. Rusty would go home, lie around and read comic books for a week, go back to school, with everything in his world normal again. My world was up-side-down. I didn't want anything my world had to offer, and I had no realistic plans to change anything. I had saved a little money from my summer's wages and my only thoughts were to pack my things and go some place far away—any place but here. Maybe I'd try to find Grandma in Dallas.

Rusty told his mom as soon as we got home. She didn't say much. She never did. I told her I was quitting school and would be leaving tomorrow. "Oh my, Dennis," she said, "you can't do that!" I could tell she was upset because she rarely said anything to me, except in a loving or teasing manner.

Rusty and I went outside and played basketball in the back yard. About fifteen minutes later, Mrs. Harrison yelled from the back door, "Mrs. Valliant wants to talk to you."

I hadn't thought about her calling the Valliants. But I didn't really care; the whole world could know as far as I was concerned. I told Mrs. Valliant I was leaving the next day. She asked me to wait until she could get to town tomorrow afternoon; she wanted to talk to me. I said, "Okay," and hung up the phone.

I slept late the next morning, ate breakfast with Rusty, and went for a walk. The whole thing about quitting school, Seymour's badmouthing, and that business about being on county welfare were starting to bother me, particularly the county welfare part. I knew what county was, but what exactly was *welfare*? I had heard the word used, but not in a good context, and if Mrs. Seymour associated it with my name, I knew it wasn't something I could be proud of.

Now that I was over most of my mad, I really didn't want to quit school. I had basketball, I was good at the high jump and pole vault, and track was starting in April. Then there was baseball and the school band, and I had a couple of friends now. If I quit and went to another school I would have to start all over. I would still be who I am, and there would be bullies in any school—maybe even another Seymour. I had a week to think about it—and I was going to think hard.

———

Mrs. Valliant arrived in the early afternoon. I met her at the door. We got in her car and sat for a long time, each looking straight ahead. When she turned toward me she had tears in her eyes, and I could see the worry in her face. "Are you all right?" she asked.

"Yeah, I'm okay." Which was another lie, I wasn't okay, not by a long, long shot. I was frightened and lonely, paddling a chicken wire canoe. Every five minutes since early morning, I choked up and stifled a cry. I didn't want to quit school, I had no place to go, and I didn't have much money to go anywhere. I didn't want to leave my friends, the Valliants, Bob and Pauline Ware, or Mr. Young, and start all over somewhere else. No. I wasn't okay, but I didn't want to cause her any more trouble by telling her how I really was, and I didn't want her feeling sorry for me.

Another long silence, then she turned toward me again, more composed now. "Dennis, you can't quit school. You've come so far. You're only fourteen; if you could somehow just make it through the eighth-grade you'll be sixteen and better able to make a decision about what to do with your life."

"I don't want to quit school, but the Seymours treat me like a criminal, and everything I do is wrong," I said.

There was another long silence, with both of us looking straight ahead. "Can you tell me what happened at school?" she asked, in such a kindly voice it made me cringe with guilt.

I'd already lost face with the Valliants, this I was sure of, but maybe there was a tiny patch left, about the size of one of my freckles, and I wanted to keep it. I had mulled it over and over in my head all day, and practiced all my excuses, but, suddenly, none of it seemed worthwhile. So I mostly told her the truth. I told her I had been skipping school, hanging out at the Hobo Pool during the day and the pool hall at night. I left out the part about smoking and stealing candy at the drug store. I also left out the part about being beaten up by the school bully. I told her I didn't know why I had been so bad and that I was sorry I had disappointed them. I told her I wanted to quit school because I hated the Seymours and they hated me. "And they said I was on county welfare. What exactly is welfare?"

"Well," she said, "Welfare is ah….when you get help from the county when you don't have any place to stay, or anything to eat."

"Am I on welfare?"

"Yes, Dennis, you're on welfare."

"Do they give you money when you're on welfare?"

"Mr. Harrison gets money for your board and room, but you don't get any."

"Where does the county get the money," I asked.

"From the people, Dennis, but it doesn't matter, it's a good thing, and it has allowed you to go to school. Why are you so concerned about welfare?"

"Because I heard some kids talking about the Penningtons being on welfare...and you know who *they* are. I don't want to be on welfare. If the kids find out they'll make fun of me."

"You can't live in town and go to school unless you accept welfare," she said.

"Then I won't go to school."

Her shoulders slumped with a sigh. We sat for a long time again without talking. "Will you keep going to school if I can find you another job on a dairy with a nice family?" she said, turning my way and laying a hand on my shoulder.

I didn't know if she had a plan or not, and I wasn't at all sure if I could go back into that school and face the Seymours again. "I don't know what to do," I said, "but I'll try."

"One more thing," she said before leaving, "I talked to Mr. Young, and Mrs. Seymour. They both want you to return to school. You know Mr. Young likes you, and Mrs. Seymour said she will be more patient with you if you quit skipping school and start turning in homework again."

The week passed. Sunday morning Mrs. Valliant called to say she was going to church and wanted to talk to me afterwards. Again, we sat in her car to talk. She was in a cheerful mood, and I suspected she had some good news for me. After asking how I was, she paused, collecting her thoughts.

"Do you remember Dawson Coleman?" she asked, laying her hand on my arm.

I told her I did.

"Well, Dennis, I talked to Dawson, and he talked to Tom Watson, and they want you to go to work for them. You can help them milk morning and night, and keep going to school. And you *won't* be on county welfare." She chuckled.

"Okay, I'll start working for them," I said, "but if it don't work out I'm gonna quit school and go back to Texas and live with my grandma."

"Fair enough," she said with a big grin.

My remark about going to Grandma's was a hollow threat, but I wanted her to know I wasn't caving in all the way. I had thought all week where I could go and came up with nothing. I knew Grandma would be in Dallas, *but where was Dallas?* I had never been in a large city and the thought of trying to find one person in a place that big made me tremble. Going to live with Clarence and Jerry was out of the question; I had lost their address. I had no place to go.

I knew Dawson Coleman. He had worked for the Valliants a week or two during hay harvest before taking a permanent job with the Tom Watson Dairy Farm. That's why I remembered him, but that isn't why I remembered him so well. From the first moment I laid eyes on Dawson, I thought about my dad, because they looked so much alike. Dawson had wild, brown hair. My dad's hair was dark red, but their body features and movements were enough alike to give me goose bumps: broad, bony shoulders, probably over six-feet tall, quick with their hands and feet, and a wild, careless look in their eyes. I remembered that Dawson was married, his wife and one kid lived in town. I recalled that he had a large gap in his face where two of his front teeth should have been. One day I asked him what happened to his teeth and he replied that he had lost them in a fight outside the Rustic Bar.

THIRTY

Mrs. Valliant dropped me off at the Watson Dairy late Sunday afternoon. The place looked deserted, except for two large dogs lying on the porch. I thanked Mrs. Valliant for everything, grabbed my cardboard box and walked toward the smaller of the two houses, where the dogs were sleeping. I sat the box down at my feet and started to knock, just as Dawson opened the door.

I could tell by his rumpled hair and sleepy gaze that he'd been napping. He stood in the doorway, forcing back a yawn. "Stow your things in the big house," he said, "Tom is in Utah, but that's where you'll be sleeping. Put your work clothes on and come on back, we'll have a roll before milking."

I guessed that Mrs. Valliant had already told Dawson all about my work experience with Boris Klein, a Grade-B Dairy, where cows were milked by hand, and the milk cooled in the creek in five-gallon cans. I didn't know what to expect here, but I wasn't worried; it couldn't be worse than where I had been.

I walked into the milking parlor behind Dawson, without a thought that anything would be different from the manure-splattered walls and the stink of days-old rotten cow shit drying on broken concrete. Standing there, beside Dawson, staring at the floor, and the walls of the milking parlor, my first reaction was simply disbelief. It didn't look like any place where cows had been, or even should be. Everything was clean and neat. Nothing looked out of place, and the floor and walls had that scrubbed look to them. Dawson didn't know what I was thinking, but he must have sensed my bewilderment, because he chuckled, and said, "Don't worry, it's easy and you'll get used to it. We can milk these eighty cows in about two hours, and everything will look just like this when we finish."

It wasn't quite as simple, or easy, as that, but it wasn't that hard either—and we *did* milk the eighty cows in two hours, using two milking machines. There were twenty stanchions in the milking parlor, where cows munched contentedly on grain, while milking machines chugged them dry. The bowl below the mechanical hands that pulled at the tits was secured by a strap fastened over the cow's back. When the bowl was removed from the cow, the milk was emptied into a large vat, strained, cooled over refrigerated coils, and trickled into five-gallon cans. When all the cows were milked, we loaded the cans into a large cooler, fed hay to the entire herd, cleaned the milking equipment and washed down the stalls. In three hours we were through and on our way to his house for supper.

Later that night, Dawson told me my job would be helping him milk every morning from four to seven, and after school. On weekends I could earn some extra money, five dollars per day, helping him haul hay and chopping feed for the cows.

He said someone had to haul the milk to the dock every morning, and, maybe, after I turned fifteen, I could drive the milk truck into town and unload before going to class. That settled it, as far as I was concerned. All of my reservations about working for the Watson Dairy vanished. I could feel the envy of all my classmates when I skidded to a stop in front of the school, sitting behind the wheel of the big yellow two-ton truck. Just before shutting off the key, I'd push the gas pedal all the way down just once, and everyone within a block would hear the roar of the crippled muffler.

That night I slept in the big house (Tom Watson's house) alone. Tom was in Utah with his wife, who was taking treatments at a special clinic for rheumatoid arthritis.

Lying in Tom's lumpy bed, thinking back over the past few months, I realized just how badly I had messed up my life. I was screwing up so terribly that I had forgotten about my real reason for wanting to stay with the Valliants. And with the stark realization that I had brought all my trouble upon myself. I was angry, a kind of angry that I had never felt before; a fierce anger turned inward. Right then I realized that if I didn't get my act together I may as well give up now, return to Texas and be a cotton-picker the rest of my life. I was crushed, thinking about my behavior—skipping class, stealing, smoking, and not turning in homework. I was almost sick enough to throw up.

Before going to sleep, I thought about why all but a few of the kids shunned me at school. I didn't go to class with cow dung on my shoes any more and I took careful pains to wash my face and hands, and I didn't stutter hardly any. *Maybe I'm really not normal*, I thought, not like other kids, anyway. Normal kids had a mother and a father, and they didn't go around feeing lost and lonely most of the time. And normal kids didn't have to put up with all the crap from the Seymours just to go to school.

Wallowing in self-pity wasn't my usual way of thinking and it didn't take me long to bring myself out of it. I had the good life. Normal kids got the tar beat out of them every day for something. They didn't have their own money to buy cigarettes, candy, pop, and ice cream, and they couldn't curse any time they wanted to. Normal kids couldn't go anywhere they wanted to go. Plus, normal kids couldn't give the Seymours the Finger, just like that, and go live with their grandma.

I didn't blame Rusty for what had happened to me, but I didn't want him to be my best friend anymore. I would always be glad to see him in school, but I couldn't sneak off the school grounds and smoke, and I couldn't even think about playing hooky with him again. I had enough trouble without trying to invent stuff with Rusty. Maybe I didn't need a close friend now; I had Mr. Young (who I was sure would accept me back as a friend), and, later, maybe Dawson and I could become friends. Anyway, I was certain that if I ever had another close friend I needed someone who wouldn't want do the things Rusty and I had been doing.

I drew blank stares as I got on the school bus Monday morning. I chose an empty seat and stared out the window, trying to prepare my mind for my first day back at school—a place I had vowed never to return.

The smell of chalk, mixed with the oily, oatmeal stuff used by the janitor to sweep, brought back my old fears and disgust associated with the Seymours and the whole school scene. I wanted to turn and run out of there, hitchhike back to the dairy, get my stuff and head south. But, I had promised Mrs. Valliant that I would try, and what was one more day?

Geography was my last class of the day. "Dennis, I want to see you for a moment before you get on the bus tonight," Mrs. Seymour said, as I rushed out of her classroom.

I didn't have time to get scared, or angry, or anything. Mr. Seymour, old Pudge-face, walked in the door as the last kid left the room. I was alone with the two Seymours. When the door closed, he grabbed my shoulders with both hands, and shoved me into a chair. "Okay, you're gonna cut the crap, straighten up and fly right, or do you know what's gonna happen to you?"

I told him I didn't. Which I knew right off was a mistake.

"I'm gonna kick your ass so hard you'll have to take off your hat to go to the bathroom…that's what," he said, shaking me as he spat the words out.

I knew he was telling the truth. I told them I would do better. But, even without thinking about it very much, I knew they didn't really care. When I got tired of them staring at me without saying anything, I said, "I'm gonna miss the bus."

"Okay," Mr. Seymour said, "get your ass on the bus; and don't you forget, we'll be watching you—and Mrs. Valliant can't save your ass next time."

My meeting with the Seymours didn't help my attitude, or shave any part of the chip off my shoulder. I felt my face get flush with a big stab of temper when I thought about them on the bus ride home. Then I closed my eyes and was struck by a vision of them getting splattered by a run-away log truck as they crossed the street.

———

I worked for the Watson Dairy until school was out in May. Dawson wanted me to stay and work through the summer, but I felt an obligation to work for the Valliants. Mr. Valliant hadn't said so, but in the back of my mind I had it figured that he valued my help with lambing more than he did his own grandkids, Mark and Craig. Mr. Valliant said if I worked for him during the summer I could join the 4-H club and he would give me two ewe lambs to show at the fair.

It was late afternoon of the last day of school. Mr. Valliant was waiting in the old black Chevrolet to give me a ride to the ranch. I shook hands with Dawson, promised him I would return in the fall and ran toward the car.

The first person I saw when entering the ranch kitchen was Helen. I hardly recognized her. This wasn't the old Helen, not the Helen from last summer, not the one with spindly legs and scrawny arms—at least it didn't look like her. This new Helen was filled out in all the right places. I couldn't stop looking at her. We hugged each other and I clung to her until she ruffled my hair and pushed me away. This was too good to be true. I was fifteen-years old now. She was eighteen, and I was sure the age difference wouldn't be a problem. It wasn't. Hank was the problem—the guy she was going to marry.

Spring and summer came and went quickly, me following Helen around like a helpless puppy, her teasing and humoring me. We had long talks, and did our evening walks, but it was never quite enough for me, not anything like my nighttime fantasies. On most Sundays, we saddled Red and Brownie, made a quick sack lunch and rode to the beaver ponds, about three miles south of the house. We always carried our fishing poles, but fishing was the last thing on my mind.

My true feelings about Helen I kept secret—afraid she would laugh at me, or she would tell the Valliants and they would tar and feather me and run me off the ranch. I loved Helen and she would never know because she was going to marry Hank, from Rawlins, who worked as a mechanic, smoked Camel cigarettes, wore a ton of grease under his fingernails, and smelled like a petroleum factory. I knew this because he came to the ranch one weekend to get Helen, and he offered me a cigarette. Hank disgusted me and I told her so. Hank ruined my dreams that Helen would some day collapse in my arms on the banks of a beaver pond and we would go at each other right there.

The first new man Grimes hired to work on the haying crew was Harold Crump, a cowboy-type from McHargs Employment agency. Harold let us know from the start that he wasn't just a common old hired man. He was a displaced saddle bronc rider, working during the haying season just for money enough to hit the rodeo circuit again. Shortly after he arrived, I told him about my experience with Sonny Boy. "Hell, that horse can't be much; I've ridden the best of them," Harold said.

Old Grimes was standing nearby and heard Harold's comment. I looked at Grimes. He was wearing an agitated expression that I hadn't seen before. "I don't think you can ride that horse," Grimes said.

Grimes looked at me and it made me a little proud, because I knew he was thinking my same thoughts: Sonny Boy had to be a fierce bucking horse to buck me off and break my leg, and we both knew, without a doubt, that this Greenhorn wouldn't stand a chance. But, Harold wanted to show us that he was a great bronc rider, and there was only one way to settle it.

Saturday afternoon Grimes and I rode to the big pasture and drove Sonny Boy and the rest of the wild herd to the corral where I had broken my leg.

Harold seated himself on Sonny Boy about dark and Jones unsnapped the halter rope. About four jumps later Harold was lying on the ground, with busted pride and a broken shoulder. Grimes drove Harold to the hospital in Rawlins that evening. I never saw Harold again.

We left Sonny Boy in the corral, and I brought out some hay and water. Before the end of the next week Grimes had sold Sonny Boy to a rodeo contractor for more money than the price of a good horse.

My two 4-H lambs placed fourth and sixth at the county fair in Rawlins. Not good, but I was happy because I had met some 4-H kids from other towns in the county, and I'd learned how to trim and show sheep.

The day before school started I moved back to the Watson dairy. Tom Watson met me at the door of the big house. Tom had returned from Utah, where his wife and kids lived. Tom Watson was a burly man about thirty-five-years old and over six feet tall. With his massive shoulders darkening the doorway, he greeted me with a comical grin and shook my hand with the biggest handle I'd ever seen on a man.

Tom and I shared the Big House. It didn't bother Tom that the house had about an inch of the barnyard on the floor, or that the rest of the place was a wreck and it sure didn't bother me. We took our meals with Dawson; there wasn't a scrap of food in Tom's house. Tom confessed to being a Mormon, but not a "Regular Mormon." He said the Brothers in his church called him a Jack Mormon. I asked him what that meant, and he laughed again.

"Jack Mormons drink and smoke and our brother Mormons mostly look the other way," Tom said, with a clown's grin, "unless we uncork a bottle and light up coming out of church."

In one short week, Tom and I had become good friends. I was fifteen-years old now, and I wasn't taking any chances on not being allowed to drive the milk truck to the dock every morning. The day before he left for Utah I asked him outright if I could deliver the milk to the dock. "Well, Dennis, let's take a drive," he responded in his usual drawl.

I had driven the truck around the farm nearly every day when I worked there before and I was sure if he would watch me drive just once it would cinch my chances. I skillfully maneuvered the truck to the main road and back while he pulled on a cigarette and observed the cows out the window as if we had been doing this every day for years.

The days, weeks, and months blended together smoothly. I milked cows, delivered the milk to the dock, went to school, and helped Dawson haul hay on weekends. I became a normal kid—almost. Clay Moser and I were classmates and we became good friends. Stephen Moser and the Valliant boys still shunned me, but, if I read them right, they recognized they could not run me off.

In January, Tom Watson made one of his rare visits to the ranch from his other home in Utah and stayed for a week. On a Friday morning, the day after Tom returned home, he told me I would need to ride the bus to school because he and Dawson were taking the truck to Rawlins to buy supplies for the ranch.

About noon that day it started to snow. I stared out the school window all afternoon, watching the blizzard build and the snow pile up. All I could think about was Tom and Dawson, out there in the blizzard, and if they would get home in time to milk. By four o'clock ground visibility was near zero, with at least six inches of snow.

I got off the bus at my regular stop and staggered through the blizzard the half mile to the ranch house. Tom was not in the house. Without removing my coat, I built a fire in the wood stove, then went to the large barn to see if the truck was there. My heart sank as I stared at the empty parking space. I went to the little house, where Bonnie and Dawson lived. Bonnie had a worried look about her, and she didn't need to tell me; they hadn't returned. I asked if they had called. "No. The phone lines aren't working," she said.

Back at the Big House, I waited by the fire until six o'clock. I was worried, not about Dawson and Tom; I knew they could take care of themselves in any situation, but cows needed milked, and it was an hour past milking time. If they weren't milked on time their milk production would fall for two or three days, and Tom wasn't a rich man. I had never milked without Dawson and wasn't sure I knew where to start. But I *would* start—they would be home soon, I told myself.

I finished milking at eleven o'clock, cleaned the equipment and washed down the barn. I was putting milk cans into the cooler when Tom and Dawson walked into the milk barn. The surprise and relief on their faces made it all worthwhile. They stood there smiling, without saying a word. "You might make a hand yet," Tom said. Then he slapped me on the back hard enough to knock the wind right out of me.

THIRTY-ONE

All along I had told everyone that I was going to finish high school. That was my dream even before my first day of school. Those were just hopeful thoughts and words. But, the first day I stepped into that class as an eighth-grader, I could feel it. This is where I belonged. I wasn't just fooling myself any more. Sure, I still had the Seymours to contend with, but suddenly it all seemed worth it. Anyway, I figured I could easily kick the crap out of old Pudge-face if he kept after me. So what if he kicked me out of school? I would turn sixteen in March, and I could go anywhere, get a job and finish school.

Mr. Wolfe was my homeroom teacher. He was new in the school, about my same height and wore a tiny little black mustache. If the Seymours had told him about me being the bad seed, he didn't seem to care. Mr. Wolfe treated me decent, like he wanted to get along with me, and that's why I didn't say anything to his face about the droplets of foam that formed at the corners of his mouth when he really got into something important. His foaming at the mouth and his little mustache gave his face a mad dog, wolf-like bearing. I wasn't the only one who noticed the likeness, and it became the major topic of conversation by most of the eighth-grade boys when his back was turned.

In May I graduated from the eighth-grade, with ceremony. Not with a cap and gown like they did in high school, but at an evening performance, in Levi jeans and a clean shirt—just like the other seven boys in the class. Mr. and Mrs. Valliant, Bob and Pauline Ware, Dawson, and even Tom Watson, attended the graduation. But the most enjoyable part of the whole thing for me was when old Pudge-face walked to the stage and announced, almost tearfully I thought, that his contract had not been renewed and he and Mrs. Seymour would be leaving to teach at another school. I had a near uncontrollable urge to clap loudly, stand on my chair and yell good-bye and good riddance, you SOB. I didn't do any of that, but I *did* keep a broad smile on my face the rest of the evening.

I was a man now, I thought, sixteen years old. No more fears about anyone shipping me back to Texas, no more worry about bullies, a place to stay or a good paying job. Word spread fast in a small community. Even before school was out, I was approached by two other dairymen, and a neighbor of Tom's, and offered a job for the summer. My self-esteem had grown tenfold in one year, my speech had improved to almost normal, Craig and Mark were grudgingly speaking to me, and I felt like the world was at my fingertips. There was no one to tell me what I should or shouldn't do, and no one to reprimand me for whatever choices I made. I could go any place, do anything I wanted to do; I had earned my way, and I earned my eighth-grade certificate. I didn't feel accountable to anyone. And I wasn't.

A few days after graduation, the high was gone. I returned to the Watson Dairy, packed my things, and, against the wishes of Tom and Dawson, returned to the Valliants to work. Throughout the summer, Craig, Mark and I worked together during lambing, rode shoulder-to-shoulder on cattle drives, fixed fence, and worked in the same field during haying season. We didn't argue, joke or play together, or pretend to be anything to each other, aside from getting the job done as fellow workers. This was frustrating to me—something I couldn't understand about myself—*why did I care so much about winning their approval? And why did they openly show their resentment toward me?*

All along I convinced myself that my real goal was to go to school and become like other kids. The school part was going great, but I didn't feel normal—not the way I thought other kids felt. No matter how good things seemed to be going for me, part of me just didn't feel right. There was always a void in the back of my mind, and an empty feeling in the pit of my stomach. For some reason, I felt the approval and acceptance by Craig and Mark had something to do with it. I wanted desperately for them to treat me as their equal—be my friends. I had a few other friends, but it wasn't the same.

———

Since the day I waved good-bye to my sister, Mary Lee, on the highway in Reliance, I had wondered and worried what had happened to her. Hoping to learn something about her, I had written several letters to Grandma the past three years, addressed to "General Delivery, Memphis, Texas." The letters came back, stamped "UNCLAIMED." I wrote three more letters during the summer after my graduation, with the same results.

That summer, Mr. Valliant raised my wages to a hundred and fifty dollars a month. By the end of August, I had saved three-hundred dollars—a small fortune. I hadn't told anyone, but I had it in my mind to buy a car at the end of haying season, drive to Memphis and look for Mary Lee. I would bring her back with me and find a job where we could both live and go to school.

On a Saturday afternoon, toward the end of August, Grimes drove me to Saratoga. I told him I was going to buy a car and asked him to take me to the River Street Garage, where I had seen several cars that looked within my price range. Grimes emitted a low, guttural noise that sounded like "Aaaah," and that was the end of our conversation. The car that struck my eye and sent my pulse racing was a 1938 Ford coupe, with a V-8 flathead engine. I wrote a check for $100, the owner gave me a receipt marked 'Paid in full,' the title to the car, and I drove away all wrapped up in a sense of wellbeing.

Grimes followed me back to the ranch, or until my car quit on top of the hill overlooking the corral where Sonny Boy had dumped me three years earlier. The gas tank showed full, and everything looked normal under the hood. I cranked the engine until the battery went dead, pushed it off the hill—still it wouldn't run. Grimes and I brought a chain back from the shop and pulled my new car back to the ranch.

The next day was Sunday, my day off. After breakfast, I jumped the battery to the old rake car, and exhausted both batteries. Suddenly I remembered Pete telling me long stories about his mechanic experiences before his sheep-herding days. I saddled Red, and galloped him most of the way to the sheep camp, where I found Pete lounging in the shade of some aspen trees. I hurriedly described the symptoms of my crippled Ford.

"It needs new points and plugs," he said, with a confident smile.

I thanked him and raced off toward the ranch, not realizing until I was nearly home that nothing was open on Sunday to buy auto parts.

A week went by, with me fussing with my new car every day after work. Saturday was forever away, and the Ford ignored my efforts after I cleaned all the plugs and points. I *had* to get it running. School was only two weeks away and I would have to leave soon if I were to get to Memphis and back before school started.

Saturday afternoon Grimes drove me to town. I bought points and plugs for my car, and we picked up the mail from the post office. There was a reply from Grandma, or someone who had written a letter for her. I tore the letter open with a rush of adrenalin.

Dear Dennis, how are you, we are fine. You asked about Mary Lee but she is not here now. She came back after going with you to Wyoming, but she left again and we haven't seen her since. Marvin, Eugene, Fred, and Melvin are all here with me. We hope you can come to see us. Love, Grandma.

The letter had a Memphis, Texas, postmark, and a "General Delivery, Memphis, Texas," return address. My heart sank to the bottom of my stomach. Grandma was my only contact with Mary Lee, and she was no help. I rode back to the ranch with Grimes without saying a word. Getting my car running again was no longer important to me; nothing at all seemed important. I cursed myself for not trying to contact her before now—now that it was too late. Now that she would probably be out of my life forever. And that was more than I wanted to think about.

I put the new parts on the Ford, pushed it off the hill, and it fired like a new engine. But, for the moment, most of the fun had gone out of owning my new toy. There would be no trip to

Memphis to look forward to, and the thought of not ever seeing Mary Lee again stifled my enthusiasm for everything else.

County Fair was the last week in August. School would start the second week in September. I had two wether lambs to show at the fair. I would show my lambs, but I still hadn't gathered my thoughts enough to know if I would start back to school.

I saw Dawson at the fair and he asked, again, if I would work for him when school started. I hadn't yet decided if I would return to school, but I wanted to cover all of my bases and told him I would—under certain conditions. If I went back to school I wanted to play basketball. I told Dawson I would work for him if I could stay after school and practice with the team when basketball season started in October. He thought for a moment. "Yeah, I guess that would be okay," he said. "I could handle the milking at night for a couple of months. You'll still be there every morning and on weekends."

Talking to Dawson seemed to help me make up my mind about school: *What else was I going to do?* I reasoned.

When regular basketball season started, I alternated starting with the first five with another freshman. This went on until the end of the season. The last game of the season was with Encampment, our heated rival, and I was scheduled to start with the first five. During the first half of the game, I got into a fistfight on the floor with one of the Encampment players. The referee kicked both of us out of the game. I showered and left the gym with Rusty Harrison, who had been kicked off the team earlier that year when the coach caught him smoking in the pool hall.

Rusty rode with me in my old Ford to Donelan's Drug Store. The kid I had been fighting with was already there, sitting in a booth with two of his friends. I started walking past the trio, looking straight ahead, when I felt a foot kick me on the chins, sprawling me into the aisle on my face. I jumped up in a rage to the smiling face of the kid I had fought with in the game. He stood up. I pushed him hard, and he fell over the booth. "Let's go outside," he said.

I had a wild temper and was raging mad when I stomped out the door and onto the street. At that moment I didn't care that he outweighed me by at least twenty pounds, or was four or five inches taller. I wanted to see him on the ground, hurting.

We danced around some, without throwing a punch, feeling each other out, which allowed me time to regain my composure. Suddenly I had this strange feeling he wanted to impress his friends and put me away with one lucky punch. I guessed right. He threw the wildest punch I'd ever seen. I ducked. He was off-balance now and I let him have it with three or four good solid punches to the face. He went to the ground, and that was the end of it. They helped him to the car, Rusty and me following, calling them chickenshits, sissies, schoolgirls, and a lot of other names.

We followed them back to the school and sat in the car for a while. Rusty offered me a Camel and we both lit up. In about fifteen minutes the town cop skidded to a stop, lights flashing. I asked Rusty to go in and see what was going on. Rusty peeked into the door of the gym, hurried back, and jumped in the car.

"Let's go….now!" Rusty blurted.

"What the hell is going on?" I asked, peeling dirt and gravel out of the parking lot.

Rusty was laughing so hard he could hardly speak. "Ol' Fat Boy is lying on his mother's lap, crying like a schoolgirl and that damn flat-foot is standing there talking to his dad," he chortled. "You better stay with me tonight; you can bet your ass they're gonna be looking for you."

They *did* look for me—all night, so I heard. The cops went to the Valliants about midnight, scaring Mrs. Valliant half to death. Mr. Valliant got mad as hell and ran them off. And who knows who how many other innocent people they brought out in their nightshirts? But they didn't find me.

Saturday morning I returned to the farm early enough to help Dawson milk. I told him what had happened. He laughed.

"I've been in lots of fights," Dawson said, "They can't do anything to you. He swung at you first. Hell, you couldn't just lie down and play dead."

Monday morning I arrived at the school and parked the milk truck two cars away from the town cop and slowly walked into the building. Greg Nielsen, our new school superintendent, met me at the door. He was smiling, but I could tell it wasn't a real smile, just a stretching of his lips enough to hide a frown, or maybe it was concern, because Mr. Nielsen was my friend. "Come to my office, Dennis," he said. "There's some people who want to talk to you."

There were several people waiting to talk to me: the town cop, the Encampment school superintendent, old Fat Boy's parents, my shop teacher, and, of course, Greg Nielsen. The cop went first, staring right at me: "I don't know all the details," he said. "But you're lucky I didn't find you that night or you would have ended up spending some time in my little jail down by the river. This boy was beat up pretty bad. His two friends said you swung first then kicked him while he was on the ground, he's a lot bigger than you, and it's my guess they're telling the truth."

Mr. Nielsen interrupted the cop by saying it was only fair I tell my side of the story before any more accusations were hailed at me.

I asked if they could get Rusty so he could confirm my story. The cop said he had already talked to Rusty, and that Rusty had apparently lied to him. "According to Rusty," the cop said, "Aaron (that was his name) swung first, then you punched him three or four times, he hit the ground, and you two walked off."

"That's the way it happened," I said, feeling a ray of hope now.

The cop walked around the room, staring at me in silence, before saying, "Well, hell, what am I supposed to do. You say one thing, they say another. There are witnesses on both sides, telling different stories. Aaron has a broken nose and chipped teeth, his parents want you in jail...but, I can't do that; there isn't enough evidence."

Another long silence, while Aaron stared at his crotch, his mom and Dad giving me the evil eye. "I can't put Dennis in jail, or file any charges on my own," the cop said. "You folks can file charges if you want...but I wouldn't. Would you be satisfied if

Dennis apologized to Aaron and wasn't allowed to play in any more games with Encampment?"

Aaron's dad stood up and looked at me with a white-eyed, crazed stare. "I don't know what we're going to do about filing charges, but I can tell you *one* thing, I'm gonna whip his ass," he shouted.

Greg Nielsen stepped between the crazed parent and me. "You *may* be able to whip his ass, but you'll have to go through me first." That was all Mr. Nielsen said.

That was all Mr. Nielsen needed to say. Aaron's father fell back into his chair. I restrained a smile. Greg Nielsen was an ex-Special Forces Marine, six-foot two, with broad shoulders, long ropey muscular arms, and a neck as thick as a gorilla's. The cop left, followed by Aaron's father, then the shop teacher, then the rest of Aaron's sympathizers.

I said, "Thanks, Mr. Nielsen," and I was sure I detected a faint smile crease his lips.

"Get out of here, and keep your nose clean from now on," Mr. Nielsen said, without a hint of emotion. I turned and walked to my first class, which was almost over.

Playing sports interfered with my job, and school was becoming routine and boring. And I didn't want to go to school three more years and be twenty-years old when I graduated. I was pulling A's & B's in English, and C's and B's in everything else, and, somewhere out of the blue sky, I got the notion I could graduate with only three years of high school. After thinking about it for a few days, I went to Mr. Nielsen with my idea.

Mr. Nielsen looked at me for a long moment. When he could see I was serious, he pulled my school records, studied them for a few minutes. "It's not impossible, Dennis, but it wouldn't hurt you to stay in school until you're twenty-years old. Tell you what, though, I'll have my secretary outline a course study for the next two years, and we'll talk some more."

The next morning Mr. Nielsen saw me in the hallway, before class bell, and asked me to come into his office. "You can do it,

Dennis, but you'll have to study your little ass off—and no more fighting," he warned.

He handed me the paper with my classes outlined for the next two years, and I left his office walking on air.

I finished my freshman year in high school, lettering in basketball, track, baseball, football, glee club and band.

That summer I worked with Craig and Mark, and, again, we had little or nothing to say to each other. I wanted to pretend it didn't matter—but it *did* matter, and I couldn't explain why to myself. I had earned the respect and recognition of almost everyone who really knew me. I was pulling good grades in school, I had broke a new colt every year (neither of them had), and I had never asked either of them for a favor. I was disappointed, but I didn't kowtow or suck up to them.

In June I bought two Southdown wether lambs from the Halston Ranch to fatten and show as my 4-H project. The Halston girls had won champion and reserve grand-champion at the county fair and state fair, for as long as anyone could remember. The older Halston sister was out of school, and not showing lambs anymore. They owned a small herd of Southdowns together, and after the younger girl, Shana (who was still showing), picked out the best of the best in the herd, she allowed me to take my pick.

My lambs won grand champion, and reserve grand-champion at the county fair. I showed against the Halston girl at the state fair, and, again, won champion and reserve-grand champion fat lambs. Added to that, I won grand champion sheep showman at both fairs.

THIRTY-TWO

I was seventeen-years old when I started my sophomore year in high school. I wasn't prepared at all for the heavy academic load heaped upon me by my decision to complete high school in three years. I was working on the Watson Dairy seven to eight hours a day, and twelve to fourteen hours a day on Saturdays and Sundays. That didn't leave much time for studying. But I managed to get through the year, with C's in everything.

About two months into my sophomore year trouble found me, or I found trouble, again. I was sitting in study hall, doing my English homework. Something caught my hair and pulled it, hard, from behind. I knew it had to be another student, and I didn't care what student. I turned and looked into the face of Mike Sweeney, the school bully. He was smiling, like it was a big joke—until I back-handed him across the cheek. Nothing was funny any more. He jumped out of his chair, grabbed me by the nap of my neck, lifted me out of my chair, and brought me around to face him. He was gritting his teeth and talking at the same time: "Let's go, you bastard. This time I'm gonna kill you." It wasn't recess or noon; we were on school time.

Without asking permission, or looking in the direction of the study hall monitor, we marched from the class, out the door, and on out to the baseball field, only a few steps from the school building. Mike was a town kid, didn't play sports or work after school. He had grown taller since our last encounter, and fatter. He was almost twice my weight, and I figured right that he was, also twice as slow. Over time, I almost forgot that he had made goulash out of my face in front of the whole school, and my grudge slowly faded into tolerance for him. But on the way out the school door all my anger and resentment returned. It was like he had just finished mauling me for the first time. Now I wanted revenge.

I was right about him being slow. It seemed like fifteen minutes after he wound up before I saw his punches coming—none of which connected. I battered him with two or three punches to the face, then stepped back—careful that he didn't get a hold on me. He was breathless before one of his wind-ups caused him to trip and fall backwards.

Mr. Nielsen stepped out the door of the school building to witness Mike's clumsy fall onto his back. Mike was bleeding from the nose, and it looked as if a black eye was coming on. Mr. Nielsen watched for a minute, until he could see Mike wasn't getting up with any steam. "Okay, you guys, the fight is over, get back to your classes," Mr. Nielsen said, guiding Mike toward the building with a hand to the nap of his neck.

That's it? I couldn't believe it!

After our fight Mike tried to be my friend, but I wanted no part of him. But thereafter, whenever he saw me, or wherever he saw me, he smiled and waved. If we were a block apart he would break his arm trying to get my attention.

THIRTY-THREE

I turned eighteen during my sophomore year. I was five-foot, eleven-inches tall and weighed 148 pounds. By the time my birthday rolled around I had been in high school almost two years and calling myself a junior, with only one more year to graduate (if I continued to pull the load and kept my grades up).

The day before school dismissed for summer vacation, Mr. Nielsen called me into his office. "Tomorrow you will officially be a senior in high school," he said, with a big grin.

Until that day I felt it could go either way. My grades were above D's, but just barely in algebra, and I was afraid Mr. Nielsen wouldn't allow me to graduate in three years with anything below B's in all my courses. It was hard for me to comprehend all at once. I needed some to time to think about it.

The following day school was dismissed for summer vacation. I raced back to the Watson dairy and was almost home when I heard a terrible noise coming from the engine of my 1938 Ford, then nothing. I pushed it to the side of the road, raised the hood, and stared at a big hole in the top of the flathead engine. It had thrown a rod. I loved that car and knew I couldn't afford to replace the engine.

A passing rancher stopped and gave me a lift home. The next day Dawson and I towed my Ford to the River Street Garage, where I traded it for a 1937 Plymouth coupe. I received twenty-five dollars as a trade-in, wrote them a check for seventy-five dollars, and drove my clunker home. The Plymouth wasn't what I wanted, but it was transportation and would serve my needs until I could make some money to trade-up.

I returned to the Valliants to work during the summer. Lambs were being born, and sheep shearing had just started. The ewes were sheared before dropping their lambs. We could always expect a late snow during lambing. With a full coat of wool they would stand out in the snow and the newborn lambs would freeze.

The lambing crew still consisted of Craig, Mark, Mr. Valliant and me. By now I had grown accustomed to feeling inadequate around Craig and Mark. Not to say it didn't bother me—it ate a hole in my guts, but I was careful to hide my feelings from everyone. Maybe if I tried harder, I thought. But deep down, I knew better. I was convinced there was a definite barrier between us that would always be there. To make up for my feelings of unworthiness around them I always tried to work harder, ride better—and keep to myself as much as possible.

Mark had graduated high school the year before, and started school at the University of Wyoming. Craig would graduate high school with me, next year.

———

It was Sunday afternoon. The hired men were just lying around the bunkhouse, and I was bored. I filled my old Plymouth up with oil (it was now using three quarts of oil per round-trip to town) and drove to the Watson place to visit Dawson. He was taking the afternoon off, relaxing in his living room before milking time.

"Hey, did the Valliants fire you?" he greeted me.

"It's touch and go," I said.

He got out of his chair, slipped on his boots, stood up. "I want you to meet the two most shiftless assholes in the world," he said, putting on his hat.

We walked to the bunkhouse, pushed the screen door open, and entered. The Assholes were sacked out on bunks on either side of the wall. Without saying a word, Dawson kicked hard at one of the bunks, nearly causing it to collapse.

"I want you to meet my friend, Dennis," Dawson said, trying to be serious.

They rose up in bed, rubbed their faces with both hands. "Oh yeah….we're just getting up—what….what time is it?" one of them said, barely audible.

Dawson turned and walked outside, with me at his heels. "Why did you do that?" I asked.

"Just a little harassment, for both of you—for them because they deserve it, and for you so you will know what you left me with."

We were standing by my car. I was telling Dawson I was buying oil by the barrels to go to town and back when the two new hands emerged from the bunkhouse and joined us.

"Nice car. Is it yours?" one of them asked.

"Yeah, but I haven't had it very long."

"Wanna sell it?" the tallest one piped up.

"Well…I guess I could, I been wanting to trade-up. It uses a little oil."

"How much?" the tall guy asked.

"How much oil or how much for the car?"

"For the car."

"Guess I could take a hundred dollars for it."

"We been working for a week, do we have a hundred dollars yet?" The shortest one asked, looking at Dawson.

"Yeah, I guess you probably do," Dawson said.

Dawson and I jumped into the Plymouth, drove back to the Valliant ranch, found my title, and filled the old junk with oil again. The Assholes (Dawson also called them The Chicago Twins), were waiting outside the bunkhouse when we returned. We exchanged money and title, they loaded their belongings in their new car and told Dawson they were through. "Ranch work just ain't our style," one of them said.

Three days later I was riding back from checking on the late-lambers in the upper pasture. Nearing the house I noticed a police car parked out front and two cops standing nearby talking to Mr. Valliant. I tied my horse to the hitching rack under the cottonwoods and cautiously walked over to them. Right off I could tell it was serious business. There were no smiles or official introductions. This was no social visit, and I knew sure as the world Mr. Valliant hadn't done anything wrong. I racked my mind for the last time I did anything that could warrant a visit from the county sheriff. I couldn't remember anything, but I still got weak in the knees.

"Dennis, these guys are sheriff's deputies from Rawlins," Mr. Valliant said. "They want to ask you some questions."

"You own a 1937 Plymouth?" one of them asked.

"No, I sold it a couple of days ago."

"Who'd you sell it to?"

"I don't know, they were just a couple of guys who worked for the Watson Dairy over on Spring Creek."

"Have you seen them since they bought the car?"

"No."

A light came on in my head. I had forgotten to take the license plates off the Plymouth. The damn thing was registered in my name and they got into trouble with the law driving *my car*. The cops had traced it to me.

"We caught two guys who were driving a Plymouth registered in your name," the tallest cop said, "and they're in a lot of trouble now. We haven't got everything put together yet, but we think we've narrowed it down to one of four things: the car was stolen, they bought the car and you didn't take the tags off, you loaned them the car, or you were with them and somehow escaped before they were apprehended. Now which is it?"

"I already told you. I sold them the car."

"Do you have any proof?"

"I'm not sure....maybe."

I didn't....or did I? Dawson wrote me the one hundred dollar check, which paid for the car, and I handed the shortest one a signed title. But I couldn't remember the names of either of them...but Dawson would know their names.

"Where've you been since you sold the car?"

"Right here on the ranch," Mr. Valliant shot back. That was the first time I had ever heard Mr. Valliant speak sharply to anyone.

"We're not going to take you in...not now anyway," one of them said. "We've got a lot of work to do on this thing yet. Don't you leave the ranch, and we'll be in touch."

The deputies drove away. Mr. Valliant and I stood and looked at each other. He knew I was innocent; stupid maybe, but innocent, and I could read a few of these thoughts in his crooked little smile. I was still sweating and too mentally exhausted to do anything but look at the ground.

I never heard from the sheriff again. Through the grapevine, the newspapers, and calls to the sheriffs department, we learned the Chicago pair had robbed four remote gas stations between Saratoga and Kaycee, Wyoming. They were caught running through a field shortly after the Kaycee robbery, when they sped away in their 1937 Plymouth, blew a piston through the engine, and set off on foot. We also learned they were ex-convicts and wanted in several other states as robbery suspects.

Several days later, I bought another clunker, a sun-scorched tan, 1934 Chevrolet, four-door, six-cylinder, with two dented fenders and mechanical brakes that didn't work. The salesman at River Street Garage was asking one hundred dollars, but he nodded quickly when I pulled out seventy-five dollars from my wallet. "That's all I have," I said, which was a lie. But that was all I was going to pay for something that looked like it had been carelessly pushed out of the city dump with a bulldozer.

I returned to the Watson Dairy in early September to work during my last year of school. I was uneasy about the new school year. I still had to work my usual shifts in the dairy barn, and my grades had suffered pretty badly last year from lack of study time. Knowing I *had* to graduate this year, I decided to try and cut a deal with Dawson to allow for some extra study time. I proposed to Dawson that I work my usual shifts morning and night, but be allowed a half day Saturday and Sunday to study. He agreed. I kept my grades above D's, played in the band, sang in the school glee club, saved some money, and the school year went smoothly—until one day the first week in May.

Saratoga was scheduled to play a baseball game with Encampment after school hours on a Friday afternoon. Tom Watson was home for a few days, and since he could help Dawson milk, I asked, and received permission to skip my evening milking duties. I didn't play baseball, and neither did three of my buddies, Boomer, Rusty, and Joe. We decided to go to the game as spectators and raise a little hell.

We'd planned this for two, maybe three days, having already stashed our beer in the Platte River—beer that Joe had paid one of his dad's hired men to buy for us. We found our beer, chugged a few before leaving the site, and wrapped the rest in wet feed sacks for cooling.

The game was already in the fourth inning when we arrived. We watched the rest of the show, making general asses of ourselves—as were most of the other kids from Saratoga. The game ended, Saratoga won, and our thirst returned. We drove a few miles out of town and finished off the rest of the beer, then drove back into town to look for someone to resupply us. The one bar in Encampment was deserted, except for two old men, neither of them familiar to any of us. We then drove the two miles to Riverside, where we hit the jackpot. Joe knew a hired-man-type sitting on a stool in the Riverside Bar, motioned him outside, and we were supplied with booze again.

It was dark when we drove back to Encampment and slowly trolled up and down the one-half block business part of town, threw a few firecrackers out the window, and harassed a couple of high school boys whom we knew to be self-proclaimed town toughs. We hadn't done anything illegal (except maybe for the firecrackers), but we didn't want to stick around anymore. The little town didn't have a cop, but who knew where the county sheriff could be lurking. We headed for the mountains west of town, bounced around and over some rocks on a little-used road until we found a suitable location to finish off our beer.

Another two hours of drinking beer, telling dirty stories, and confiding nasty experiences we had had with girls, and we were brave enough to go back into town and look for some action with the Encampment town toughs.

We had taken a little walk to finish the last few cans of beer and were returning to the car. "Hey, Stud, you got a flat tire," Rusty shouted, falling to the ground with laughter. Everyone roared with drunken merriment. They didn't know there wasn't a spare tire, jack, or lug wrench in the old junk heap.

We could sit for a month on this road without anyone passing by. Joe (who had drunk less than the rest of us) said he would walk the mile or so to the main road and flag down some help. Another two hours passed before we saw headlights crawling toward us. As soon as they stepped out of the pickup, Rusty exclaimed, "Wow, it's Smitty!"

Smitty (Rusty told me later) worked as a trucker hauling logs from the mountains to the mill in Saratoga. Smitty had a spinner-type lug wrench, but no jack. I grabbed a nearby log and dragged it to the back of the car, then we all picked up the rear end of the car and pushed the log under the differential. Now we could take off the tire, but what then? It was late at night and nothing would be open in town.

I told Smitty I didn't care about fixing the tire tonight; if he could just take us all home, I would return tomorrow for my car. We removed the wheel from the car and tossed it in the back of Smitty's pickup. Rusty jumped in front and Joe, Boomer and I rode in the back with the spare tire. I was the first one to be dropped off by Smitty—about the time I started to feel the first signs of a hang-over.

Early the next morning I confessed my misadventure to Dawson and Tom. They had a good laugh before Tom offered to give me a tire he had taken off an old wagon. We removed the ruptured Chevy tire, replaced it with the smooth wagon tire, and Tom drove me to my car. By the time we arrived back home, I was more tired than I could ever remember. I helped with the milking and crashed into bed.

Monday morning. I walked into the school building a few minutes after the bell. Mr. Nielsen caught me in the hallway before I got to my first class. "Dennis, come to my office," he said, touching my shoulder, without looking directly at me.

Joe, Rusty and Boomer were already seated in the superintendent's office.

On the other side of the room sat Wheaties (that's the only name I ever heard him called), the Encampment baseball coach, Mr. Sternin, the Encampment Superintendent, and sitting next to him was one of the toughs we had harassed after the baseball game.

But that didn't complete the complement of visitors. Just as I was taking my seat against the wall with the other three fugitives, a county sheriff's deputy walked in, followed by Mr. Nielsen. *All of these people have come to punish us for throwing firecrackers onto a deserted street in a little burg only a half block long?* I wanted to laugh. We didn't hurt the little punk seated next to Mr. Sternin—maybe scared him a little; that wasn't a crime.

When everyone was in the room, the little red-faced superintendent from Encampment rose to his feet. Without being introduced, he started to rant: "You hoodlums can save us a helluva lot of time by just admitting your guilt. You can all go to jail and we can go back to doing what we're paid to do. And…"

"Mr. Sternin, Mr. Sternin," the deputy interrupted. "Let me handle this." The little superintendent sat down, exhausted.

"Okay, guys," the deputy started, "We all know why we're here, but I think it's only fair we inform the accused—these four boys—of the charges against them."

"What charges?" I asked, louder than I should have.

All the faces from the other side of the room looked at me with disgust.

"Let's start over," said the deputy. "On the outside chance you *are* innocent, I'm gonna tell you what these folks are charging you with. Last Friday night someone broke into the Encampment Grade School and vandalized the whole place, causing thousands of dollars worth of damage. Calvin here says he saw you boys driving around town after dark, about the time the vandalism occurred, raising hell and throwing firecrackers."

"Bullshit," Boomer said, "We didn't come close to your damn school!"

"Just shut up and listen," warned the deputy.

"Now, if you can't convince me where you were during the time the vandalism took place I'm gonna have to take you to jail until the judge can decide what to do with you. Is that clear?"

"Yes sir," I said, and gave Boomer a "keep-your-damn-mouth-shut" look.

"Now, here's how it's going to work," the deputy explained, choosing his words carefully. "One at a time I'm going to take each of you into a separate room and you're going to tell me where you were during the time this crime was committed. If I'm not satisfied with your answers you're all going to jail...now. Just remember, telling the truth can't do anything but help you, no matter what you did."

Rusty was first, then Joe, then Boomer, then me. I kept my head in my lap while waiting my turn. I knew the other side of the room was looking at me with a "we-got-you-now" look and I didn't want to see it. The fact that I knew we were innocent didn't diminish my anxiety much. And everything just got worse when Boomer returned to our crowded little room red-faced and subdued.

The deputy led me to an empty room with a desk and a chair behind it. There were no other chairs in the room. He pointed to the chair and commanded, "Sit."

"I'd rather stand," I said.

"Sit!"

I sat. Now I was more angry than nervous. This was ridiculous.

"Why did you do it, Dennis? And what do you think your punishment should be for doing something like that?" The deputy was standing, pressing his face close to mine.

"I told you we didn't do it!" I said, in as normal a tone of voice as I could manage.

"Then, suppose you tell me exactly what happened, or where you were during the time the school was vandalized."

I didn't tell him about the beer, and maybe some other small details, but I told him as much as I thought he needed to know, and I was hoping none of the others mentioned the beer part. After I told him my story, he got nice again, saying things like:

"I can't tell you what the others said, but if you just tell me the truth I can maybe vouch for you in front of the judge and he may give you a lighter sentence." This was the first time I had been alone and seriously questioned by a cop, but anyone could read this guy like a *Dick Tracy* comic book. He was trying to handle me and I was tired of it.

"Look, I've told you everything I know. If you want to know something else you're gonna have to ask me some different questions," I almost shouted.

He stared directly at me for a long minute or two. "Okay, let's join the others," he said, clomping out of the room ahead of me.

Everyone sat down again, except the deputy. He fixed his stare on our opponents. "Their stories are almost all the same...and almost believable," the deputy said, measuring his words, again. "They had a flat tire in the mountains. A fellow by the name of Smitty—they don't know his real name—came along and gave them a ride home. They say Smitty, whoever he is, can verify their story. I'm not going to arrest them until this Smitty fellow can be found and questioned. They all said Smitty hauls logs to the mill, and that's where I'm going now. You can all go home, or you can stay here. I don't know how long it will take me to find him." He turned and stalked out without looking back.

Nobody moved for a long time—maybe a minute or two, but it seemed a lot longer. Mr. Nielsen stood up. He hadn't said hardly anything until now. "I realize the severity of the crime these boys are accused of, but don't let anyone forget they're innocent until proven guilty. I don't know how long it's going to take for the sheriff to find Smitty, but these boys are free to go."

Mr. Nielsen turned and looked directly at the four accused. "You boys aren't suspended from school," he said, "but I think it's best for you and everybody concerned if all of you just go home until we get some word from the sheriff."

He didn't need to say it twice. The four of us hurried out the door and gathered in the parking lot to compare stories and smoke cigarettes.

I went home that morning and told Dawson and Tom what had happened, which was a mistake. For the next two days they made my life miserable, ragging me something wicked. One, then the other: "We'll bring you cigarettes, and cake to the jail, maybe every week. Hell, in a couple of years you'll be out; your job will still be here," and on and on. I didn't think any of this was funny and told them so. Three short weeks until I would be graduating high school…My mind was working overtime. Six years working my ass off trying to get through school, and now this…No graduation and maybe a jail sentence for something I didn't even do.

For two days I lived in a state of silent panic.

Dawson and I were finishing hosing down the milk barn. I looked out the window and saw Tom coming toward the barn. He'd barely hit the door before he started talking. "Well, Dennis, I have some bad news and some good news. What do you wanna hear first?"

"Give me the bad news."

"I just talked to Greg Nielsen. He said you ain't kicked out of school. Wanna hear the good news?"

"Hell, you just gave me the good news."

"Damn too bad about the other news, though," Tom said, slowly shaking his head. "I just talked to a guy who looked like he'd be a pretty good hand to replace you. Now I gotta tell him you ain't going to jail after all."

When he quit laughing he told me the rest of the story. Seems a few Encampment eighth-graders thought if they wrecked their classrooms it would save them from going to school the rest of their lives. One of them confessed even before the deputy found our friend, Smitty. I was so relieved I didn't know whether to laugh or cry.

THIRTY-FOUR

All that was left to earn the right to that cap and gown was take a final test in all my subjects. And for once I wasn't worried about flunking any courses. Even if I flunked the algebra final, my average for the year would pull me out of it. *Then why wasn't I excited and feeling like I was walking on air?* I asked myself. Maybe it just hadn't hit me in the right places yet. Or maybe I'd been excited all along without knowing it and was still excited. Or maybe I was just overwhelmed because I was graduating high school after only going to school for a total of six years. Or maybe it was because I had heard Pete had taken sick and wouldn't be around to herd sheep this summer, and maybe I suspected who his replacement would be.

Graduation night and I still didn't feel any differently. The relief was there alright, and handshakes and smiles from Tom Watson, Bob and Pauline Ware, and my other friends felt good, but my life still didn't seem like it was under control. The excitement and good feeling finally overtook me when I walked upon the stage to receive my diploma, but it wasn't like I felt like crying, as I saw some of the girls do when they walked off the stage. I was thinking all night that I would have plenty of time to feel whatever I was supposed to be feeling while sitting on a rock in the mountains, watching the sheep graze.

Saturday morning. I returned to the Valliant ranch where my worst nightmare was confirmed: Pete's health hadn't improved and I would be his replacement, herding sheep and living in the sheep camp—alone. I expected Craig and Mark to offer to spell me from time to time, giving me a day away from the sheep camp. But I wasn't going to hold my breath until that happened.

During lambing I herded sheep within a mile of the ranch headquarters and was allowed to return home at night and sleep in my own bed. About the middle of June we moved the sheep to the mountains, where the sheep wagon became my home. Pete was never allowed to take his car near the sheep wagon, but I argued that if I could drive my car as far as the forest boundary fence I could come back to the ranch for supplies a couple of times a week and supply my own camp.

My motives for having my car near the sheep camp weren't entirely honest. I was dating a girl in Saratoga, and I knew some back roads that led from the boundary fence to the Spring Creek road. Several times a week, after the sheep were bedded down, I left a cloud of dust that anyone could see for miles, dragging myself back to camp before daylight.

Herding sheep did have its advantages, though. I had lots of time to think and daydream, and in my wildest dreams I never pictured myself as a sheep herder. The French Foreign Legion, mining coal, picking cotton, anything but the sight of a sheep appealed to me after two weeks of herding. Something had to change, but Mr. Valliant seemed perfectly happy with the arrangement.

I'd been giving some thought about college, too. Mark already had a couple of semesters of school under his belt, and Craig had been accepted for the fall semester. I hadn't been encouraged by the Valliants, or any of my teachers, but I'd done a lot of things without encouragement. I didn't have any money saved for college, but from Dawson, who was an Army veteran, I learned about college benefits from the GI Bill of Rights. Lately I had visions of becoming something other than a sheepherder or an ordinary ranch hand. I was excited again.

During the second week in July, I drove to the ranch one night and told Mr. Valliant I needed a day off to visit the draft board. The Korean conflict had ended, but kids were still being drafted at age nineteen and I wanted to find out where I stood with their numbers—all the time hoping my "Greetings" letter was already in the mail.

The next day Mark came to the sheep camp. "You better be back here tonight," he said, scowling as he rode off. I smiled and galloped off toward my car. Someone had told me the draft board was in Rawlins, but I didn't know what it was, where it was, or who it was. I located it in a tiny building on Main Street, in downtown Rawlins.

I expected to find a group of old men sitting around debating who should be called next and drawing names out of a hat. What I found was one old woman sitting behind a tiny desk just big enough for her manual typewriter. After introducing myself, it took me awhile to get the information I needed. She told me draftees are called by numbers and there were over one hundred names waiting to be called.

"How soon will I be called," I asked her point blank.

She nervously fumbled through some papers, as if she had never been asked the question before. "I can't really say, maybe sometime in November," she finally replied.

"I can't wait that long, I'll be in college," I lied.

"Too bad," she said, shaking her head helplessly, "lots of boys are in college when they're drafted."

"Listen, I need to go *now*," I begged.

She looked at me as if I had gone crazy. "Well, Sonny, there's two ways you can go *now*," she said, tapping her pencil on the manual typewriter. "You can enlist for four years, or you can volunteer for the draft. If you volunteer for the draft you will only serve two years, just like being drafted."

"I'll volunteer—only I want to go *now*; tomorrow if possible."

She shoved me some forms that I hurriedly made out and gave back to her, said good-bye, thanks, and went back to the sheep camp, expecting a "Greetings" letter in the mail within three or four days—no more.

I sweated, and cursed the draft board until that wonderful day, August 15th, when Mr. Valliant rode up to my camp on Brownie, handed me a letter and grinned. "Guess you got what you wanted," he said.

THIRTY-FIVE

I'd been riding bulls and bareback horses in local rodeos since age sixteen (after I bought my first car), not making much money, but enough to keep my interest and excitement high. The weekend before the Monday I was to report to the Army, I entered Carbon County Fair Rodeo in Rawlins. My rides were scheduled for Saturday and Sunday. On Saturday I made a qualified ride on both bareback and bull, but not good enough to get in the money. Sunday I rode my bareback first—again a good ride, but no money. Finally my bull, the last bull I would ride for at least two years, I thought. My bull ride was a disaster. I was bucked off, kicked in the head and stepped on. I gained consciousness with several cowboys standing over me asking if I were all right. I wanted to say, "Yeah, I'm all right," but I couldn't say a word. All my conscious energies went to worrying if my injuries were serious enough to keep me out of the Army.

Monday morning I boarded the bus for Denver, with an elephant-sized headache, bruises, and eye-lids that weighed several pounds each.

Two days later I was in Fort Leonard Wood, Missouri, with a bunch of other inductees, for orientation, indoctrination, uniforms, equipment and haircuts that left us nearly bald. Everywhere we went they told us we are sorry pieces of maggot dung, a disgrace to the human race, lazy ass-dragging dropouts. And it got worse when we were sent to Camp Chaffee, Arkansas, for eight weeks of infantry basic training.

Hup ho hup ho hup hup, get in line soldier, straighten up, stick out that chest, suck in that belly. This ain't no damn grade school fire drill. You're gonna be a soldier or you're gonna die.

Come on sing it, sound off.

I know a girl from Santa Fe
she don't do it like her sister Kay

Sound off
One two three four
After eight weeks of basic infantry training, they sent me to Fort Sill, Oklahoma, where I attended sixteen weeks of Radio Maintenance school. The day I finished my training I picked up my papers for an assignment in Berlin, Germany—along with a two-week furlough.

I had applied for Europe as a first choice to serve the rest of my Army hitch, and was thrilled at the Berlin assignment. But I was more excited about getting away from an Army base for two weeks. I'd had enough of their in-your-face, hup ho one-two-three-four crap, and I was more than ready to go *anywhere* to escape Army routine—but *where?* I thought. I had no real home, unless I considered the Valliant ranch home, and I had to remember they weren't real pleased when I volunteered for the draft and left them without a sheepherder. I thought about looking for my sister, Mary Lee, but *what could I do in two weeks without a car and no addresses?*

Shortly after arriving at Fort Sill, I wrote to Mrs. Valliant to give her my new address. Several weeks later I received a reply from her: *Pete was back on the ranch after responding well to a new, experimental treatment for ulcers. Mark wasn't going to the Army after all, and Craig was going to college after receiving a draft deferment. Everyone else was doing fine. Craig and Mark had asked about me.* I had an urge to laugh aloud. I was happy for the mail, but disappointed she didn't ask when I would be getting leave, or ask me to visit.

Saturday morning. I rode the Army bus into town, found a phone booth and called the Valliant number. Mrs. Valliant answered. She was overwhelmed, almost to tears, and begged me to get on a bus. She promised to have someone meet me in Rawlins. I said I would come, gave her the bus schedule (which I had checked before calling) and hung up the phone.

Why not visit the ranch again? I asked myself. I wasn't the same tin-horn boy who graduated high school nine months ago. Some of my friends may not even recognize me; I had gained forty pounds and had grown at least an inch in height. I had a GI haircut, my broad shoulders were balanced on a one-hundred-eighty pound, six-foot solid frame, and I didn't act like a school boy anymore.

It was ten o'clock in the morning. My bus wasn't scheduled to leave until four in the afternoon. I wandered the streets until I came to a clothing store, where I bought a new shirt and socks. At the store I changed into my Levi jeans, western boots, and stuffed my Army uniform into my duffel bag. I walked the streets some more until I met up with another GI who was going to Laramie, Wyoming, and waiting for the same bus. He was a city boy and we didn't have much in common, but I was glad for the company.

The bus was on time, and the Laramie soldier and I found a seat together. We had tired each other of talking by now, and we sat in silence for a long time.

This was my first long bus ride since that day, almost seven years ago, when a scrawny twelve-year-old, seventy-pound boy got on a bus almost like this one—a boy with two dollars in his pocket, and scared as a rabbit—a boy anxiously holding onto a dream of escaping the tyranny of an alcoholic father, learning to read and write, and starting to school for the first time. The bus had the same sweaty people smell, dirty head rests, dark places on the seats, where chewing gum had been scraped off, and candy wrappers scattered in the aisles. The drone of the bus engine sounded familiar, and for one short, eerie moment I became that frightened little boy again—the boy who had no past and no future. The boy who had a bad speech impediment, the twelve-year-old boy who couldn't distinguish road signs, and who couldn't read a simple comic book to while away the long hours ahead of him.

Now, sitting in almost the same seat as seven years ago, I felt invincible, just like any other normal teenager—the teenager who had a seven-year past and everything in the world to look forward to in the future.

Five o'clock the next morning, it's still dark, and we're in Laramie. The city boy bade me good-bye, good luck, and stepped off the bus, leaving me with a full seat. I leaned back and tried to go back to sleep; I didn't want to think about how I would kill time for two weeks on the ranch.

I gave some thought to Craig and Mark. I recalled what a threat they had been to my self-esteem for so many years, and wondered why I had tried so hard to win their friendship and acceptance, and why, just seven short months ago, I was still begging for approval and acceptance from them and everybody in the world. *I'm bigger, stronger and smarter than either of them now,* I told myself. *I've done things they couldn't dream of doing. So why do I bother to clutter my mind with bad memories? I don't need their respect and recognition—they need mine.*

The bus slowly braked to a stop in Rawlins. I waited for the familiar sound of the air brakes being set before standing in the aisle to work my way to the front. With my heart in my throat, and without looking up or ahead of me, I cautiously stepped out of the bus.

As I walked away from the bus, I quickly scanned the small group of people waiting to pick up passengers, doubting if I would see a familiar face to meet me this early in the morning. I was looking straight ahead, working my way toward the little restaurant. "Hey Soldier Boy, looking for a ride?" a voice sounded, over the mixed chatter of the other passengers.

The voice wasn't familiar, but I was sure I was the only solider on the bus. I looked to my right, and there stood Craig and Mark, not four feet away, with outstretched hands—Craig with a mouth full of teeth, and Mark with a pleasant, wry smile. We stood there and shook hands as if we had been friends forever.

"You traveling light, Soldier?" Craig asked, looking at the shaving kit I carried in my left hand.

I pointed to the belly of the bus, where the driver was busy unloading bags. "I've got a bag under there, somewhere," I said.

We stood like deaf mutes, watching the bus driver sort through baggage. A lone Army duffel bag was tossed onto the sidewalk. Craig looked at me and I nodded. Without saying a word, he grabbed the bag, hoisted it onto his shoulders and ambled off down the street, me following, then Mark. No one said a word. At the end of the block, Craig tossed my bag in the back of a new, 1954 Chevrolet pickup. Mark eased himself under the steering wheel, Craig slid in the middle. I took the outside seat and closed the door.

Mark started the engine. "I'm starved," he said, turning his head, looking for on-coming traffic. "Let's go to the truck stop and chow down. Either of you yahoos got any money?"

Craig turned to me with raised eyebrows, and a wide goofy smile. I shrugged my shoulders.

"Hell, you're the only one who has a real job," Craig said.

"Shit, why did I even ask?" Mark grumbled, trying to sound disgusted.

Mark eased the pickup down the street, past the bus stop. Passengers were starting to get back on the bus. I turned my head and watched the big greyhound emblem glide past my window. I caught my breath and felt an unfamiliar sensation well up in my chest. I could feel a smile break across my face, and caught the look of a tall, curvy blonde waiting in line to board the bus. She waved and returned my smile.

———

It had only been six months since I had left the ranch, but nothing seemed the same. I mean, everything *looked* the same, the building, the pastures, the houses, but the social atmosphere was completely different, with everyone treating me as if I were someone special. I was confused. I hadn't changed, except for gaining some weight and height—still the same old Dennis. But it was like they had me mistaken for someone else.

I shook hands with Richard first. He held my hand with a firm grip, smiling, at first not saying anything. Then he said, "You've done well for yourself, Dennis. We're proud of you. You can be proud of yourself, too."

Ellen came to me giggling like a schoolgirl and wrapped her arms around me. Ellen had never really hugged me before, so I didn't have anything to compare it to, but I could feel the warmth, genuine concerned warmth. "Oh, Dennis, I can't believe it." She backed off and held me at arms length, really looking at me. She had quit giggling, but the happy face was still there. "Dennis, we are *so* glad you're home. We're planning a little party for you, but now you better get on over to the other ranch; Anna and Booth can hardly wait to see you."

About that time, someone darkened the doorway. It was Spike, or so I guessed. It wasn't Spike the little kid, though. He was man-size now, almost as tall as me, and a little heavier. We shook hands and looked each other over, before we had a good laugh. "You gotta get going, pardner," Spike said. "Gram and Grampa called just a few minutes ago."

Craig dropped me off outside the gate at the old ranch. Mr. and Mrs. Valliant, with Grimes looming behind them, stood outside the door, waiting on the rickety old porch. I could see Pete standing off to the side, pulling on a cigarette. My heart did a little leap, because I could see the happiness in their smiles, and I knew instantly that nothing had changed here.

But I was wrong. When we entered the kitchen, Mrs. Valliant said, "Let's all go in by the fireplace where it's warm. I want to know everything about your new life, Dennis. It's so wonderful what you're doing." Trailing the others out of the kitchen and into the large living room is when I first noticed the change in Mr. and Mrs. Valliant, and a strange feeling came over me—like a sad omen. Mrs. Valliant shuffled along, watching her feet, as if she were directing the movement of each step, and Mr. Valliant holding on to things, chairs, the door frame, anything to help steady his arthritic legs. I tried to remember if they had always been this way.

Grimes went off to his room. Mr. and Mrs. Valliant sank heavily into the same old worn couch. I grabbed a wooden chair and moved it around to face them. Mrs. Valliant reached over and held onto Mr. Valliant's hand while we talked. They wanted to hear all about my life as a soldier, but I knew their body English; they had important things to tell me, too.

I talked for maybe fifteen minutes, telling them all about what I had been through in basic training, and the communication school that I had just finished. I told them my new assignment was Berlin, Germany, and that I planned to use the Service library to help jump start my first year at the University of Wyoming.

When I finished, we sat for maybe a minute or two without speaking. Mrs. Valliant moved her mouth to adjust her bridgework, as she always did before starting to speak. "When you get out of the Army, are you coming back to work for the ranch?" she said.

"Maybe. It's still a year and a half away, but I'll for sure need a job during the summer."

"I know Richard will hire you in a minute, Dennis. You will always have a home and a job here. He told you about buying the ranch from us, didn't he?" *So that's what it was all about. I should have guessed from the start.*

"No. Richard didn't say anything. Are you moving to town?"

Mr. Valliant chuckled. "The Missus says they'll have to carry me out of here on a board, but I don't think we'll wait that long." He shrugged his shoulders. "We don't get along like we used to, and maybe it *would* be easier if we lived in town."

It wasn't even noon yet, but I hadn't slept much, and I was tired from the long bus trip. Maybe they hadn't slept well either, because I could see the weariness in their faces. I wanted to just go to my old room and take a long nap. But I had something more to say, and I couldn't let the opportunity slip. I wanted to tell them how I felt about them, how much I appreciated what they had done for me. I had been thinking about it. I was going away to a strange place. Maybe there would be a war, or maybe something would happen to one of them. Maybe it would never be this perfect again, ever. I wanted them to know that I cared deeply for them, not only because of how they treated me, but just because of who they were. All of these thoughts were right there, welled up in my chest, ready to come out, but I couldn't say them—not in those exact words. What I said was, "I don't guess I ever told you in so many words how much I appreciate you taking me in like you did. I don't want to even think about where I would be today if you hadn't helped me. Guess I'd probably still be picking cotton and stealing chickens in Memphis, Texas." They both smiled when I said that, and I wanted to believe they understood about all those other things that I couldn't say.

My two-week furlough passed too quickly, driving around the country visiting classmates, a Saturday night dance at the Fireman's Hall with Craig and Mark, and a big house party at Richard and Ellen's. All of this gave me a good feeling, but I was still confused and overwhelmed. *Why now?* I thought, all the while wondering if it were possible that I could return their outpouring feelings of goodwill. I had returned prepared to fight, with the same old grudges and resentments as the day I left six months ago. All of a sudden making my feeling do an abrupt about-face was more than I could handle.

The air was still, but it was cold and cloudy, with about six inches of snow still on the ground from the last snowfall. Tomorrow, Mr. and Mrs. Valliant would drive me to Cheyenne to catch a plane to New York City for the first leg of my trip to Germany. After the noon meal, Pete went off to the bunkhouse, and the others settled down in the living room to enjoy the warmth of the fireplace. I bundled up and walked out toward the horse pasture to see my old horse, Red, and to just be alone. I had a lot on my mind—torn between the need to forgive and the need to keep on hating.

I had thought about it every night before going to sleep, and decided that, even after all the love and friendship shown to me by those from whom I least expected, I still didn't know if I could put it all aside just like that.

Trying to make some sense of everything, I reasoned that some of the treatment handed out to me and that I gave back would have happened to any new kid on the block. And when it came right down to it, I really didn't want to leave here all welled up inside with that same old feeling. I had so much emotion welled up in me, with such violent force, that I knew I had to let some of it go. There was no reason to keep the feelings, I finally decided. Maybe I could be part of something now…

I could see my old horse, Red, with his head high in the air, staring at me a short distance away. He nickered, and I slowly walked toward him. I was taking deep breaths, allowing my chest to relax, and willing myself to just forgive them for what they had done or had not done, and to forgive myself for all my mistakes and the things I had done to hurt other people.

Maybe it would have been easier if Bob Ware had been there to say a little prayer, full of divine guidance, but just willing myself to erase all the bitterness in my heart, and doing it, was something quite different.

I wish I could say, at that moment, I suddenly forgave the world for all the bad things that had happened to me, and forgave myself for causing part of it. But I would be a liar, because it didn't happen like that. Only fairy tales end that way. But I can tell you that I knew it was time to stop dwelling on the past and make another new start. And I can tell you that, right then, I breathed a big sigh of relief and my whole mood changed.

I walked over to Red and ran my hand along his neck and mane. He pawed at the pile of hay he had been munching on, and threw his head into the air. I grabbed a handful of mane with my left hand and threw my body onto his back. He lifted his head high and tore off toward the barn at a dead run, just like always, except now we were both free as the cold wind in our faces.

www.ingramcontent.com/pod-product-compliance
Lightning Source LLC
Chambersburg PA
CBHW071320090426
42738CB00012B/2741